I0770340

Leaders on every food-growing continent warn of future conflicts over **food, water and climate change.**

"Accelerating climate change impacts will cause more than 100 million deaths and knock off more than 3% of GDP by 2030."
– **DARA** and the Climate Vulnerability Monitor

"The threat from climate changes is serious, it is urgent, and it is growing, as more frequent droughts and crop failures breed hunger and conflict." – U.S. President and Nobel laureate **Barack Obama**

"We know that a peaceful world cannot long exist, one-third rich and two-thirds hungry." – **Jimmy Carter**

"The war against hunger is truly mankind's war of liberation." – **John F. Kennedy**

"If you desire peace, cultivate justice, but at the same time cultivate the fields to produce more bread; otherwise there will be no peace." – **Norman Borlaug**

"The U.S. intelligence is preparing for the threat of a global war for water, which they believe is likely to occur by 2030. – Global Water Security, **U.S. intelligence Assessment**

"For all the anxiety about the scarcity of oil, gas and vital minerals, the fiercest fight in the coming decades will involve food and the land it grows on." – **Michael T. Klare**, The Race for What's Left: The Global scramble for the World's Last Resources

"Man seems to insist on ignoring the lessons available from history." – **Norman Borlaug**

"Everybody thinks that the future is going to see fights over energy, it's far more likely to be primarily over food." – **Thomas Barnett**, *The future of Fifth Generation Warfare: Follow the food!*

"Over the next decade, water problems will create instability and state failures in countries important to the U.S. national security interests." – *Global Water Security*, **U.S. intelligence Assessment**

Ana Feeds our World by 2040

Ana Cultivates Miracles with Nature's Nano Cell Biofactory

Mark R. Edwards

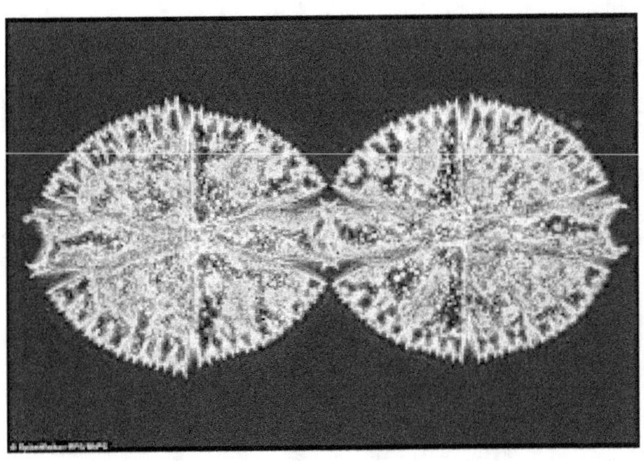

How nano single-celled organisms will transform the future of food.

The Green Algae Strategy Series

AlgaeCompetition.com

Ana Feeds our World

Consider joining the Algae Biomass Organization.
- Expand your horizons.
- Educate yourself about our world future.
- Enhance your knowledge of sustainable systems.
- Engage with aligned smart people, who want to improve our world.
- Use the promotion code "Ana" for a 10% new member discount.

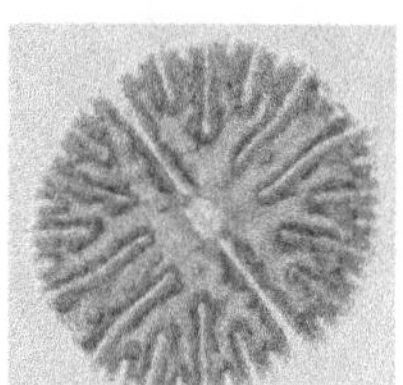

The Spanish meaning for **Ana**: Grace or favor.

ISBN-13: 978-1979212861
ISBN-10: 1979212864

Dedication

To hundreds of my delightful students over 39 years at ASU who gave me the privilege of teaching and who sparked my curiosity for sustainable systems for business, agribusiness and our world. May Ana's insight engage you and your friends to assure sustainable and affordable food for all our children and their children.

To my fabulous life-partner, Ann Ewen, a master of the culinary arts, who consistently brings joy with her music, gardening and passion for community and social justice.

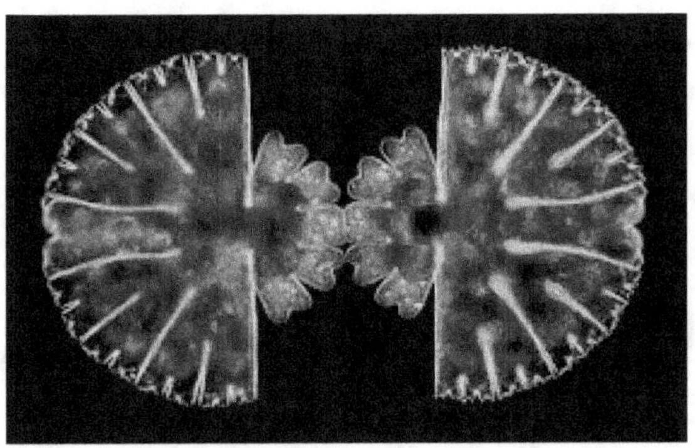

Ana's Quest

Ana, a foodie, grew up in food paradise, San Francisco, which is one of the wealthiest, most beautiful and innovative cities in the world. She was shocked to see the *San Francisco Chronicle* headline in May 2017 that 1 in 4 people in San Francisco are food insecure and hungry. How could so many people suffer from hunger in a land of plenty?

She found that San Francisco made #6 on the USDA's list of the unhealthiest food deserts. Families in food deserts have access only to processed, calorie-dense foods high in sugar, fat and salt. Junk food leads to obesity, diabetes and other serious health issues.

Ana's passion about food extends to food justice; democratic access to affordable healthy food. She learned that the rest of America and the world also suffered food injustice. Over 50 million Americans are food insecure. Over 20% of the children in 22 states live in food-insecure households. Ana's present world has 7.3 billion mouths to feed, but modern industrial agriculture has failed. The UN WHO estimates that 3 billion people, are malnourished; deficient in calories, protein, micronutrients or vitamins. By 2040, Ana's world will have over 9 billion hungry people on our perilously hot, dry and hungry planet.

Ana studied sustainable systems in graduate school at Arizona State University, where she fell in love with algae. She worried about what her children would do for food and wondered if microcrops might deliver. Her professor ignited her life's mission with a simple parable.

> *Give Ana food and resolve her hunger for a day.*
>
> *Teach Ana to grow abundant food in Peace Microfarms,*
>
> *And she can feed her family and community forever.*
>
> *Allow Ana to share her knowledge, and Ana can feed the world.*

This is the fascinating story of Ana's path forward to apply her ingenuity and to engage her social network in her quest for food justice – locally and globally. Ana's passion for eco-smart, single-celled organisms forms the foundation for her incredible journey.

Our Nanocrop Path to Eco-Smart Foods

When has the global need for a miraculous "thrive package" containing all the essential proteins and nutrients to sustain life ever been greater? Over half our world's people are hungry and a billion are malnourished. We have more migrants, homeless and hungry people now than any time in world history. Half our global neighbors will go to bed hungry tonight.

Modern food production has become dependent on increasingly scarce fossil natural resources. "Fossil food" produced by industrial scale agriculture placed a huge bet on a few monocultures that survive only in good weather and then, only in the absence of serious pest vectors.

We need solutions that resolve hunger with methods that provide for both our rich and poor, and our rural and urban communities. The solution should maximize the sustainability triple bottom line. Ana's solution addresses many constraints and grows good food that:

1. Enhances health and vitality for every plant, animal and person.
2. Is affordable and sustainable so that it creates food justice – access to good food by everyone.
3. Reduces the physical risk of food production and enables social justice – good jobs independent of gender, race or religion.
4. Preserves, protects and replenishes fossil resources and natural ecosystems for our following generations
5. Thrives with magnificent biodiversity independent of altitude, latitude, geography, politics or climate.
6. Is carbon neutral or negative and moderates rather than accelerates climate change and global air, water and soil pollution.
7. Produces local to consumers to minimize transportation.
8. Creates a positive eco-footprint while improving the health of local, regional and global ecosystems.

Microcrops are astonishing nano-cell factories with extraordinary capabilities to elevate industrial agriculture crop and animal production. Microcrops will grow superior nutrition for the strong cellular metabolism of plants, animals and people.

Algae and her cousins, other nano-sized single-celled organisms, will transform modern industrial and organic agriculture more in the next 20 years than the 65-year Green Revolution. That revolution was not green. Productivity came from fossil sources; massive expansion in cropland, irrigation, fossil fuels, chemical fertilizer, pesticides and poisons, as well as new hybrid and transgenic modified seeds.

The next food renaissance will engage green biotechnologies that produce healthier foods with minimal or no fossil resources. Freedom foods liberate growers from fossil resource consumption and deliver superior nutrition and taste without pollution and waste. Nutrient cycling with single-celled organisms will replace "one-and-done" fossil agriculture with its constant extraction, consumption and pollution.

Freedom foods made from microcrops will redesign our food supply from the foundation of the food chain, made with both single and multicellular organisms. Freedom foods free consumers for smart food choices, free growers for eco-smart production, and free ecosystems of waste and pollution.

Abundance growing methods free farmers from reliance on fossil resources because growers can recover and repurpose precious nutrients from waste streams to grow clean, healthy food. Farmers will embrace an efficient net-zero carbon food production system that preserves rather than consumes natural resources.

Algae nano cells offer an array of advantages that are unavailable in land plants. Each tiny algae cell packages the essential nutrients for multi-cellular life – plants, animals and humans. All plants evolved from algae 500 million years ago. All the nutrition, colors and healthy compounds in modern crops and vegetable produce are also available in algae.

Microcrops grown in Peace Microfarms flourish with biodiversity 100 times greater than industrial agriculture. Microcrops offer far more cultivar choices for growing food, biofeed, biofertilizer and other bioproducts. Microcrop nano-cell biofactories can produce excellent food, significantly faster, independent of weather or climate.

Peace microfarms liberate growers from dependence on increasingly expensive cropland, fresh water, fossil fuels, chemical fertilizer and other non-renewable resources. Peace microfarms avoid conflict, and possibly war, over diminishing natural resources by using abundance methods that cycle nutrients to grow microcrops.

Natural resource over-consumption and pollution cannot be addressed without engaging the agribusiness community. Microcrop nano cell biofactories will make the biggest impact to world food supplies by providing stronger nutrition for plant and animal production in existing industrial farms.

Abundance growing methods reduce risk, costs and pain for modern industrial farmers. Algae biofertilizer improves yields while reducing farmers' dependence on chemical fertilizer. Algae biofertilizer ends hidden hunger by increasing field crop nutralence – nutrient quality, density, diversity and bioavailability. Algae biofertilizer also improves crop stress tolerance to weather and pests, while substantially reducing fertilizer and pesticide pollution. Abundance methods clean degraded and polluted ecosystems. In some cases, algae biofertilizers can bring abandoned cropland back to life by restoring soil fertility.

Algae biofeeds deliver similar benefits for animal farmers. Biofeeds enhance animal growth and development, improve survivability, and reduce waste because the feeds deliver higher nutralence. Field tests have shown animal products and meat grown with algae biofeeds have superior color, texture and taste, while delivering more protein and other nutrients per bite and healthier fats.

Microcrops, the foundation of this food renaissance, includes the full spectrum of microorganisms including algae, yeast, fungi, bacteria, archaea, plankton and many others. The focus here will be on algae, but these other microcrops offer similar benefits.

Food grains (e.g. rice, soy, corn and wheat) make up about 80% of the world's food supply today. I predict that by 2040, algae-based foods will replace 60% of the food grain products. Algae texturized meats, (think tofu vegiburgers) will replace 40% of the meat products and provide enhanced nutrition, texture and taste with 90% less pollution and waste. Algae protein bars, power drinks and food additives will give consumers stronger nutrition, more nutralence, at substantially lower cost than today's protein products.

Algae biofertilizer will replace 70% of the inorganic fertilizer currently applied to field crops. Algae biofeed will replace 30% to 60% of animal feed, depending on the animal, and 90% of fish feed. Plants and animals are what they eat, so the resulting foods will contain various expressions of algae nutrients.

In a broader context, algae bioproducts will replace large numbers of products that today are made from plants and animals, including 50% to 90% of cosmetics, nutraceuticals, pharmaceuticals, vitamin and mineral supplements, medicines, green chemicals and plastics.

These changes will occur because algae nano cell biofactories provide higher quality target compounds substantially faster than industrial agriculture. Bioproducts contain fewer contaminants, at lower cost.

Algae's tiny cell size create an ideal delivery system for bioproducts such as cosmetics, nutritional products and medicines. Consumers want the best functionality, which they will get with the multiple sustainable competitive advantages provided nano biofactories. When consumers have a choice of two similarly priced items, they will make climate and eco-friendly choices. Their choice will be made easier with healthier products at lower cost.

Agriculture emits nearly 20% of the global CO_2. The algae microcrop food revolution will cut pollution by half, which will moderate climate chaos. Abundance methods recover and reuse carbon and other nutrients rather than polluting the atmosphere and local ecosystems.

Fossil agriculture currently consumes 92% of all fresh water globally. Abundance methods can cut fresh water consumption for food production by at least half. Peace microfarms can use non-potable water for safe and healthy biofeed and biofertilizer production. Other microfarms can clean wastewater, as algae has done for decades. Clean water may contribute more value to the community than the rich, nutritious biomass.

Peace microfarms produce 30 to 72 times more food per section of land every year than modern agriculture. Microfarms do not require cropland and scale to any size. Microfarmers may produce food practically anywhere, including cities. Microfarms with nano-cell biofactories will enable Beijing, New Delhi, New York, Jakarta, Buenos Aries and Athens to grow 80% of their food in the city.

Microfarmers recover low cost nutrients from sterilized waste streams and transform them into freedom foods and other valuable bioproducts. Growers use abundance methods to assure a sustainable food supply for many generations. Microcrop bioproducts can transform our food future from extractive to sustainable, but the transition will not be simple. If supplying Ana's world with abundant good food were easy, it would already have been done.

Single-celled organisms will leverage the future of our food, but only with the cooperation of industrial and organic farmers. The keys to engagement lie in creating strong benefits in bioproducts to improve yields and quality of legacy food crops, while reducing costs. Algae nutritional bioproducts will upgrade health and vitality for plants, animals and humans and lead the way to our shared future with net-zero carbon food production.

Mark R. Edwards, drmetrics@gmail.com

Our eager Algae Foundation students will receive a free color PDF of *Ana Feeds Our World* as part of their educational curriculum in algae's promise to improve society and our planet Many students are Millennials and bring an expectation of immediacy. The protocol here uses hyperlinks rather than footnotes. Hyperlinks allow instantaneous access to journal articles, key websites and educational videos from students' electronic devices.

Additional supportive resources are available at the Algae Foundation, *Algae Industry Magazine*, *Algae 101*, Smart Microfarms, Spirulina Source, and the Algae Competition.com.

The Algae Foundation led by Ike Levine, promotes the power of algae to transform the human race and the environment upon which it depends. The Algae Foundation facilitates a future in which algae are a fundamental source of energy, nutrition, bioproducts and ecological services for sustainable societies globally. To accomplish its mission, the Algae Foundation engages in and funds educational outreach. *Ana Feeds Our World* assists in our educational mission.

Attention young scientists

Metrics provide your best scientific guidance for solving challenges and selecting the best alternative. Nature's most common metric, a 20% difference, occurs in many natural settings. Scientists call it a significant difference. You will see many comparisons here between terrestrial plants and single-celled organisms. One may display a 10x advantage, which is 1,000%, but may be referred to as an "order of magnitude." By 2025, algae will enjoy a 100x productivity advantage over field grains including corn, soy, wheat and rice for protein, oil, sugar and essential nutrients. Algae foods already deliver 100x the nutralence available from land-based foods. Improvement in abundance growing methods will produce algae foods with 1000x more nutralence than legacy crops.

Some of these projections for algae's ability to recover and cycle nutrients, to reduce waste and pollution and to improve health and vitality may seem like science fiction. They are not fantasy because they are backed by empirical evidence from years of scientific R&D. Algae has successfully cycled nutrients from commercial wastewater systems in the US for over 50 years.

Algae have already performed over 25 amazing miracles that improve societies, which are listed in Appendix I. Algae have performed only about 5% of her miracles to date.

She needs **your help to create her next miracles**. We look forward to your engagement in nanotechnology to make Ana's quest for food justice a reality for your family and for our global community.

CHAPTERS

1. How will Single-Celled Organisms Transform Food?

I am here to sound the alarm about our direction as a human family, especially global warming and rising food prices.

– Ban Ki-moon, U.N. Secretary General

By 2040, Ana's world will have over 9 billion hungry people competing for nourishment on our increasingly hot, dry and crowded planet. What will Ana's children do for food? To provide abundant affordable and sustainable food for everyone, we need a plant that works miracles. This is the story of that single-celled plant.

Many young scientists want to change our world for the better. Please consider this advice: "When planning to orchestrate miracles, choose something that dependably produces miracles. Past behavior provides the best prediction of future behavior. Choose your miracle worker carefully, based on past demonstrated talent and performance."

The plant in the spotlight here has already delivered **five incredible miracles** that have substantially changed our world. Algae generated the O_2 that enabled life on earth. Then algae became the foundation of the food chain, providing nutrition for all living organisms.

About 500 million years ago, algae experienced an astonishing evolution event that propagated the terrestrial plants that we use for food today. Algae become the mother of all our foods. Algae wisely reserved one miracle for herself – the ability to grow healthier food, significantly faster than terrestrial plants. More recently, algae developed more nutralence than any other plant on our planet. Algae's cellular biofactories provide more protein, nutrients and medically bioactive compounds than any other plant on our planet.

Please consider solutions to these questions, which are vital if we are to provide sustainable and affordable good food for our children.

1. What is the most important energy stored on earth? What is both the first living organism on earth, the most abundant today, and also the youngest?

2. Visualize a magnificent 300-foot Sequoia redwood tree that weighs 2.7 million pounds and is 100 feet wide. From where did the giant Sequoia get its biomass?

3. Was corn ethanol biofuel a wise strategy for America?

4. If you could design an energy storage system from scratch, what is the most efficient, clean and sustainable way to produce affordable stored energy?

Energy stores. The most important energy stored on earth = **FOOD!** Without food, plants, animals and humans lack the nutrition necessary for energy cellular metabolism and die – quickly. Fossil fuels are useful, but humans lived for thousands of years without burning fossil energy and polluting our planet with greenhouse gasses.

Fossil fuels are simply fossilized algae that settled to the bottom of ancient oceans. The rich biomass folded into the earth and was transformed over eons by extreme pressure and heat into coal, shale, petroleum and natural gas. Now, we burn fossilized ancient algae at our peril since global climate chaos threatens food production.

First, most abundant and newest life. The first living organism on earth were single-celled microorganisms that lacked a cell nucleus or cell membrane, known as prokaryotes. Archeologist have found individual fossilized microbes, probably cyanobacteria, blue-green algae in rocks 3.5 billion years old. Every minute when the sun shines, algae produce mega-trillions of offspring globally, making microbes the most abundant and the youngest life on earth.

Tree biomass. The giant Sequoia get its mass from the same place as a blade of grass, the air. If the tree used nutrients from the soil for building mass, then there would be a big hole when the tree fell over. The tree absorbs CO_2 and water to make hydrocarbons that grow the tree's mass. Photosynthesis, possibly the most important formula to human, animal and plant life, is beautifully simple.

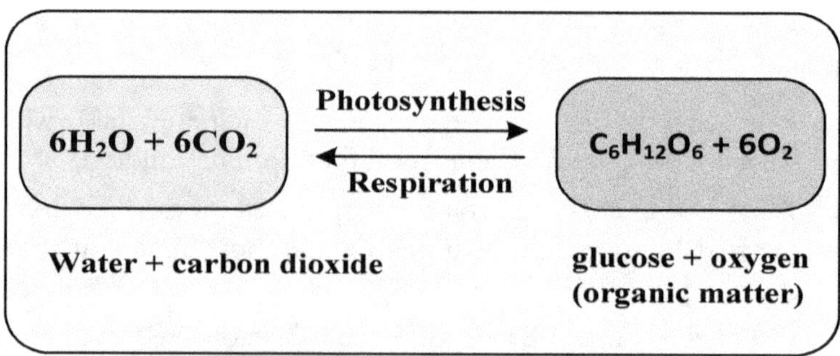

Solar energy powers photosynthesis

What makes Single Celled Organisms Special?

U.S. Biofuel strategy. The 2008 Energy Act funded $288 billion in transfer payments to biofuel producers over five years. The Act was possibly the most foolish and environmentally disastrous decision ever made by the US Congress. *BioWar I: Why Burning Food for Fuels Leads to World Hunger*, follows the substantial money trail, which led to a few be ag companies that bought Congressional votes to enrich themselves, especially ADM and CEO Dwayne Andreas.

Throughout military history, burning food was an offensive act of war designed to punish the opposition. The US became the first country in history unwise enough to burn its own food. Biofuel production did indeed lead to world hunger. Reducing world food stores by burning US corn caused price increases of 50 to 120%, and led to more than 40 food riots globally. The food riots left hundreds of people dead but many millions were still unable to afford sufficient food for their family.

Biofuel production from corn robbed our next generation of billions of tons of natural resources – topsoil, water, fossil fuels, inorganic fertilizers and agricultural chemicals. When, in the next generation the Ogallala aquifer, the Midwest's largest, goes dry, many residents will have to move to other regions, because no fresh water will be available. Our children's assessment of this US biofuel strategy will be much harsher than current critiques.

Sustainable energy storage system. An ideal eco-smart energy system would mimic nature and cycle nutrients as many times as possible. The storage system would use the power of the sun in photosynthesis for energy production. The system may grow single or multicellular organisms that grow quickly and efficiently in non-potable water. The process should recover and reuse waste stream nutrients from air, water and solids, while producing nutritious and healthy food.

The energy system should consume minimal or no fossil resources, fertile land, fresh water, fossil fuels, chemical fertilizers, pesticides or poison. Photosynthesis allows the system to be energy neutral. Nutrient cycling provides the system with a positive carbon and ecological footprint.

A global food model, developed by a team at Anglia Ruskin University's Global Sustainability Institute in the UK, shows that business-as-usual agriculture is unsustainable. The model concludes that failing a change in course by 2040, the global food supply system will face catastrophic losses, with an unprecedented epidemic of food riots, and possibly wars.

Other credible models predict food disasters between 2030 and 2050 due to the combined impacts of population increases, climate chaos and natural resource extinction.

Industrial agriculture

FAO scientists predict the world will need 70% more food production by 2040. The foundation of modern industrial agriculture (MIA) rests on fossil energy. Unfortunately, MIA consumes over 10 times the energy that it returns in food. Does the planet have enough fossil fuels to double food production? What will happen to MIA food production as the cost of fossil energy increases? How will farmers be able to afford crop inputs that are becoming increasingly scarce and expensive?

Our planet may not have the remaining natural resources to sustain current food production, let alone increase food substantially. The best chance we have to assure the survival of our next generations are major changes in MIA methods. Algae-based bioproducts can assist with this transition by cycling nutrients, cutting fossil resource consumption and repairing degraded ecosystems. Step one is provision of nutrients.

Nutrient deficiencies not protein

During the 40 years following WWII, nutritional scientists believed that protein deficiency was the most serious and widespread dietary deficiency in the world. The World Health Organization (WHO) made its prime objective improving protein nutrition. The condition was called "kwashiorkor". The word came from the Ga language of West Africa that means "the disease of the deposed child".

Medical science discovered that protein deficiency was not the problem. When it occurred, it was caused by a simple lack of food, rather than food with low-protein content. The major challenge for resolving world hunger is not more protein, but a solution to the seemingly intractable problem, nutrient deficiencies.

Algae provide an uplifting model for human food because these nano-plants can provide the protein and micronutrients to resolve the most serious cause of global malnutrition – nutrient deficiencies. The four most prevalent deficiency diseases are: malnutrition, nutritional anemia (iron and B12 deficiency), exophthalmia (vitamin A deficiency) and endemic goiter (iodine deficiency). Some digestible algae such as Spirulina, address each of these issues through the production of high protein, iron and B12, vitamin A and iodine. The Kanembu tribe in

What makes Single Celled Organisms Special?

Chad has been harvesting naturally occurring spirulina from lakes and eating about 10 grams per serving with most of their meals for centuries, with positive results.

Algae produces protein substantially more efficiently than conventional food grains. Algae produce a higher protein yield per unit area, 15 tons/Ha/year compared to terrestrial crops, such as soybean, pulse legumes, and wheat that produce only 0.6–1.2 tons/Ha/year. Superior protein production is only one benefit.

Due to their harsh environment and phototropic life, algae are often exposed to high oxidative and free-radical stresses. Algae have evolved natural protective systems, such as the production of pigments, (e.g., carotenes, chlorophylls, and phycobiliproteins) and polyphenols (e.g., catechins, flavonols, and phlorotannins), which impart health benefits to plants, animals and people when eaten.

Spirulina, the most highly consumed algae food, provides the highest protein content of any whole food, plus many additional nutritional benefits. Adding Spirulina to a diet provides anti-hypertension, anti-hyperlipidemia, renal protective, and anti-hyperglycemic benefits.

Spirulina provides a rich source of proteins, 63% by dry weight (dw), and contains high levels of hypocholesterolemia γ-linoleic acid, (GLA), B-vitamins, and free-radical scavenging phycobilins-proteins. Spirulina's high nutralence has earned the label of a 'super food' by the WHO. NASA sent Spirulina to space to support astronauts' diet for its high nutralence and ability to clean wastewater.

Algae acting alone?

Could Ana possibly feed the world with single-celled organisms such as algae? These unique cells form the foundation of the food chain and they grow so fast they *could* feed the world. But prior experience show acting alone may not be the best solution. The idea to cultivate enough algae to feed the world has been proposed by dozens of scientists and science fiction writers since 1898. Four times countries have seriously examined algae production for food: in 1898 after severe global famine; after each of the World Wars when millions of people were displaced, poor and hungry; and then again 1996. The last bubble centered on growing algae for biofuels.

Algae acting alone to provide food for the world was the plot for the 1973 science fiction movie *Soylent Green*, set in 2022. *Soylent Green* anticipated the challenges industrial agriculture has imposed our world today: widespread hunger, pollution, overcrowding, high unemployment, and global warming. Algae food production became the solution. Soylent Green was a green wafer advertised to contain "high-energy plankton" from the firm World Ocean. In the movie Charlton Heston's character discovered dead people were being recycled to make Soylent Green, and he led the team that stopped the big machine making it. A remake of *Soylent Green* would set the algae industry back a generation.

Real-life solutions need to be far broader than simply creating a single food for billions of hungry people. The food system needs to employ biodiversity, with single and multi-cellular organisms. Biodiversity will reduce food production risk and increase sustainability. The system must engage global farmers in a symbiotic fashion that leverages the benefits of single-celled organisms and makes industrial agriculture better. The first challenge is understanding the novel benefits available from these organisms.

Botanic Gardens Conservation International estimates there are about 350,000 species of land plants. The best-selling algae textbook, estimates there are over 10 million species of algae. Fewer than 10% of all algae species have been discovered or analyzed. Therefore, extraordinary entrepreneurial opportunities exist for microfarmers willing and dedicated to growing algae.

Algae lifts agriculture

Algae will make the strongest impact on existing industrial agriculture. **Algae microfarms** using **abundance** growing methods will provide multiple solutions for each of fossil agriculture's dilemmas. Bioregeneration gives many options to farmers for new bioproducts. Restoring the captured nutrients to manufacture value-added products flips farmers' waste-stream costs to a valuable new revenue source. The bioproduct choices with algae biomass are practically infinite.

Farmers can give their precious nutrients a second, (and 3rd, 4th, ...n) life. Cycling nutrients may be the #1 benefit algae delivers to farmers. Algae solves the non-trivial waste and pollution challenge with algae's unique bioremediation ability to cycle nutrients. Nutrient recovery not only ends waste but also reduces farmer's costs. The combination of bioremediation and bioregeneration can assist farmers to move from industrial farming to organic production.

What makes Single Celled Organisms Special?

Algae Food Pyramid

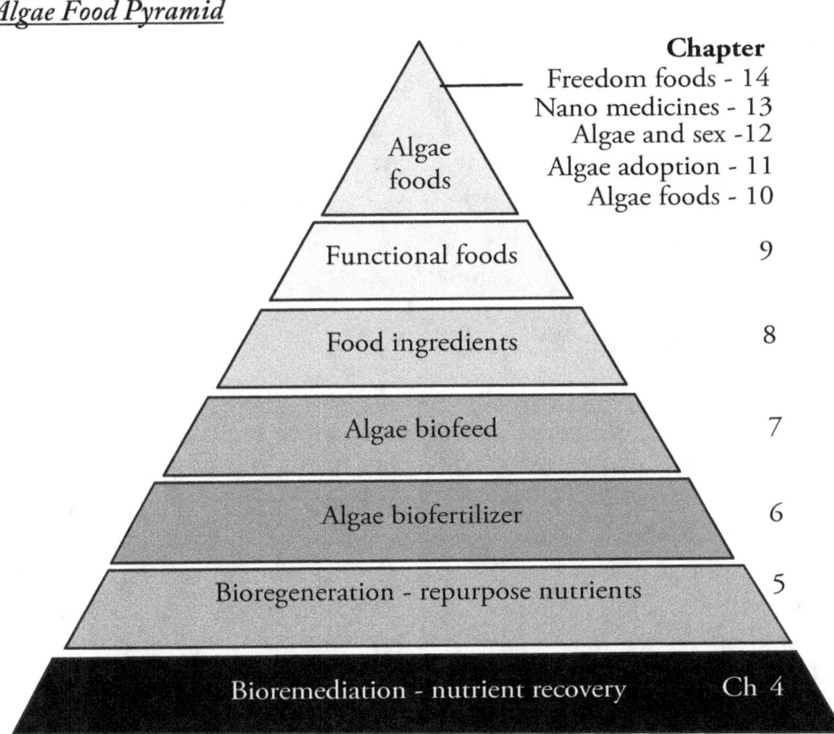

Algae's contribution to the global food system — by Chapter

Farmers can use their own waste streams to cultivate algae biofertilizer. Algae biofertilizer improves farm yields and quality for commercial crops as well as increases the nutralence of farm produce. Equally important, algae biofertilizers substantially reduce waste and pollution. Algae's unique talent for cycling nutrients and enhancing cellular metabolism make significant contributions to the global food system, on which we all depend. The Algae Food Pyramid, (next page), lays out the chapters that describe Ana's quest to supply world food.

Fortunately, cellular metabolism in animals responds as positively as plants do to algae nutralence. Algae biofeeds improve the health, speed of growth and stress tolerance of farm animals — dairy, meat, poultry and fish. Biofeeds enhance the color, taste, texture, color and nutralence of animal products. Farmers can reduce their cost of production by using abundance methods and cycling nutrients for biofeed rather than continually buying new animal feed.

Algae components serve as ingredients for many modern foods. As supply increases, more foods will improve taste, texture, color, odor, and astringency. Algae can amplify basic tastes, including sweet, sour, bitter, salty and especially umami, (wholesomeness, brothy or meaty).

Many Asian recipes add algae to amplify the umami taste. The umami taste bud is so significant, it lies at the center of the tongue. Algae ingredients also upgrade the kokumi taste, which translates to mouthfulness or heartiness. Similarly, algae ingredients can enhance, piquancy, (spicy taste), coolness, and new tastes that are waiting for discovery and classification.

Algae's incredibly high nutralence will fortify and transform many modern foods into functional foods. Functional foods enhance health and vitality by providing benefits beyond that of the traditional nutrients it contains. Functional foods may include cereals, breads, beverages, bars, soups, stews or meats that are fortified with vitamins, herbs, and nutraceuticals. Healthier algae oils with omega-3 fatty acids will replace seed and olive oils. Algae-based functional foods will allow people to consumer their entire set of nutritional supplements in the food they eat.

Pure algae foods will find large niche markets. Algae will replace soy, corn, wheat, barley and other food grains to make healthier foods without the allergens. Algae protein bars, beverages and vegetable meat replacements will deliver a higher density of nutrients per bite and more nutrient diversity, along with enhanced bioavailability. The broader nutrient diversity includes many micronutrients not available in today's conventional foods, especially vitamins and minerals. These products will be marketed as plant-based, vegan, Kosher, no gluten, no soy, no dairy, non-GMO and non-allergenic.

At the apex of the algae food pyramid, **freedom foods** will improve nutrition and taste without pollution and waste. Freedom foods are algae-based products grown with no or minimal fossil resources. This new food category will be superior to organic because freedom foods delivery higher nutralence and taste with a fraction of the ecological footprint associated with industrial or organic foods. Freedom foods preserve the earth's natural resources for future generations.

What makes Single Celled Organisms Special?

Present state

The algae industry today is so tiny, it cannot yet lift agriculture. The good news is that every solution Ana intends to use, (and is described here), has been invented and tested, at least at the laboratory level. No one has produced a single meal of freedom food, using no or minimal fossil resources. We are working to produce net-zero carbon foods without consuming fossil resources. When freedom foods are demonstrated, everyone will want eco-smart foods that are healthier and deliver better taste and higher nutralence.

As demonstration projects convey the substantial value proposition, more farmers will engage, diffusing microfarm installations. As the market reports success, algae bioproduct market share will flip from zero, in 2017, to the following predictions for 2040:

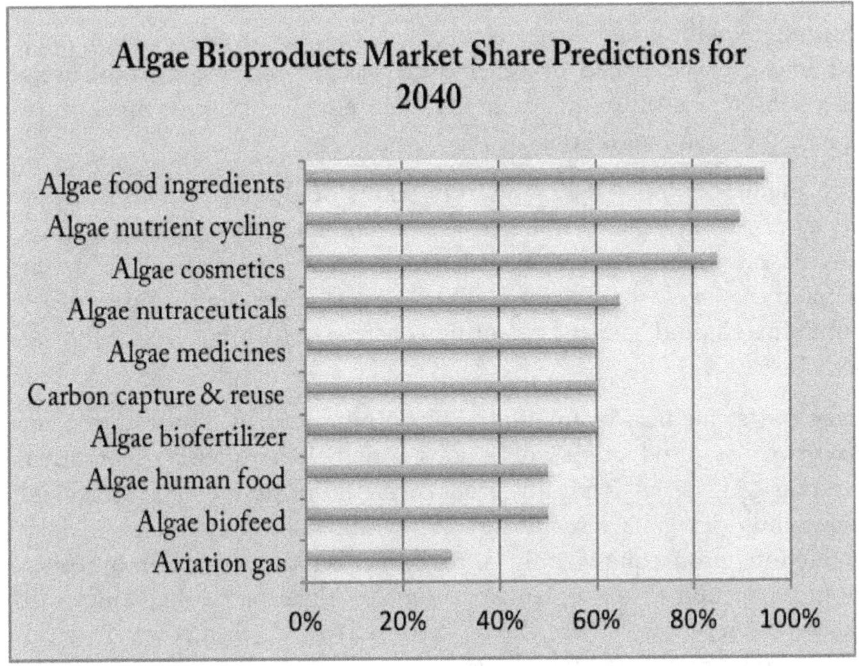

Future state

Algae solutions will first lift fossil food agricultural modestly, because most the solutions are not yet commercially available. As demonstration projects show the substantial benefits, entrepreneurs will embrace the opportunities and supply scalable solutions for diffusion. The path will follow the R3D model – R&D, demonstration and diffusion.

Algae's rich nutrients will fortify conventional foods, e.g. food grains and meat, with higher nutralence. People will be ecstatic when they can have their cake and eat it too – because the cake tastes great, yet has substantially fewer calories and minimal fat. Algae ingredients will flip calorie dense foods to nutrient dense, adding nutrient diversity and improved bioavailability. The impact on human health and vitality will be significant.

Adoption of algae nutrient cycling will occur quickly as cycling with solar energy and photosynthesis provides a game changer for farmers and the environment. Consumers will convert to algae cosmetics quickly as people learn algae offer a denser, healthier nutrient package. Algae nano-cells provide an ideal cosmetic delivery package that easily penetrates skin and hair. Algae's strong antioxidants repair skin damage and soften wrinkles.

Consumers will prefer vegetarian-based nutraceuticals. Algae's high nutralence is unmatched by other nutraceutical options. Fish oil users will celebrate the substantial benefits of omega-3 fatty acids made from algae, rather than killing the fish.

Most medicines today are made from plants or animals, which is costly and takes a long time. Often, massive amounts of the plant or animal material must be produced in order to get tiny amounts of the target compound for a medicine. The target compounds are often contaminated and must be purified before becoming an approved medicine.

Algae target medical compounds can be produced in days rather than months. Algae production will be substantially less expensive than other materials. Algae will typically produce far more of the target medical compound per kilo, with no or minimal contaminants. Algae production also requires only a tiny fraction of the space or other resources needed to grow plants or animals. Algae-based medicines will take off as medical science moves hundreds of algae-medical in-vitro studies from animals to human trials.

Carbon capture and reutilization will find an expanding niche in agriculture, as well as all the fossil fuel industries. Photosynthetic algae provide the lowest cost method to capture carbon for sequestration or for reuse. Algae biofertilizer will replace over half of the chemical fertilizers use today. MIA farmers are driven by yields and costs. Algae's high nutralent package for crops improves yields and produce quality.

What makes Single Celled Organisms Special?

Biofertilizer cycles carbon and other nutrients, avoiding the high costs associated with mining and transporting agricultural chemicals long distances. Cycling nutrients makes algae biofertilizer sustainable.

Biofeed diffusion will occur more slowly due to the variety in animal nutrition. Ruminants, such as cows, bison, sheep and goats each require different feed formulations. Algae biofeed for farmed fish will probably approach 95% by 2040, because wild fish feed on algae in their natural habitat. In 2017, roughly 33% of algae production goes to aquaculture. Algae biofeed will save billions of fish from extraction from the sea to feed carnivorous fish, such as salmon, in aquaculture.

By 2025, chefs will be using 3D printers to construct algae based meats, tasting like beef, lamb, pork, goat, chicken, turkey, fish and new taste choices. When consumers can select healthier and tastier steaks that do not sacrifice animals, they will choose algae-based meat products. It will also help that the algae product costs half as much as the legacy animal meat.

The first algae-based human foods will be functional foods that deliver healthier proteins, oils, carbohydrates and bioactive compounds. Compared with conventional products, healthier and more nutritious algae oil, colorants and flour entered the market in 2017. Of course, consumers will have additional choices. Some people may select tissue cultured meats, but those products will have the same health issues that accompanies meat consumption today. Others may choose insect protein foods, but marketers must overcome a non-trivial gag factor.

The great irony may be that both tissue culture and insect meats will need nutrients to grow. Both will probably use the highest nutralence source – algae.

Compromise for roots

Terrestrial plants made two enormous sacrifices after they evolved from algae, one caused by nature, and one caused intentionally by humans. Nature required plants to support several new energetically demanding features – roots, stems, leaves and a sexual apparatus. A plant has only the limited energy it can capture from the sun.

How the precious solar energy becomes distributed, determines its growth and food production efficiency. Land plants sacrificed efficiency in capturing photons from the sun because prior cells shaded new cells. Their ability to grow food efficiently tanked, because they had to distribute their limited energy among competing tasks, most of which had nothing to do with food production. Roots demanded energy for deeper growth and still more energy to pump nutrients from the roots through the plant. Stems commandeered energy as they made demands for vertical growth. The leaves called for energy so that they could expand and capture new photons. On top of all these demands, the plant had to invest about a third of its total energy into sex; both the physical sexual apparatus and preparing for mates or pollination.

The sacrifice created by human-directed hybrids was simple, but had significant impact on food quality. Humans have been growing plants as food crops for over 11,000 years. Farmers' primary goal has been higher yields, which produces more food. Seldom have farmers been willing to sacrifice yield for nutralence. For nearly all of human history, food nutralence was not measurable. Farmers are smart and saved seeds from the strongest or largest plants for next year's crop. Plants were bred for size or yield weight, with almost no consideration for nutralence.

MIA farmers know the value of nutrient density. However, in order to maximize profits, they grow crops to maximize yield, not nutralence. The next generation of consumers will change the status quo and demand high nutralence foods.

Nutralence

Algae-based foods have a compelling set of competitive advantages over land plants and animal products, which is apparent in nutralence metrics. Succulents are plants that selectively absorb water. Plants high in nutralence aggressively absorb, manufacture and store protein and a diverse set of other nutrients. Algae waste no energy on superfluous body functions. All their energy focuses on nutrient production.

Nutralence includes five important food compositional attributes: nutrient quality, density, diversity, bioactive compounds and nutrient bioavailability. People and animals are what they eat, so the composition of their food plays a significant role in their health and vitality.

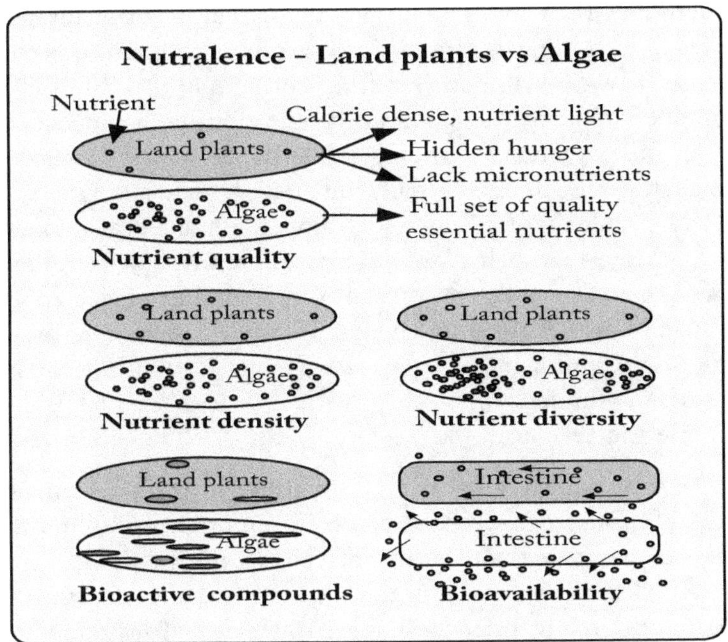

Nutrient quality includes the full set of nutrients provided per bite. Both land plants and algae may contain incomplete proteins due to a lack of certain amino acids, so that metric is important. Typically, algae foods provide 10 to 100 times more micronutrients than land plants.

Algae based foods also have 10 to 100 times more **nutrient density** than land plants. This may seem impossible except for the inconvenient truth about MIA's problems of nutrient dilution and hidden hunger.

Three recent nutrient dilution studies examined by Donald Davis at the University of Texas Biochemical Institute, looked at historical food composition data and found declines of 5% to 40% or more in some minerals in groups of vegetables and fruits. Another study evaluated vitamins and protein with similar results.

Another telling nutrient dilution metric is the high-water content of fruits and vegetables. Most fruits contain over 92% water, as do many vegetables. Cucumbers, lettuce, zucchini, tomato radish and celery are comprised of 95% water. Other veggies containing over 90% water include cabbage, cauliflower, broccoli, eggplant, peppers and spinach. After accounting for the considerable non-edible cell wall material, fruits and vegetables simply have little physical material to provide nutrients.

Many modern processed foods are calorie dense, but nutritionally poor, which causes hidden hunger. Hidden hunger causes children to become obese because they are malnourished from consuming the wrong types of foods. Hidden hunger robs billions of people globally the opportunity to reach their full potential. According the FDA, 85% of Americans do not consume the recommended daily intakes of the most important vitamins and minerals necessary for proper physical and mental development. More than half of American children do not get enough of vitamins D and E, while more than a quarter do not get enough calcium, magnesium or vitamin A, according to a recent Journal of Nutrition study. Hidden hunger can result in a compromised immune system, stunted physical growth, reduced mental ability, chronic disease and even death.

Moreover, algae-based foods have 10 to 100 times more **nutrient diversity** than foods made from land plants. The nutralence in Spirulina is evident when compared with terrestrial foods with the highest levels of key nutrients. Bite for bite, Spirulina has 180% more calcium than milk, 670% more protein than soy tofu, 3,100% more β-carotene than carrots, 2,200% more vitamin C than tomatoes, and 5,100% more iron than spinach. Algae based foods can provide up to 77 different macro and micronutrients, vitamins, trace elements and over 200 bioactive compounds. Plant-based foods are afflicted with hidden hunger and generally provide only a small fraction of nutrient diversity delivered by algae.

Bioactive compounds are produced in plants as secondary metabolites. These are not essential for the daily functioning of the plant, such as growth, but play a significant role in competition, defense, repair, attraction and signaling. The plant's bioactive compounds pass the bioactive benefits to the consumer, which may be another plant, animal or human. These substantial benefits are covered in later chapters.

Izabela Michalak and Katarzyna Chojnacka at the Department of Advanced Material Technologies, Wrocław University of Technology, Poland, published an excellent article describing the diversity of bioactive compounds that algae produces. Bioactive compounds provide both protection from health threats, (viruses and bacteria), as well as treatments. Algae produce pigments, such as carotenoids, (carotene, xanthophyll), chlorophylls and phycobilins, (phycocyanin, phycoerythrin). These pigments contain a variety of antibacterial, antiviral, antifungal, antioxidative, anti-inflammatory, and antitumor properties. Algae manufacture large quantities of antioxidants, polyphenols, tocopherols, vitamins and mycosporine-like amino acids that provide vital cellular protection and repair.

Eating high-nutrient foods is a waste of energy if the nutrients are not **bioavailable** for absorption in body tissues. A major problem with many nutraceutical supplements in pills, bars or shakes is that the nutrients are not bioavailable, and they cannot or do not pass through the intestinal wall. Algae cells are tiny, 5 μ, and flow through the intestinal wall easily. Plant cells are 2 to 20 times larger, and many nutrients may not be absorbed by the body at all. Algae foods may require pre-processing to break down strong cell walls in order to achieve high bioavailability.

Validity – Real or fake claims?

Validity is critical in the algae industry. Scientists use various forms of validity to determine whether something is true or not. Unfortunately, many claims about algae are exaggerated and invalid. The Algae Biomass Organization chartered the Technical Standards Committee with Lieve Laurens, (Chair), Keith Cooksey, Jim Spears, Craig Behnke, Amha Belay, and others. The committee examines valid metrics and creates a biannual report; Industrial Algae Measurements.

Several types of validity are used for different purposes. **Predictive validity** measures how close a prediction was to the actual event. My predictions in the previous chart, "Algae bioproducts market share in 20 years," will be determined to be correct or not by phycology and food technology scientists in 2040.

Construct validity evaluates the degree to which an assessment measures what it claims. Nutralence provides a good example of construct validity. Nutralence is a new construct in food science because it was only invented in 2011 to explain the nutritional attributes of algae that are different from land plants or meat. Several years of testing algae based foods, biofeeds, and biofertilizers will determine the degree to which this nutralence construct serves as a valid measure. Scientists often tweak new constructs around the edges to make them better.

Face validity measures the extent to which an assessment is subjectively viewed as covering the concept it purports to measure. It refers to the transparency or relevance of a metrics as it appears to those who use it. An example is a NASA analysis that concluded that one kg of the algae food, Spirulina, contains more nutrients than an assortment of 1,000 kg of fruits and vegetables. The fact that this claim resides on several hundred web-sites does not improve its face validity, or its credibility. It appears on its face, to be an exaggeration. Mahasin Tadros, at Alabama A&M University, who wrote the article did not explain how he came to his ebullient conclusion.

The only way the 1:1000 metric works is to divide by zero. He may have compared the substantial number of bioactive compounds and enzymes in Spirulina to all the land plants that contain none of those specialized compounds. He could have reported that one kg Spirulina exceeded a million kg of vegetables and fruits, but that would undermine the face validity. Who would believe such an extreme metric?

Summary

The extraordinary nutralence algae provide serves as the springboard for algae's contribution to agriculture and world food. Neither terrestrial plants nor animal products provide more than a minute fraction of the nutralence algae delivers. Modern industrial foods lack nutrient density and nutrient diversity. As a result, current foods impose nutrient dilution and hidden hunger on people, creating the costly and painful epidemic of obesity, diabetes, heart and many follow-on diseases.

Modern foods provide practically no bioactive compounds because they have been hybridized, (or genetically engineered), to maximize produce yield, with a metric for weight; not nutrient quality, density, diversity or bioactive compounds. Without sufficient nutrients or bioactive compounds, more than 70% of US consumers eating the "western diet" are overweight or obese. Substantial biomedical and clinical evidence suggests that chronic overconsumption of a foods consisting high levels of sugars and fats, but low in nutrients results in obesity. Algae foods provide superior food low in fat but nutrient dense.

Algae can produce healthier protein and other nutrients many times faster than terrestrial crops. Algae offers the unique advantage of nutrient cycling, which not only preserves increasingly scarce natural resources, but also reduces the cost of production for farmers. While algae deliver healthier food, this incredible plant can clean and repair, rather than degrade and pollute ecosystems.

The next section examines the unique attributes that will enable single-celled organisms to boost global food production.

2. What makes Single Celled Organisms Special?

The whole of science is no more than a refinement of everyday thinking.   *– Albert Einstein*

Ana knows that tiny single-celled organisms have extraordinary properties. Her favorite, algae, is the mother of all land plants. Terrestrial plants, with roots, evolved from algae about 500 million years ago. Algae comes in all shapes and sizes from tiny to macro. Some algae species group and form communities of single cells that are visible to the naked eye.

Ana wears her passion

Typical microalgae cells measure only about 5 microns across, (0.00004 inches). They are similar in size to a human red blood cell, or about 1/15th the diameter of a human hair. Algae display beautiful colors, textures and shapes when viewed under a microscope. Some microalgae aggregate in colonies that form chains or groups. Other microalgae, such as Spirulina, create colonies of single cells that string together and are visible to the eye.

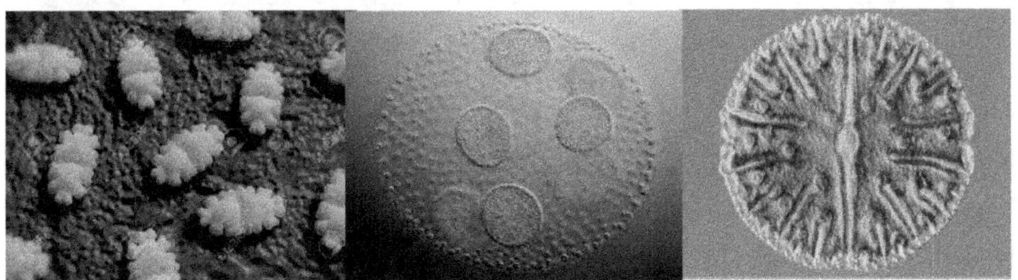

Algae nano cells under a microscope

Even though algae are tiny, each day algae produce 70% of the world's oxygen, far more than all the forests and fields combined. Algae grow so fast that each day they produce 40% of the new biomass.

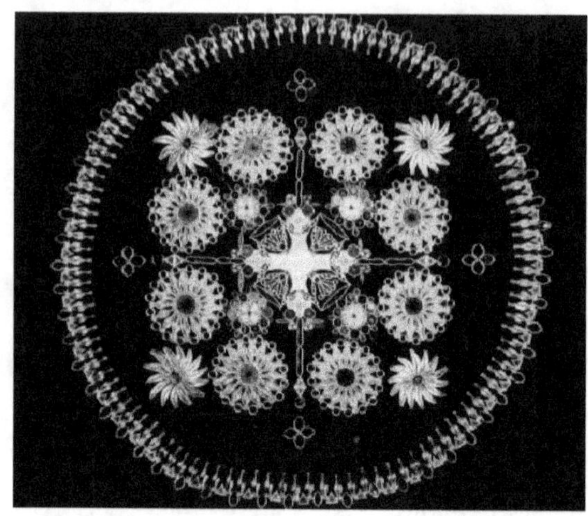

Algae are beautiful. British biologist Klaus Kemp is one of the last practitioners of the Victorian art of diatom arrangement, (at left). Diatoms are single-celled organisms found in oceans all over the world. There are estimated to be 100,000 species of these micron-sized creatures. They play a crucial role as one of the main food sources for marine organisms, including fish, mollusks and tunicates, such as sea squirts. The New York Times hosts a beautiful video on diatom art.

Algae offer the highest **nutralence** – nutrient density, diversity and bioavailability – of any plant or animal. High nutralence makes algae so attractive that nearly every animal on earth eats algae, from the tiniest shrimp, krill to the massive great blue whale. A 3-gram algae serving of algae provides the equivalent of at least one 3.5-oz serving of common vegetables or fruits, plus about 2 grams of protein – far higher nutralence than other plant foods, animal meat, or fish.

Phycology, the study of algae, includes the study of prokaryotic forms known as blue-green algae or cyanobacteria. Terrestrial algae live in or on soils and others live in symbiosis with lichens, corals and sponges. The basic single-celled organism, algae, has the general appearance illustrated below. The University of Montreal, U.C. Berkeley, University of Texas and others host culture collections of algae samples for sale and offer descriptive details and pictures.

Eukaryotic green algae, (Greek for "true nut") plants have cells with their genetic material organized in organelles. They create discrete structures with specific functions and have a double membrane-bound nucleus or nuclei. The prokaryotic cells of blue-green algae, cyanobacteria, contain no nucleus, cell walls or other membrane-bound organelles.

What makes Single Celled Organisms Special?

The following graphic shows the powerhouse behind an algae biofactory – photosynthesis in each cell.

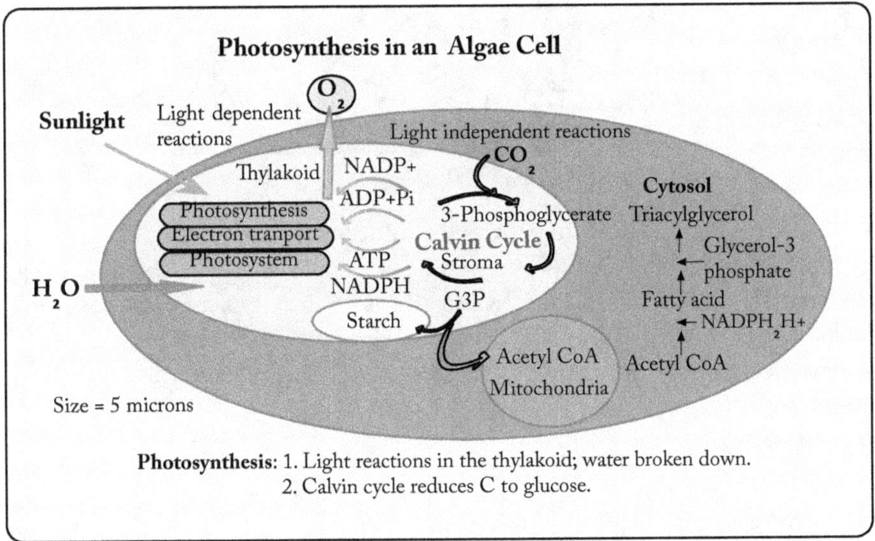

Algae Cellular Biofactory

The major groups of algae have been distinguished traditionally on the basis of pigmentation, shape, structure, cell wall composition, flagellar characteristics and products stored. Algae display so many variations, even within each species, that they express exceptions to nearly every classification rule.

Algae can be such lively little critters that some scientist consider them animals. Many can swim such as dinoflagellates that have little whip-like structures called flagella which pull or push them through the water. Some algae squish part of their body forwards and crawl along solid surfaces.

Other species are made of fine filaments with cells joined from end to end. Some clump together to form colonies while others float independently. Seaweeds may grow in nearly any shape such as cones, tubes, filaments, circles or may imitate the shape of land plants. Seaweeds developed in parallel evolution with land plants.

Major steps in cell complexity occurred with the evolutionary progression from a virus to bacterium and then from the prokaryotic cells of bacteria to the eukaryotic cells of algae. Cell walls enable algae to protect itself from the surrounding environment, typically water and pressure, called osmotic pressure.

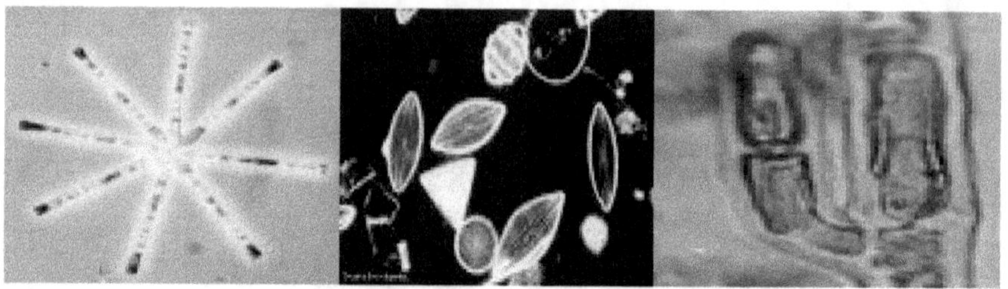

Algae Cell Walls

Cell walls regulate osmotic pressure produced by water trying to flow in or out of the cell through its semi-permeable membranes due to a differential in the solution concentrations. Algae typically possess cell walls constructed of cellulose, glycoproteins and polysaccharides, while some species have a cell wall composed of silicic, (silicon) or alginic acid.

Red algae, for example, are a large group of about 10,000 species of marine algae, including seaweed. These include coralline algae, which live symbiotically with corals, secrete calcium carbonate and play a major role in building coral reefs. Red algae such as dulse *(Palmaria palmata)* and laver (nori/gim) are a traditional part of European and Asian cuisine and are used to make other products such as agar, carrageenans and many food ingredients.

The broad algae classification includes:

Bacillariophyta – diatoms	Cyanobacteria – blue-green
Charophyta – stoneworts	Dinophyta – dinoflagellates
Chlorophyta – green algae	Phaeophyta – brown algae
Chrysophyta – golden algae	Rhodophyta – red algae

Oxygen and nitrogen

Green algae evolved with chloroplasts, which enables photosynthesis and enhances available O_2 in the atmosphere. *Prochlorococcus*, a blue-green alga, is among the smallest organisms on earth at 0.6 microns, (millionths of a meter), but is one of the most abundant organisms on the planet. A single drop of water may contain more than 100,000 of these single-celled organisms. Trillions of these minute cells make up invisible forests and provide about half the photosynthesis in the oceans.

Even though all algae species combined represent only 0.5% of total global biomass by weight, algae produce about 70% of the net global production of oxygen on Earth – more than all the forests and fields combined. Algae use nitrogen to manufacture amino acids, nucleic acids, chlorophyll and other nitrogen compounds. Cyanobacteria are able to fix nitrogen absorbed from the air, as well as from water, in a process known as diazotrophy. Since the atmosphere is nearly 80% nitrogen, nitrogen fixing is a strong competitive advantage for growth because water-based nitrogen is often limited.

Diatoms, stoneworts and dinoflagellates

Nitrogen fixing also means that algae biomass has significant value as a low energy input, high nitrogen fertilizer. Algae fixes nitrogen naturally without added energy. About 90% of the cost of commercial synthetic fertilizers comes from the energy used to extract nitrogen from the air.

Algae, often called microscopic phytoplankton, grow in most bodies of water, moist places, on and in trees and even in rocks. This little plant provides the foundation for the marine food chain, feeding both microbial and animal plankton; zooplankton. Subtract algae and phytoplankton from the water column and fish, shellfish, reptiles and many other aquatic creatures could not survive.

Algae History, Tiny Mighty Al

Tiny Mighty Al shares the story of how this 3.5-billion-year-old single-celled alga saved our planet not once, but twice. First, Al ate the predominately CO_2 atmosphere and burped enough O_2 to support life on earth. After supplying the oxygen, our planet lacked food. Al became the favored food for every plant and animal. Algae became the #1 snack for dinosaurs and all their relatives. They in turn, fossilized into coal and oil. What was algae to do, faced with a world where everyone around them was a predator?

Algae created a brilliant strategy. The tiny plant learned to grow faster than its predators could eat. Although human history is very short compared with algae, but no humans have employed a smarter survival strategy than algae. In fact, nearly every military strategy throughout recorded history can be found in algae behavior on offense as predators or on defense, as the hunted. Algae have invested 3.5 billion years of evolutionary opportunity to develop very clever survival strategies.

Algae history provides fascinating insight. Algae evolved in ancient oceans, estuaries and puddles where extreme electrical storms, temperature spikes and drought were common occurrences. When conditions were good, early algae thrived. When the local ecosystem became unstable, algae learned to go dormant.

Algae are extremely adaptable because they either adapted to the hostile conditions they encountered on early earth or they died. Algae did adapt and found a home in nearly every niche microclimate on earth. Algae can be found thriving in crusts and lichens on the hottest deserts, in and around active volcanoes, and in the boiling water of geothermal geysers. Algae grow under the polar ice caps, on and in mountaintop glaciers and they ride on ocean icebergs.

Our ancestor's attraction for the sweet taste of algae may have played a significant role in our becoming human. Strategically placed evidence on our tongue provides a fascinating clue that science has so far missed. Our pre-human ancestors made a significant, possibly accidental decision to ingest algae. Algae nutrients, especially long-chained fatty acids, omega-3s, may have led to the evolution our large brain and enabled *Homo sapiens* to evolve, thrive and rise to the top of the food chain.

Brain enlargement differentiates *Homo sapiens* from our ancestors. Our pre-human ancestors evolved from chimpanzees around 8 million years ago (mya) but very little happened to the brain for the first 6 million years. About 2 mya, brain enlargement began and by 1.5 mya, the humanoid brain was three times the size of chimpanzees. What happened to our ancestors during this half a million years of evolution? Humanoids survived their first million years with larger brains before cooking fires or hunting weapons were invented.

Rather than moving up the food chain to hunt and eat game meat, early hominids' first step may instead have been down the food chain where they ingested algae in their drinking water.

A hominoid tribe on the lee side of an algae lake may have ingested several grams of algae daily in their drinking water, similar to the algae matt on the right. These few grams of algae would have acted as a natural food supplement to supply the essential nutrients, vitamins and antioxidants, especially omega-3s that provided the green spark for brain enlargement.

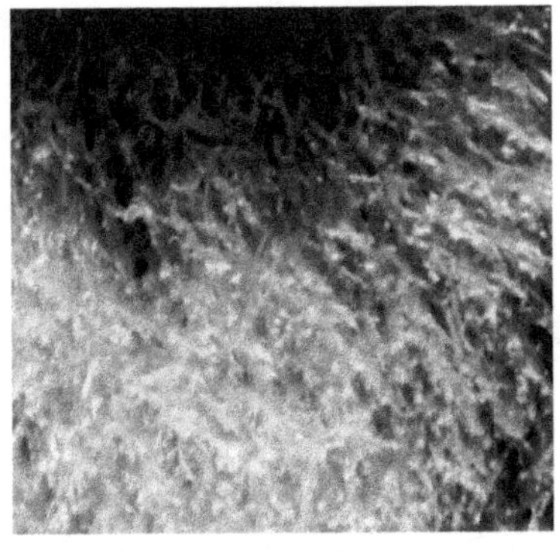

Proof for this theory lies on the human tongue, which has specialized taste bud receptors for a fifth taste – umami. Umami is a savory flavor constituent found in some protein-rich foods, especially algae.

First convenience food?

Algae provided our ancestors with the original convenience food. Terrestrial foods were dry, hard, bitter and starchy. Land plants were difficult and risky to gather. Stealth predators were better at stealth than our ancestors were at gathering. Algae offered a fresh, soft, delicious sweet taste that was unavailable in land-based foods.

Early humans probably rubbed algae oil on their skin for sun protection. Algae add moisture and speeds the recovery from wounds, burns and bruises. Algae's high antioxidant activity protects the skin from inflammatory reactions and sun damage. Pacific Rim societies have used algae for natural foods and remedies for centuries because they are effective. Organic chemists, biologists, and scientists are developing new anti-inflammatory, anti-viral and anti-cancer medicines from algae.

As early humans migrated out of Africa, they followed coastlines where sea vegetables – were plentiful. At low tide, hominids could harvest algae easily and dry it quickly in the sun.. Algae foods and algae eaters – water plants, fish and reptiles – in local aquatic ecosystems were easily accessible. In many locations, algae were harvestable year-round, which would have been a tremendous advantage when terrestrial crops were dormant. Dried algae were light and probably served as the first wampum in trade, because it was easily transportable. Algae wampum offered a side benefit; a hungry trader could eat the product.

White lichen, Manna?

Algae may have a Biblical history too. Aglae101 posts suggest that the "manna" of the wandering Israelites in the *Bible* may have been Spirulina and lichen, an alga - fungi symbiant. The product appeared miraculously each morning on rocks with the dew, where it was harvested by the women.

Women made a flour and cooked flatbread. Manna was described as tasting "like wafers made with honey." This is consistent with the taste of Spirulina scrapped off hot rocks, (that have cooled). Algae's extraordinary history contains many fascinating elements, but algae's future promises to be even more captivating.

The Aztecs used algae for food, medicine, trade and religious ceremonies. Indigenous people along coastlines or lakes have harvested natural stands of algae for millennia for use as food, feed, medicines and trade. Algae probably protected our ancestors against many diseases including scurvy, xerophthalmia, (blindness from vitamin A deficiency), goiter, arthritis, diabetes, mental retardation and others. Many indigenous societies have used algae for medical purposes for centuries because these natural remedies were safe and effective.

Abundance growing methods leverage an array of elements from algae's growth strategy, especially direct nutrient absorption and growth speed. Direct nutrient absorption allows abundance growing methods to recover and repurpose nutrients from air, water and even solid waste streams. Of course, the solids need to be pulverized before algae can absorb the nutrients. Fast growth allows abundance farmers to grow high nutralent foods substantially faster than industrial agriculture methods.

Single-cell growth advantage

Algae are aquatic microscopic plants with chlorophyll-a and a single-cell body not differentiated into roots, stems or leaves. Algae include some photosynthetic bacteria, the cyanobacteria. Algae's photosynthetic mechanism is similar to land based plants, except they are far more efficient in converting solar energy into biomass. Algae has a very simple cellular structure, live in an aqueous environment where they have efficient access to water, CO_2 and other nutrients, and an extraordinary capacity to adapt.

Terrestrial algae have adapted to live on land, and exhibit robust growth in moist environments. Algae crusts cover global deserts and get their moisture from morning dew. Algae grow on any surface, alive or not, and grow on and in the bark of trees and the roots of plants. Legumes use algae in root nodules to harvest nitrogen from the air. Algae and fungi are symbionts in lichen. Algae supplies the pigments and food, as well as sugars, while the fungi grow on the outside and protect the algae from desiccation in the sun. Algae also grow in symbiosis with moss, coral, sponges and many aquatic animals.

The energy available to each cell constrains growth, for both single and multicellular organisms. Available nutrition dictates how much energy an organism can make using cellular metabolism to either use immediately or to store. Multicellular organisms expend roughly 85% of their energy on non-growth functions. Therefore, they have only a tiny energy reservoir, and only modest energy for growth and development.

Many unicellular organisms reproduce asexually, which can take the form of binary fusion, fragmentation or spores. They do not have to waste energy and resources on a sexual apparatus, but many can reproduce both asexually and sexually. Avoiding a sexual apparatus saves 35% of the energy over multicellular plants. Asexual reproduction allows single-celled organisms to multiply at very high rates. Corn plants create 640 seeds in its one-year of life. (Actually, corn matures in about 120 days, but grows only during the summer growing season each year). Algae can double, triple and even quadruple its biomass in a single day.

Unicellular organisms have the ability to absorb energy and nutrients by diffusion or osmosis. Almost anything makes a potential food source for a unicellular organism. This eliminates the necessity for roots, which consumes about 30% of the energy for land plants. Single-celled organisms do not waste energy finding digestible food or expending their energy on a digestive system.

Terrestrial crops such as food grains must build structures that can withstand the harsh effects of wind and rain, which saps another 10% of their energy. Unicellular organisms also have no need for circulatory or excretory systems, saving another 10% of their cellular energy.

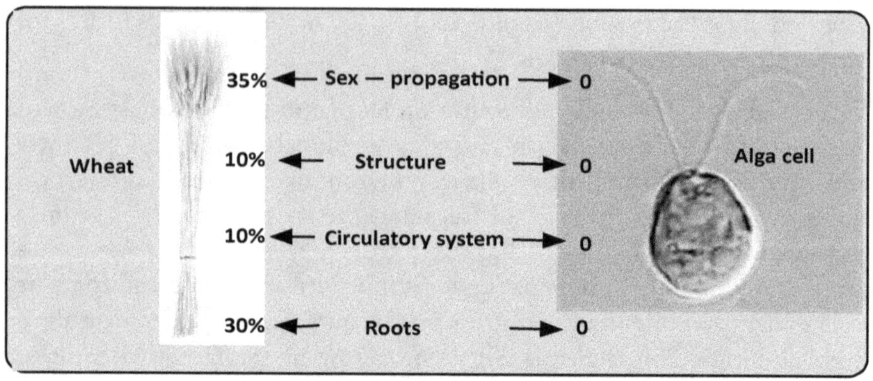

Percent of cellular energy invested in various cellular functions

Algae sustain a substantial competitive growth advantage over terrestrial plants. Algae cells waste no energy on functions that are vital to land plants, which retains all their energy for growth. In addition, nearly the entire algae biomass contains valuable nutrients.

Grain farmers must invest enormous resources to grow food grains that are more than 90% non-digestible cellulose in roots, stem, leaves and husks. Farmers harvest the fruit of the vine, typically the seeds, which is often less than 10% of the plant. In contrast, Microfarmers harvest algae that is nearly 90% food. Ash, the only non-nutritional residual in algae, accounts for less than 10% of the dry biomass.

Many green microalgae are asexual and divide by multiple fission. Most share one common feature: under optimal growth conditions, they can divide into two or more daughter cells. The number of daughter cells, also known as the division number, is relatively stable for most species, and ranges from 4 to 16.

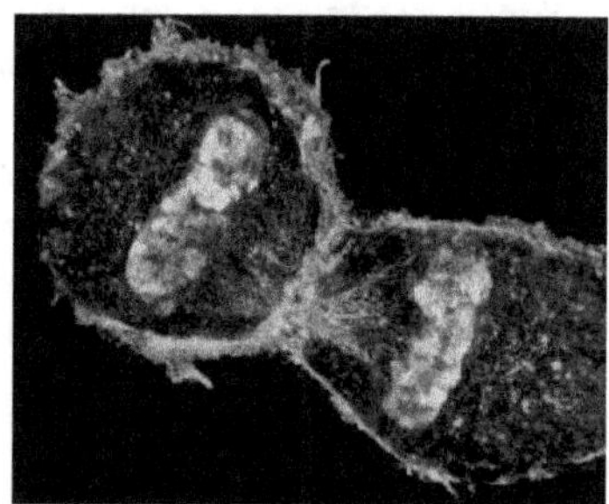

Algae fission

Light, nutrients and temperature dictate the number of daughter cells. Cells normally divide twice or three times during a single cell cycle. Cell-cycle progression starts with a period of growth, the G1 phase. During this phase, the cells increase their volume until they roughly double the volume of the daughter cell, coenobia. A coenobia is a colony of algal cells, where the cells are arranged in a constant form and number and are surrounded by a gelatinous matrix.

What makes Single Celled Organisms Special?

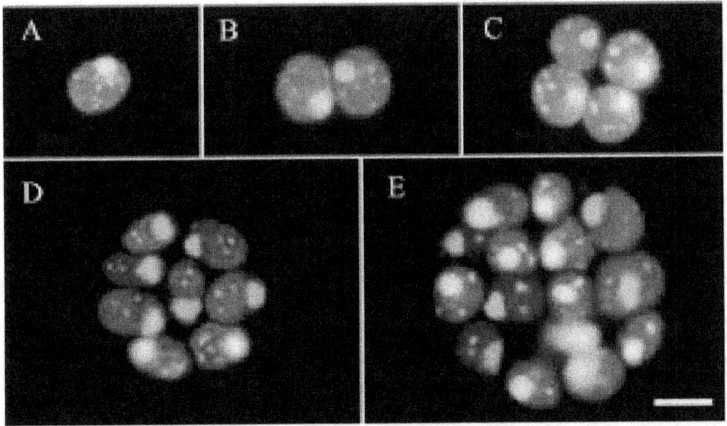

Algae can create coenobias of up to 16 daughter cells

When the cells have doubled their volume, the cell cycle approaches the commitment point (CP). When the CP is reached, the cell commits to triggering and then terminating the DNA replication–division sequence, followed by mitosis and cell division.

Scientists are actively study the CP with the plan to trigger quicker cell cycles. Another production strategy involves finding a pathway to increase the division number and create more than 16 daughter cells in each cycle. Both strategies have the potential to significantly increase algae productivity.

Algae's tiny cell size create the ideal nutrient delivery system for plants and animals. Each tiny algae cell packages the essential nutrients for multi-cellular life – plants, animals and humans. The algae nutrient packets are so small the algae nutrients are immediately bioavailable to the plant or animal.

A food grain such as corn grows primarily in one direction, up towards the sun. Algae grow in all directions, 360°, which allows considerably more freedom to multiply quickly. Terrestrial plants are locked by its roots to one location. If the nutrients available to its roots are plentiful, the plan grows. If nutrients are not within reach, the plant dies. If moisture is not within reach, the plant dies. Moisture is necessary to dissolve the nutrients for biosorption. Food crops also need microorganisms, such as algae, to break down chemical fertilizer to make the nutrients bioavailable.

Algae displays extreme biodiversity. A handful of dirt may contain several million algae cells and several hundred-different species. A cup of pond water will contain even more algae cells and more species.

Terrestrial algae thrive on land when moisture is available. They go dormant during dry times, then re-energize with rain or irrigation. Each cultivar evolved locally over eons and adapted to the unique characteristics of the *in-situ* microclimate. Most species can adapt to various microclimates, but typically thrive in the area where their ancestors have lived for millennia.

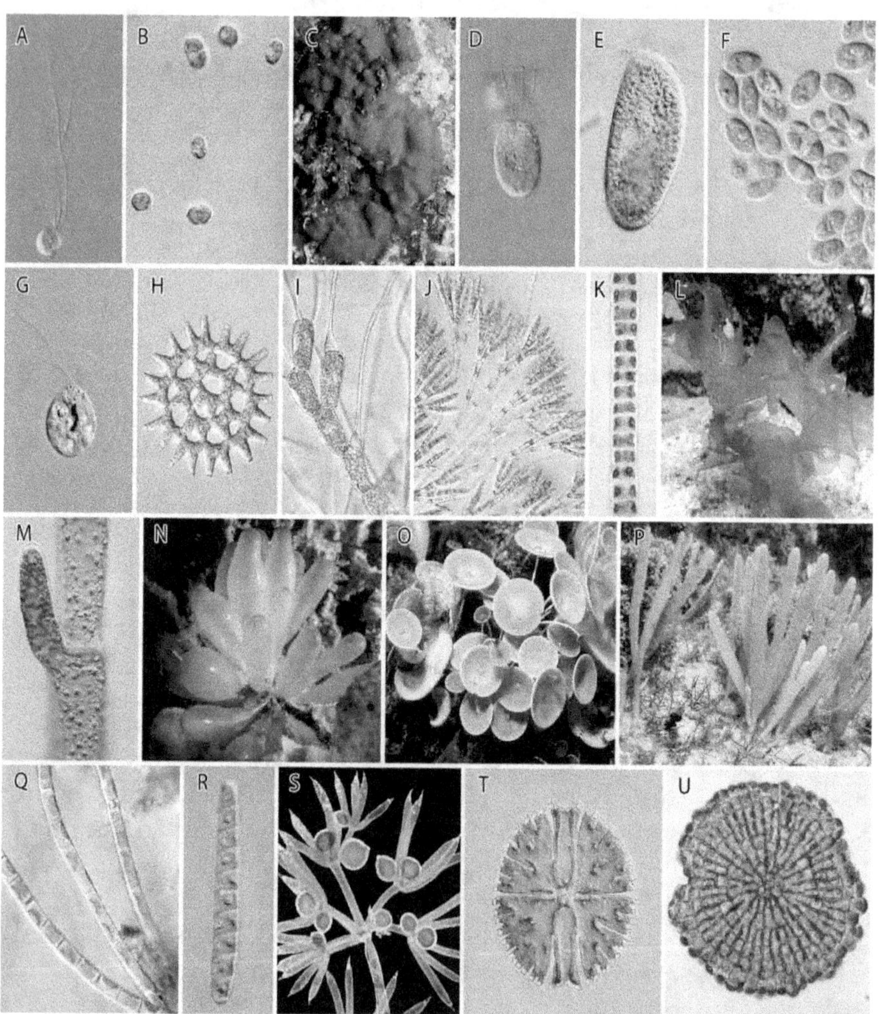

Algae grow in spectacular natural biodiversity

What makes Single Celled Organisms Special?

Algae Secrets

Algae typically do not have to move, since the nutrients flow naturally in the water to them. Algae do not need rigid structures since they are supported by water. Amazingly, algae developed the ability to swim.

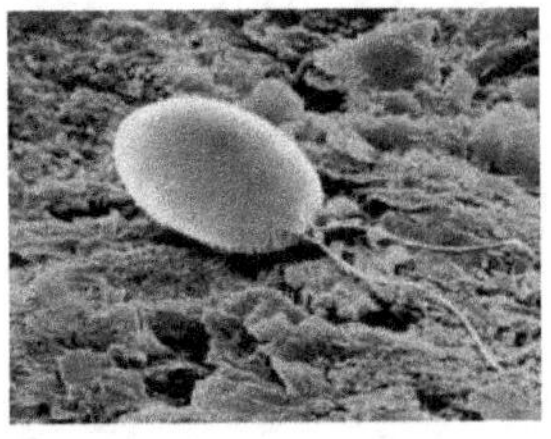

Sometimes single-celled algae grow whip-like appendages called flagella, (right), which coordinate their movements towards light for energy or to other parts of their ecosystem for nutrients. A little mobility gives them great advantage over plants with roots.

A recent discovery, published in Proceedings of the National Academy of Sciences, shows that despite their simplicity, microalgae can coordinate their flagella into leaping, trotting and even galloping gaits.

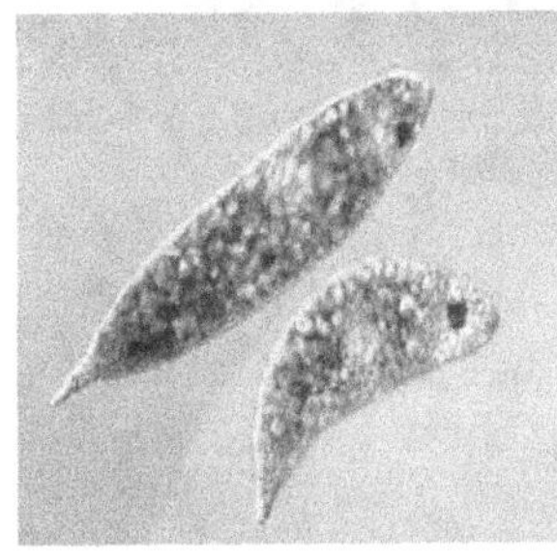

Some motile algae that can move with flagella also develop a photoreceptive organelle called an eyespot, (left). The eyespot uses the omega-3 fatty acids, DHA and EPA, to carry the signal for the light to the cell. Algae are highly light sensitive and vulnerable to photoshock with too much light. They swim away from the bright light.

The human brain uses the same omega-3 fatty acids to transfer information. Animals do not synthesize omega-3 fatty acids, they must get it from their diet. Many people take supplements labeled "fish oil," omega-3 to improve their brain function. The fatty acids do indeed come from fish, but the fish obtained their omega-3's from their diet – algae. Some algae companies are growing algae and extracting the omega-3s, which leaves millions of fish alive in the sea.

Ken-ichi Wakabayashi at the Tokyo Institute of Technology discovered that algae cells change their swimming directions upon sensing light; a response referred to as phototactic behavior. Algae's eyespot mediates light perception and allows each cell to swim in their environments for optimizing photosynthesis by swimming towards or away from light.

Single-celled organisms exhibit parsimony. They are so simple and frugal, there are very few things that can go wrong with them. Unicellular organism may miss out on some of life's higher pleasures, but they have evolved the ability to grow quickly and thrive

Algae compete for light and each cell absorbs light with pigments. Therefore, in the algae milieu, whichever algae species has the most pigments wins the competition for light, and can grow faster. All the beautiful colors in land plants and flowers are available in algae pigments, which absorb light at different parts of the sunlight spectrum. Among the advantages of algae pigments are greater color diversity and color density. Unlike commercial pigments, algae pigments provide nutralence.

Fast growth in algae cells create a challenge. The offspring tend to shade the mother cells from the light necessary to power photosynthesis. Algae have evolved several very effective adaptive strategies for acquiring enough light for photosynthesis.

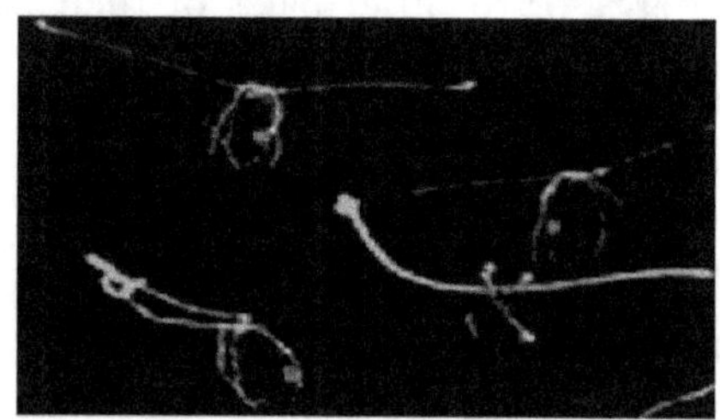

Light sensing pigments

Algae can both **adsorb** elements on their surface and then **absorb** some of those adsorbed nutrients into the cell. Some algae companies are working on a process to remove heavy metals through algae adsorption. They plan to recover the heavy metals attached to the cells before they are absorbed. This strategy could clean mine tailings and allow the company to sell the pure metals back to industry.

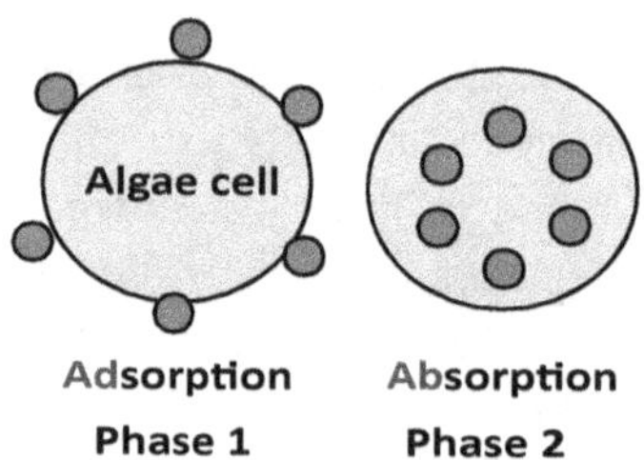

The quantity of nutrients and metals removed by absorption is usually much less than the quantity of surface adsorbed ions. Intracellular accumulation process, biosorption, takes place in two stages: first, a very rapid surface adsorption followed by a much slower intracellular diffusion or absorption. Among algae's smartest survival strategy is something land plants cannot do; go dormant in bad conditions. Desert-adapted species thrive in normal years yet survive when their moist habitats evaporate. Rather than die when conditions degrade, algae cells simply shut down metabolism and enter an inactive state.

Algae can survive on rocks as hot as 70° C, (160° F). In extreme heat stress, the naturally blue-green algae turn a frosty white cake and develop a sweet flavor, (e.g. manna). Intense heat transforms algae's 70% protein structure into polysaccharide sugars.

Summer temperatures at Arizona State University's outdoor algae production center, AzCATI, can hit 120° F, which would kill most algae. A research team found that when they placed new algae cultures in the raceways in the early morning, the cells could double before peak heat in late afternoon. The most amazing finding was that some of the new cells had already adapted to the extreme heat.

Joan Myers, a phenomenal National Geographic photographer, documents extreme environments such as ice floes and volcanoes. Her latest book, *Fire and Ice* brings to environments to life. Joan tells a fascinating story. She and a scientist were pulling cores from below the ice sheet in the 17-million-year-old Beacon Valley in Antarctica.

When they returned to the lab, they removed a million-year-old rock and cracked it open. What did they find? Dormant blue-green algae. When they added water, the algae came to life. Algae exhibit an ability to learn or adapt quickly to environmental changes. Algae survived billions of years of early earth when fierce electrical storms, temperature swings and drought were common.

Emiliania huxleyii

A team in Germany studied the tiny marine algae Emiliania huxleyii. This phytoplankton grows in groups that congeal into large floating masses and serve as food to a wide variety of fish and birds. They chose this algae because of its naturally fast reproduction rate—up to 500 generations in a single year, or more than one a day.

Algae scientists use algae's ability to adapt quickly to "train" algae with mutagenesis. DNA may be modified, either naturally or artificially, using a variety of physical, chemical and biological agents, resulting in mutations. Scientists examine the mutants to find which best express the desired characteristics. Mutation or variation breeding create crop hybrids among land plants. Successful hybridization may take a decade for land plants because they mature so slowly and then each hybrid must be tested for generations to insure it passes on the desired traits.

The team found that algae evolved quickly to survive in their rapidly changing environment, including extreme heat. The individual algae cells became smaller, but they also grew faster. This behavior suggests they might form even bigger or denser plumes in hotter oceans.

Algae produce so quickly that **mutagenesis** often yields a variety of offspring with suitable features each day. Phycologists use mutagenesis to modify algae cells for higher production of target compounds, such as specialty oils, long chains of amino acids for proteins or medically desirable ingredients. Algae can also be modified effectively with a variety of genetic engineering tools.

Some algae species, such *H. pluvialis,* react to environmental stress by metabolizing valuable oils, such as astaxanthin. The cells spontaneously produce the oil to protect itself from too much sunlight. Astaxanthin can significantly reduce free radicals and oxidative stress and help the human body maintain a healthy state. Astaxanthin provides healthy oils to animal feeds and gives the beautiful pinkish-red color to farmed salmon, shrimp and shellfish.

James Umen at the Danforth Plant Science Center discovered that algae can signal their community. Some species have evolved the ability for "nutrient sensing" to control growth and lipid metabolism.

The team found that one signal is tuned to match the cell growth rate with nutrient levels in the environment. The other system involves proteins that produce small phosphorylated molecules that are thought to act as intracellular signals. By altering the intracellular signaling, the team has increased oil yields. Algae signaling may make algae better oil producers.

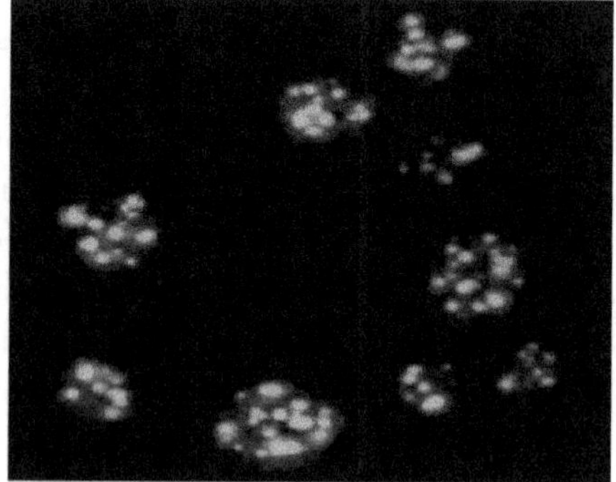

Algae cells containing oil droplets

Algae metabolize nutrients into many bioproducts and store energy in the form of oils, proteins and carbohydrates. The oil is valuable for food, feed, biofuels and nutraceuticals. Algae producers can grow algae and harvest the Omega-3 fatty acids, which is fish-free fish oil.

Algae must compete for sunlight. They use an ingenious go-to-light strategy by manufacturing oil, which is lighter than water and makes the cell buoyant. Some algae species make 80% oil in their biomass, but they grow very slowly. Many varieties make oil at about 20% of their biomass. Algae biologists like Andrew Ayers in Arizona have trained algae to double and even triple their oil composition.

Rich Michod, a University of Arizona evolutionary biologist discovered that algae display altruism. He noted that, "You don't need a brain or nervous system to be cooperative." When stressed with heat, some algae species go into a programmed death spiral. Darwin's natural selection theory posits that nature is raw in tooth and claw, with competition driving everything. Instead of competing, algae cooperate.

Some algae cells act altruistically and commit suicide so that others in their community can live. They chop up their DNA in a regular pattern called DNA laddering. This programmed cell death provides life-saving food for other algae cells in their community. Algae show that cooperation is fundamental to the diversity of life. Mochod believes that programmed cell death in single cells may be a precursor to multi-cellular life.

Land plants cannot fix nitrogen from the air. Legumes claim that talent, but closer inspection reveals that the modules on the roots of alfalfa, soy beans, lentils and peanuts that fix N_2 are filled with cyanobacteria. The blue-green algae, cyanobacteria have the ability to fix both CO_2 and N_2, from the air or water. Fixation of N_2 comes at a high metabolic energy cost, but cyanobacteria are phototrophic organisms that use sunlight to fulfill their energy demand.

Nitrogen fixation bacteria in the soil produce nitrogenase enzymes to pull N_2 from the air and transform it to plant bioavailable NH_3. The ammonia is subsequently converted to nitrate by other bacteria in the soil so that it can be used by plants. Algae biofertilizer offer a sustainable approach to synthesizing ammonia by allowing the crops to do the work. Algae biofertilizer will revolutionize agricultural fertilizer production providing a sustainable solution that cycles nutrients and reduces production costs, waste and pollution. Farmers will benefit from algae biofertilizer with higher crop yields and better quality produce.

Miracle compounds

Algae evolved in so many different competitive environments that the organisms built incredibly sophisticated defensive shields. Imagine each algae cell trying to survive and grow surrounded by a milieu of predators trying to eat it and billions of bacteria, viruses, molds and other microorganisms trying to use it as a host. Algae had to figure out how to become inhospitable to all the infective agents. As a result of eons of natural evolution, algae contain more valuable medical bioactive compounds than any other plant.

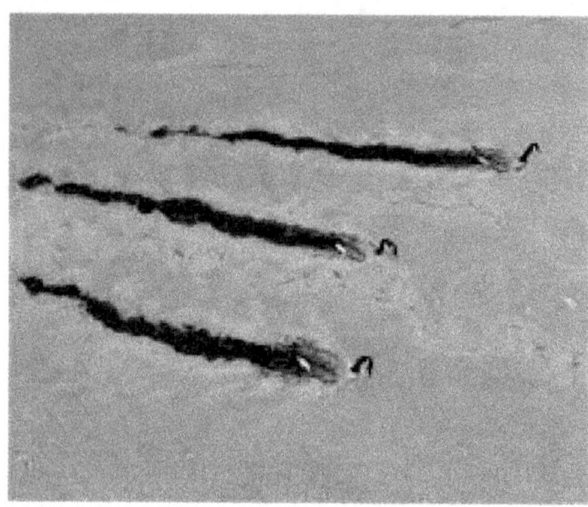

Algae growing on a pond may look tranquil, (left). The algae provide lots of oxygen and great food for ducks and other aquatic life. Under the surface, the teaming microorganisms fight millions of pitched battles for survival. Hungry predators attack, parasitoids and viruses search for hosts. Millions of microbes fortify their defense.

Algae contain bioactive substances like polysaccharides, proteins, lipids and polyphenols. Bioactive compounds include antibacterial, antiviral, anticancer and antifungal properties, as well as many others. These compounds not only improve algae's own defenses but pass those capabilities on to the animal or plant that consumes algae.

Macroalgae – sea vegetables

Algae form unicellular, colonies, filamentous groups and multicellular communities, such as sea vegetables, that can grow to 90 meters. Seaweeds or sea vegetables are macroalgae that make up about 10% of all algae species. Sea vegetables have pseudo stems and leaves that are tough enough to absorb the pounding of the surf. Similar to microalgae, macroalgae have no circulatory or digestive system, and no roots. Some species have a tiny holdfast, to anchor them to rocks, and protect them from raging tides and surf.

Giant kelp is harvested as a source of algin, an emulsifying and binding agent used in the production of many foods and cosmetics, like ice cream, toothpaste and cereals. More than 95% of global sea vegetable production, (approximately 21 million metric tons a year) is farmed.

Beautiful sea vegetables

Monterrey Aquarium studies demonstrate that the majestic giant California kelp forest, (right) grows faster than tropical bamboo, 10 to 12 inches a day in natural stands. Under good cultivation conditions, giant kelp can grow up to two feet each day.

Production occurs primarily in the Asian Pacific rim. Sea vegetable compounds today improve thousands of human food products, especially ingredients such as agar-agar, carrageenan and alginates. Sea vegetable phytochemical compounds are extensively used in food, textiles, dairy, paper industry and confectionary. Sea vegetable extracts are an important component of biostimulants known for their richness in polysaccharide, minerals and vitamins. Phycologists are studying and cultivating sea vegetables for food, feed, nutraceuticals, cosmeceuticals, medicines and other valuable bioproducts. They provide a source of dietary minerals such as sodium, potassium, iodine, as well as fiber. Sea vegetable supplementation has gained popularity to improve the taste, color and texture of foods.

Sodium alginate from sea vegetables is used in culinary physics, or molecular gastronomy, at some of the best restaurants in the world. Molecular gastronomy investigates the physical and chemical ingredient transformations that occur while cooking. The study includes the social, artistic and technical components of culinary and gastronomic phenomena such as spherification of juices and other liquids. Sodium alginate is combined with calcium lactate to create spheres of liquid surrounded by a thin jelly membrane. High-end restaurants present these spheres with different internal liquids for cocktails, appetizers, side dishes and desserts.

Path forward

Can Ana feed our world by 2040? Transforming food production from unsustainable to sustainable will require some heavy lifting. The bio-machine that makes this revolution possible is so tiny, it cannot be seen with the naked eye. These tiny single-celled organisms have evolved to mighty, thanks to the eons of advancement by single-celled organisms.

Possibly their signature skill may save mankind from wars, pestilence and hunger. Algae are endowed with a miraculous ability found in no other plant – to recover and recycle nutrients.

Food supplied by modern industrial agriculture is built on a foundation of fossil resources. It is sustainable only as long as those resources are available and affordable. Several fossil resources will go extinct in the next generation. What will our children do for food?

No, Ana cannot save modern industrial agriculture (MIA), from itself. MIA consumes far too many nonrenewable resources, uses them very inefficiently, and only once. The residuals leak to create massive waste streams that erode, degrade and pollute not only its own ecosystems, but the air and water for millions of people.

The FAO projects that our global food supply will need to double by 2050, to close the gap between food supply and demand. The earth simply has too little remaining fertile soil, fresh water, fossil fuels, fertilizer, (especially P), and ag chemicals to sustain current production.

Several models predict MIA will crash around 2040, give or take one-half a generation. The well-researched Lloyds of London analysis predicts that "A systemic shock to global food production will have acute economic, political and social impacts, including food price rises, food riots, and substantial disruption to economic markets." Nations and states have gone to war many times of food and resources. History will repeat unless Ana delivers miraculous solutions.

Two critical factors that are not included in the models that predict an impending food supply crash also deserve serious consideration; monocultures and mono-farmers. Monocultures put the entire food supply at risk and mono-farmers defeat social justice.

Monocultures

The severe threat of monocultures to the global food supply are a direct result of GMO crops. The value proposition for GMO crops seemed too good to be true as they became available in 1996. Monsanto promised these weed and pest resistant seeds would revolutionize industrial agriculture by improving crop yields while reducing the need for cultivation, fertilizers, pesticides and herbicides.

None of these promises have been realized. In addition, the EWG discovered GMO crops actually require more fossil resources, including water, fertilizer and pesticides with no productivity increase.

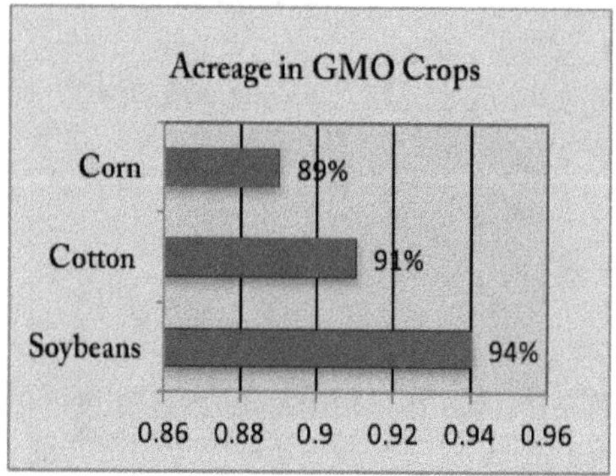

Monocultures, cultivation of a single crop over a large area, puts the entire food supply at risk. Twenty years ago, there were no GMO seeds. Now US farmers plant 9 out of 10 acres in GMO crops. Many weeds and pests have developed resistance to GMOs, making farming problematic.

The severe risk from GMO crops stems from the fact that farmers are forced to grow monocultures. GMO crops are monocultures because the incredibly high cost of acquiring FDA approval for GMO seeds means that only a single cultivar is approved. Farmers can increase profitability dramatically with monocultures. But the short run advantage may be outweighed by intermediate term risk of catastrophic crop failure. Large plantings of homogeneous crops enable parasites – bacteria, viruses, fungi and insects – to specialize on one specific host, increasing the chance they will mutate into a more pathogenic form. Farmers tend to choose the same crop cultivated by neighboring farms because of efficiency gains (e.g. spraying, cultivation and harvesting). The same crop in the next field makes it easier for a disease to spread – quickly. A single pest vector could abruptly wipe out an entire crop over a huge area. Food security depends on crop diversity.

A 2016 National Academies of Sciences, Engineering, and Medicine, (NAS), study examined the economic, agronomic, health, safety, or other impacts of genetically modified organisms, crops and food. The empirical research examines both the benefits and risks of GMO crops. The NAS posted an excellent video summary.

The health risks from GMO crops are extensive, including allergens, pesticide residues, carcinogens and others, which are covered by the Environmental Working Group (EWG). Two of the nation's most respected experts on pesticides and children's health called for the FDA to require mandatory labeling on GMO food. Titled *GMOs, Herbicides, and Public Health*, Landrigan and Benbrook examine the widespread adoption of GMO crops, resulting explosion in the use of toxic herbicides. These poisons pose extreme risk to human health, especially pregnant mothers and children. They argue that labeling GMO foods is critical for protecting public health.

Mono-farmers

Crop scientists have known for decades that plant diversity provides many benefits for the soil and for crops. Social scientists have proven that diversity in any industry provides a host of benefits.

Industrial agriculture cannot approach food justice unless women are empowered to grow crops. The challenge of allowing women access to food production is a global issue, but the US may display the ugliest metric on women and farming at only 7%.

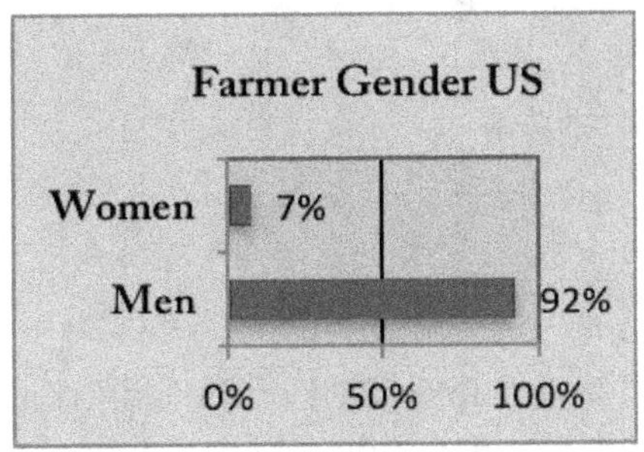

The 2012 Census of Agriculture revealed that more than 92% of the 2.1 million US farmers are non-Hispanic, white men. In Iowa, the second largest producing agriculture state, 99.3% of farmers are non-Hispanic white men. Women own only 7% of U.S. farmland and account for only 3% of sales. Not only do US farmers discriminate against women, but also against young people and non-white men. In 2012, the average farmer in American was 58.3 years old.

Dependence on fossil resources

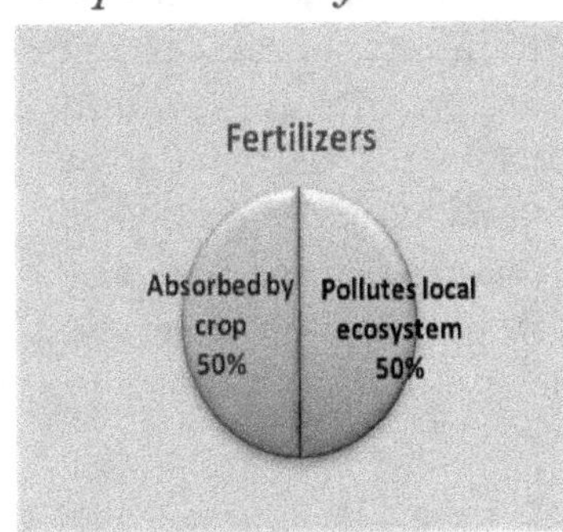

MIA cannot produce food economically without massive consumption of fossil resources that are inefficiently used once, and then replaced. Fertilizers are expensive and often represent 35% of a farmer's cost.

Yet, fertilizers are used very inefficiently, as only about half is absorbed by the crop. The other 50% pollutes air, water and soil. MIA's total dependence on fossil resources makes global societies vulnerable to a food crash. A food production system built on a foundation of fossil resources cannot sustain itself.

MIA has already consumed too much fertile soil, fresh water, fossil fuels, fertilizers and agricultural chemicals. More than a third of all raw materials and fossil fuels consumed in the US are used in animal production. Producing a single hamburger uses enough fuel to drive 20 miles and causes the loss of five times its weight in topsoil. It takes more than 2,400 gallons of water to produce one pound of meat and only 25 gallons to produce one pound of wheat.

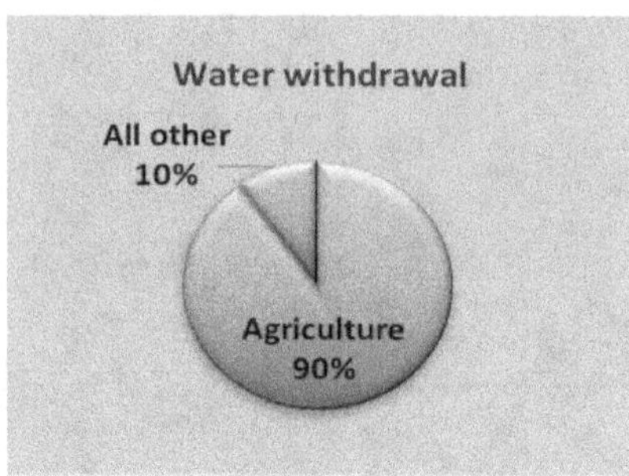

While billions of people struggle to get sufficient freshwater for daily needs, MIA consumes 90% of global freshwater. MIA needs far more freshwater to increase production, but there are no drops to spare. Many critical aquifers globally and in the US will be extinct by 2040.

MIA produces 24% of the all greenhouse gas emissions and creates smog and air pollution. The massive amounts of excrement produced by livestock farms emit toxic gases such as hydrogen sulfide and ammonia into the air. Roughly 80% of ammonia emissions in the US comes from animal waste. MIA uses 37% of earth's non-ice landmass and systemically degrades those ecosystems with erosion and pollution. Animals raised for food produce approximately 130 times as much excrement as the entire human population. Animal farms pollute our waterways more than all other industrial sources combined.

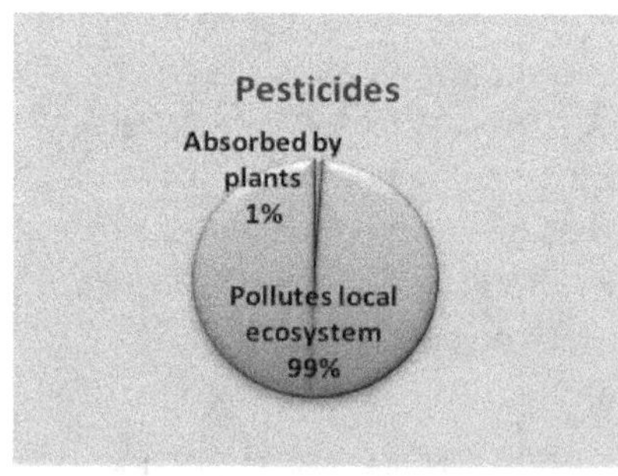

Run-off of animal waste, pesticides, chemicals, fertilizers, hormones and antibiotics are contributing to dead zones in coastal areas, degradation of coral reef and health problems. Pesticides cause havoc and impose severe health penalties on farm and rural families.

Climate chaos risk

MIA farmers face substantial risks, including economics, health, physical labor, dust, pesticides, and heavy equipment. Their largest risk, climate chaos, puts their entire farm at significant risk.

Climate Chaos Impacts

- Warmer lows
- Heat spikes
- Cold spikes
- Hot dry winds
- Heat stress
- Earlier spring
- Later fall
- Unpredictable weather
- Water scarcity
- Drought
- Faster evaporation
- Irrigation salt invasion
- Seawater salt invasion
- More water conflicts
- Drier air and wind
- Higher temperatures
- More thunderstorms
- More & fiercer storms
- New rain patterns
- Massive dust erosion
- Devastating floods
- Hot land surface
- Energetic atmosphere
- Snow pack, glacier loss
- Rivers run dry
- Amplified wildfires

Farmers have to make a full investment in their crop and pray that severe weather events, drought or pest invasions do not destroy their crop. A single storm, such as hurricane Harvey or Irma, a temperature spike or pest invasion can destroy crops. MIA ignores biodiversity and grows only a relative few different crops, often chosen because they are immune to Monsanto's Round-Up.

Crop failure that results from climate change and diminishing non-renewable resources can cause food wars. Bad weather for crops causes price spikes, fear, food riots and war. The French Revolution in 1784 ignited due to escalating food prices. *"Qu'ils mangent de la brioche,"* (Let them eat cake) uttered by Marie Antoinette, was in response to the poor demonstrating for bread to eat. Crops across Europe failed due to extreme weather from El Niño, amplified by the 1783 volcanic activity at Laki and Grímsvötn, Iceland.

The 2011 Arab Spring parallels the revolutions across Europe in 1848. The "Spring of Nations" experienced a year food riots that escalated to revolutions throughout Europe following a decade of weather that caused failed harvests. Climate chaos threatens to destroy many harvests in the near future.

A United Nations Development Program report estimates that failure to address climate change by limiting global warming from CO_2 and other GHG pollution would cause the world's gross domestic product to fall

$33 trillion. The report says that addressing global warming will save $12 trillion (about £9.6 trillion), which represents about 10% of global GDP.

Is man stupid?

Pope Francis said that political leaders and others who denied climate change reminded him of a passage from the psalms about man's stubbornness. Pope Francis was flying over the Caribbean islands devastated by Hurricane Irma when he said to journalists: "Man is stupid, the Bible said. It's like that, when you don't want to see, you don't see."

Pope Francis urged those who denied climate change, such as United States President Donald Trump, to consult scientists who had clearly determined anthropogenic climate change was real. Pope Francis warned that humanity would "go down," if global warming was not recognized and addressed. The Pope said about President Trump: "Decide and history will judge your decision."

During Mr. Trump's May 2017 visit to the Vatican, the pope gave President Trump a copy of his 2015 encyclical letter, "Laudato Si," which called for a human response to global warming, and top Vatican officials appealed to the president not to withdraw from the landmark Paris climate accord.

Devastation from Hurricanes Harvey and Irma

The 2017 severe hurricanes and wildfires did not motivate the President or Congress to address anthropogenic climate change. By more than 5 to 1, voters say the US should participate in the Paris Climate Agreement.

Cut rainforests

Farmers are both the cause and the victims of climate chaos. Farmers want to expand production. They greedily convert huge tracks of carbon-rich rain forests and savannah grasslands with biodiverse natural ecosystems to cropland. Forest-to-field conversion provides short-term crop yields, which quickly drop. It accentuates anthropogenic greenhouse gas emissions and climate forcing. MIA production, including indirect emissions associated with land-use change, accounts for about 25% of the total anthropogenic greenhouse gas emissions. Poor land management contributes to land degradation, further reducing soil and water productivity. Globally, the land used, abused and abandoned is about equal to the land in use for MIA today.

Degradation risk

Systemic cultivation, nutrient extraction, chemical fertilizers, pesticides and poisons degrade and eventually destroy cropland and neighboring ecosystems. Food crops systematically extract humus and nutrients from the soil, seriously degrading cropland over multiple harvests.

The International Food Policy Research Institute reports that each year an estimated 20 million hectares, (50 million acres) of cropland worldwide are abandoned due to soil erosion, irrigation salts and exhausted soil. The USDA estimates 5 million cropland acres must be abandoned and go fallow in the US each year due to exhausted soil. Abandoned land is referred to as dead because it lacks the rich microbial communities and humus. Algae biofertilizers can perform a miracle by restoring fertility and bringing dead soil back to life.

Water risk

Producing food grains to feed animals for meat requires 100 times more water than producing food for vegetarians. Meat production consumes 1,000 times more freshwater than using protein from algae. Algae do not require freshwater or arable land to grow, maximizing resources that can be used for additional food production or other cash crops. The water saved can be traded to serve thirsty people in urban markets. Numerous sources predict future wars will be fought over water. Wars are not a difficult prediction because history from tree rings proves the relationship between water and war.

Food and war

Failed harvests destroy food supplies and cause people to get angry. Those angry, hungry people staged food riots and insurgencies that toppled governments across North Africa in 2011. The UN Refugee Agency calculates that more than **65 million people,** the largest number in human history, are now either refugees or internally displaced due to conflict or poverty. Conflict, migration and drought are tightly interwoven. Drought contributes to conflict, which leads to poverty, displacement, migration and more war.

Add to the 65 million hungry migrants, more than 40 million Africans that are trying to survive on severely degraded or worn out land. A *New York Times* report by Jeffrey Gettleman observes that population swells, climate change, soil degradation, erosion, overgrazing, poaching and global food prices are exerting incredible pressure on African farms. Degraded land is fueling conflicts across the continent. Farmers from one destroyed area attack their neighbors, killing animals and stealing food. Land disputes are fierce and are driving farmers off their land. NASA satellite images reveal overwhelming land degradation throughout Africa. Gettleman's report does a good job describing the farmers' pain and suffering, but the pictures of dead animals and dead cropland are quite disturbing.

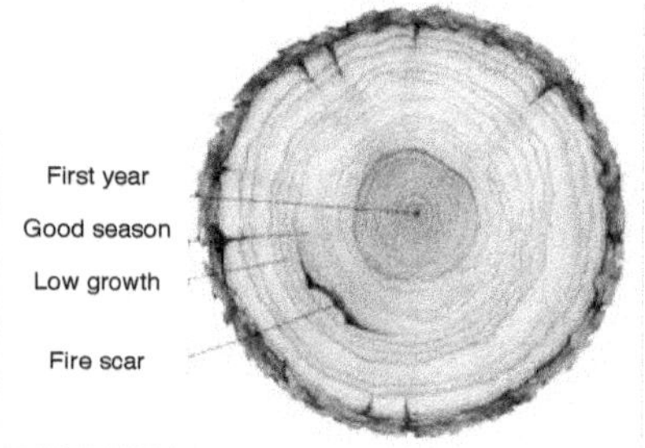

A team led by David Zhang analyzed tree rings in order to estimate the swings of temperature in China over the last 1,000 years. They reviewed 899 wars fought in China between 1000 and 1911 and found a strong correlation between warfare and temperature change.

Records showed that weather changes resulted in food price inflation, followed by war, famine and population decline. The findings suggest that worldwide price cycles in recent centuries have been driven mainly by climate change. A second team led by David Zhang examined temperature data and climate-driven economic variables during the "golden" and "dark" ages in Europe and the Northern Hemisphere during the past millennium. Their findings align with the China studies. The data indicated that climate change was the ultimate cause, and climate-driven economic downturn was the direct cause of large-scale human crises in preindustrial Europe and the Northern Hemisphere.

A series of extreme El Niño weather events in 2015–16 caused severe droughts throughout Africa, Asia and the Americas. Many countries had to import emergency food for their citizens. Much of the conflict and forced migration from North Africa is occurring now due to extended heat and drought.

Unfortunately, rising temperatures amplify drought conditions. Excess heat spawns fierce storms that destroy crops and the ag infrastructure. NASA scientists calculate the chances for a 35-year or longer "mega drought" striking the America by 2100 are above 80% if the world stays on its current trajectory of GHG emissions. This conclusion sounds eerily similar to Food System Shock predicted by Lloyds of London.

Health risk

Roughly 99% of pesticides are not absorbed by crops and pollute local ecosystems. Pesticide pollutants cause diseases of major organs, including the brain, heart, lungs, respiratory and vascular system. Dust, fertilizer, pesticides and ag chemicals make farming and living in farm communities dangerous to health. Farmers, ranchers and agricultural managers are among the top five most dangerous jobs in the US. They suffer a fatality rate of 26.7 per 100,000 workers.

Dust, pesticides and poisons make farming dangerous

Animal production, which the Bureau of Labor Statistics defines as raising and fattening animals on ranches, farms, and feedlots for eventual sale, ranked #1 in the US for injuries. Animal production experiences a serious level of 66.6 injuries per 100,000 workers. Farm workers make the most dismal jobs list because they require intense physical labor under harsh conditions – and receive very low pay.

Farmers must work long hours in all types of weather, perform heavy labor and work on and around heavy machinery. Many farmers are regularly exposed to dust, agricultural chemicals, pesticides and other poisons. Available labor for food production will decline even further as young people leave rural areas for better jobs and lifestyles in cities.

Half the world lives in urban settings now, and 75% will be urban by 2050. MIA farmers must live in rural communities, distant from cities, shopping and entertainment. Young farmers find it difficult to attract a wife. She must be willing to put up with the rigors and isolation of farm life – which requires long hours and considerable independence.

Peace microfarms using abundant methods provide solutions to reduce each farmer risk, except finding a farm wife. Farmers will have to rely on their own DNA ingenuity for attracting and sustaining a spouse.

Algae lifts MIA

How Algae can help Agriculture

	Algae's contribution
Cropland. Food production consumes about 50% of the planet's land surface globally, and about 50% in the US. Agriculture threatens to consume the remaining forest land.	Reduce by 50%
Animal production. WHO calculates that growing livestock consumes 80% of the world's total agricultural land.	Reduce by 60%
Water consumption. A recent comprehensive study, *The Water Footprint of Humanity*, reports that agriculture accounts for 92% of freshwater used globally.	Reduce by 70%
Fossil energy. The FAO reports that agriculture consumes 30% of global energy.	Reduce by 40%
Fertilizer. WHO reports that global fertilizer use is above 200 million tons, with 23 million tons in the US.	Reduce by 60%
Phosphorus. P shortages threaten food production. Less than 20% reaches food crops. Waste degrades ecosystems.	Reduce by 60%
Dead zones. Ag pollution causes 400 zones that expand 10% a decade. Eutrophication costs the US $2.2 B a year.	Reduce by 50%
Pesticides. Over 2.2 billion pounds of pesticides are used in the US each year, and 5.6 billion pounds worldwide.	Reduce by 70%
Greenhouse Gasses. Agriculture produces 33% of all anthropogenic emissions that add to global warming.	Reduce by 60%
Greenhouse Gasses. The livestock sector produces 18% of greenhouse gas emissions; more than transportation.	Reduce by 70%
Water pollution. NOAA estimates that 80% the pollution to the marine environment comes from agriculture.	Reduce by 60%
Water pollution. The USDA reports that over 46% of US surface waters are too polluted from agriculture for fishing, swimming, or aquatic life.	Reduce by 60%

Can Ana Save Modern Industrial Agriculture?

Fossil vs abundant agriculture

Two forms of agriculture: industrial, (fossil) and abundant

Modern industrial farmers face a nasty set of pain points as they struggle to maintain productivity, profitability and health. Farmers must endure increasing costs for scarce fossil resource inputs, especially water, fuel and fertilizers. Abundant agriculture will reduce farmers' production risks, reduce costs and improve health for farmers and consumers. Ana knows that our food production system needs novel eco-smart solutions. While Ana cannot save MIA, she can use her miraculous single-celled friends to enhance legacy agriculture.

Improve farm profitability

While algae biotechnologies are busy reducing MIA overconsumption, waste and pollution, algae will improve farmers' economics, health and social factors. For example, avoiding massive fossil resource consumption, saves farmers millions of dollars. A farmer who can cut fertilizer use by 50% may save 20% on the total cost of production, from fertilizer cost alone. The same logic applies to cropland, freshwater, fossil fuels, pesticides and agricultural chemicals. Algae's lift to MIA creates many benefits to farmers, society and ecosystems.

Triple bottom line

The sustainability triple bottom line, (3BL) provides a useful framework to examine MIA that depends on fossil resources. The 3BL model incorporates three performance dimensions: environmental, social, and economic. The model's 3Ps are referred to as people, planet and profits. MIA fails to provide healthy or sustainable solutions for the environment, human societies or the economics of food production. The 3BL model provides strong constructs for comparing MIA with abundance methods. The comparison will come later.

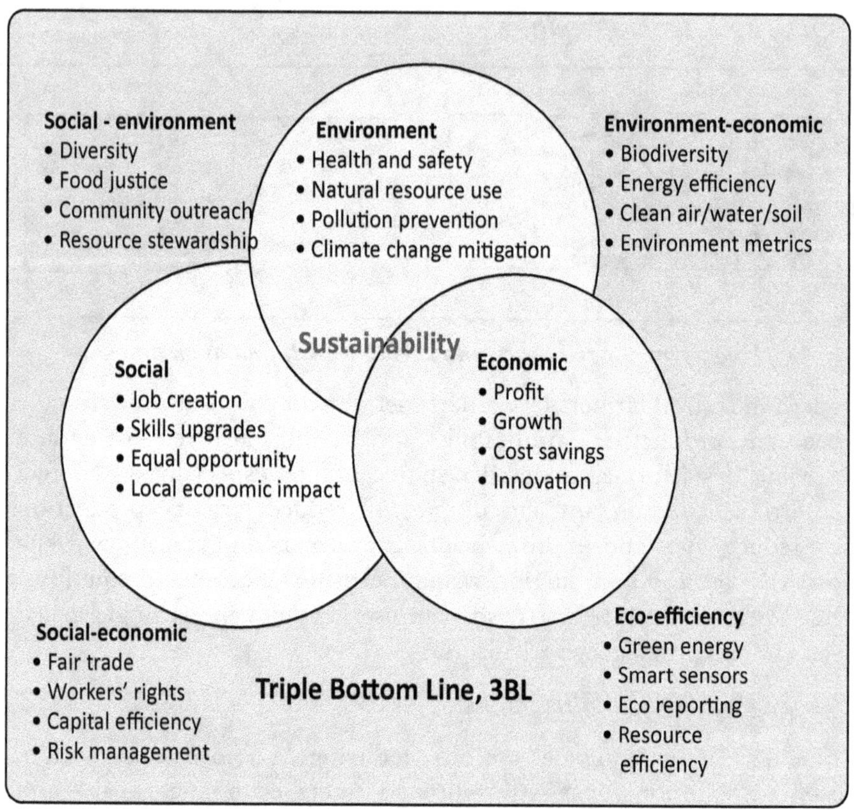

Green solution

People need access to lower cost fresh local foods that are packed with nutrients. Peace microfarms use abundance methods that cycle nutrients and assure sustainable food production for many generations. Growers produce freedom foods that free consumers to choose healthier foods.

Algae biosystems can do something that MIA desperately needs, cycle nutrients. The next section drills down on how nutrient cycling occurs and why nutrient cycling will transform MIA.

4. How Important is Nutrient Cycling?

Photosynthesis is simultaneously the cheapest and most efficient known solution of all nutrient cycling technologies.

Nutrient cycling provides the foundation for Ana's quest to supply good food for hungry people. Nature wastes nothing by maintaining a closed nutrient loop. Each plant lives with nutrients passed down from organisms that lived earlier. When the plant or animal dies, it's nutrients cycle to provide energy for following generations. Nutrient cycling has sustained ecosystems for eons.

Nutrients are chemical elements that an organism needs to survive and grow. Several nutrients required for food production are becoming increasingly scarce and expensive. Failing sufficient nutrients delivered at just the right time, cellular metabolism shuts down and fails.

Macronutrients provide most the energy for cellular metabolism. Micronutrients provide the necessary cofactors for metabolism. Both macro and micro nutrients usually can be acquired from the environment. Macronutrients are converted to energy to power the organism. Micronutrients drive several cellular functions, including building and repairing tissues and regulating body processes.

The nutrient cycle includes the use, movement, and recycling of nutrients in the environment. Valuable elements such as carbon, oxygen, hydrogen, phosphorus, and nitrogen are essential to life and must be recycled in order for organisms to exist. Nutrient cycles include both living and non-living components, as well as biological, geological, and chemical processes. These nutrient circuits are also known as biogeochemical cycles.

MIA has disrupted nature's sustainable cycling process by growing field crops in a manner that requires massive cultivation, compaction, irrigation, chemical fertilizers and pesticides and poisons. Growing field crops systemically extracts soil nutrients.

Farmers typically replace only the top three macro-nutrients, NPK, with new chemical fertilizer, due to both cost and availability. Nutrient extraction depletes soil and leaves crops with hidden hunger and produce with empty calories – very few nutrients per bite.

Elements:
- Carbon (C)
- Hydrogen (H)
- Oxygen (O

Macronutrients:
- Nitrogen (N)
- Phosphorus (P)
- Potassium (K)
- Calcium (Ca)

Micronutrients:
- Boron (B)
- Copper (Cu)
- Iron (Fe)
- Chloride (Cl)
- Manganese (Mn)
- Molybdenum (Mo)
- Zinc (Zn)

Repeated use of chemical fertilizer and pesticides degrades and eventually destroys the soil making it sterile. The other actions lead to serious erosion by wind and water that not only wastes precious nutrients but pollute ecosystems.

Fossil agricultural chemicals

MIA farmers currently use over 207 million tons of mined inorganic fertilizers annually, which is sustainable only as long as all the ingredients in fertilizer are economically recoverable. Fertilizer production accounts for about 35% of farm energy use in the US. Fertilizer also represents about 35% of the production cost for field crops.

Thoughtful farmers rotate crops to replenish nitrogen and minimize pathogens. MIA farmers replant the same crop, such as corn, year after year to maximize profits. They apply inorganic fertilizers to approximate the soil's natural fertility. Both crops and pests develop resistance. Food crops require increasingly more fertilizer to sustain the same level of production. Repeat plantings encourage invasive weeds and pests to propagate, which creates a substantial drag on crop growth. The desire to improve crop productivity combined with rising pest resistance demands more fossil intensive fertilizers, herbicides and pesticides.

MIA skips the replacement of soil organics with compost because substituting fossil fuels and mined compounds is less costly, faster and enables higher productivity – in the short term. Each year a farmer begins preparing the land for a new crop by replacing last year's lost nutrients. The additional agricultural chemicals are sourced from mines that are depleting quickly. Each year, fertilizer tends to cost more because chemicals easy to mine have already been removed. Mining becomes increasingly expensive as more material must be removed each year. As a result, fertilizer quality continually diminishes.

Fossil nutrients create a resource sink due to MIA's one-and-done behavior. A farmer may apply 100 pounds of P, (or other fossil resource) per acre, but loses about 80 nutrient pounds each year. The crop harvest removes about half, as that P enters the human or animal food chain. Another 30 pounds are lost to erosion from wind, rain and irrigation. Those nutrients move from the soil to nearby waterways, where it stays in dilution and poisons people or aquatic animals. In both cases, harvest and erosion, the nutrients are lost to the field.

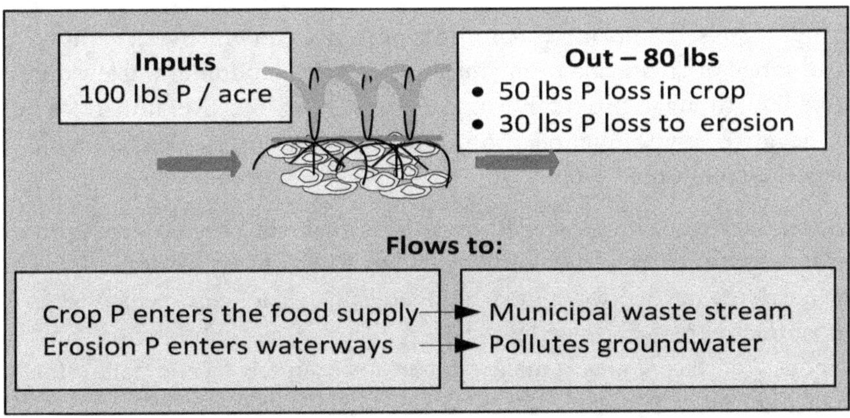

Loss of Fossil Nutrients – Resource Sink

Every year the farmer must begin again with an increasingly degraded field, using more fossil fuels to cultivate the field, inflicting more soil erosion and consuming additional fossil chemicals for fertilizers, herbicides, pesticides and fungicides. Algae bioremediation provides a cost-effective solution to nutrient loss and chemical pollution.

Algae growth

Algae need a source of energy and a source of nutrients to survive. Algae evolved over eons using a variety of strategies for surviving, even when conditions became unfavorable. In the puddles of early earth where algae evolved, conditions often became extremely hostile. Algae are naturally phototrophs and capture photons from sunshine or artificial light sources for the energy they need for growth and development. Phototrophic algae do not need a supply of organic carbon in their culture because they use light energy to power metabolism.

Many algae species can switch to heterotrophic energy production if light is not available, but they need an organic nutrient source. Mixotrophs can use a mix of solar energy and carbon sources and can grow in the light or dark, with an organic carbon source.

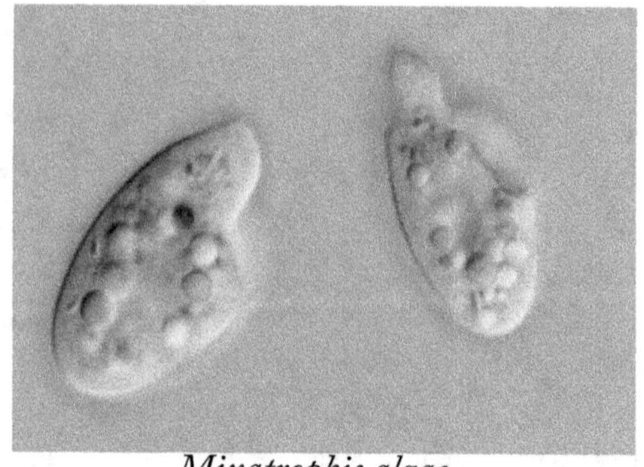

Mixatrophic algae

Through algae's various modes of nutrition, algae can effectively remove a broad range of chemicals from aqueous matrices. Coupling wastewater treatment with algae production makes sense. Algae can eliminate the large negative environmental footprint and pollution associated with industrial agriculture.

Algae are incredible single-celled organisms that not only absorb light, or in heterotrophic mode absorb sugar, but also directly absorb all the other nutrients needed for cellular metabolism. Algae nano-cells offer a huge surface area for nutrient adsorption. Direct absorption and enormous surface area make algae a superb candidate for bioremediation.

Algae's nutrient recovery ability

Why are algae so adept at nutrient recovery? The short answer is their tiny cell size. Algae cells must take in supplies of essential nutrients from outside to meet their energy needs. Cells also have to move wastes from inside to the outside. A high surface-area-to-volume ratio favors efficient uptake and output. As cells get larger, the ratio becomes lower and nutrient exchange less efficient. Algae retained its nano-size, (3 to 40 μ), so that their surface areas are large enough to let in essential material fast enough to meet their needs. Yet cells are small enough to allow waste materials to diffuse out quickly to avoid being poisoned by their own wastes.

In a *Scientific American* article, R. Kolkwitz counted about 400,000 algae cells per cubic centimeter. That means an algae screen for bioremediation the size of a cubic postage stamp has more surface area than four football fields. Interestingly, some new graphene filters that are fabricated one atomic layer at a time, to create a honeycomb filter with similar surface area. Graphene has a theoretical specific surface area (SSA) of 3,523 m²/g. These filters are being designed to capture CO_2 directly from the air.

Bioremediation

Bioremediation, nutrient recovery, serves as the critical first step in nutrient cycling. Most bioremediation research focuses on the capture of nutrients harmful to the environment, animals or people such as excess CO_2, nitric oxides (NO_x), polluted wastewater or toxic heavy metals. Bioremediation can also recover scarce nutrients that are expensive and in danger of extinction, such as phosphorus.

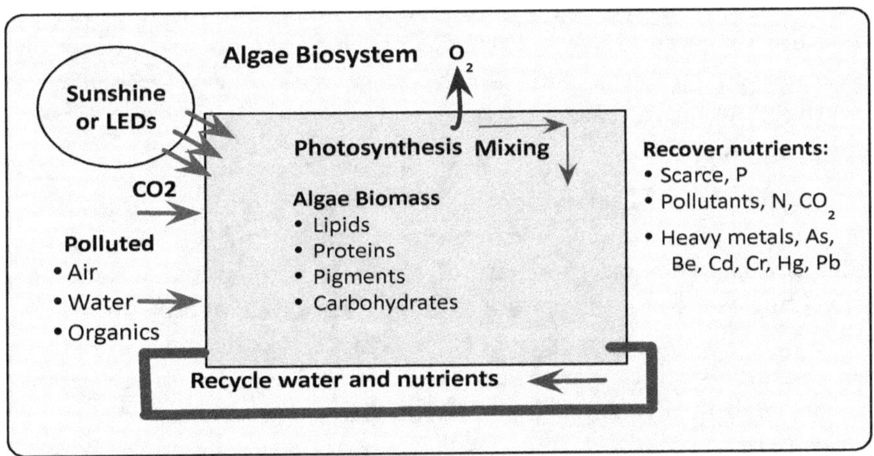

Nutrient cycling in an algae biosystem

Bioremediation uses naturally occurring organisms to recover nutrients and other elements. Bioremediation provides three ecosmart solutions. Algae biosystems can recover scarce waste nutrients such as P in polluted water and organic solids. Some nutrients, such as CO_2, CH_4, and N, are polluting air and waterways. Algae biosystems can recover those nutrients and at the same time as capture P. Industrial practices are releasing massive levels of heavy metals, which can also be remediated with algae biosystems.

Algae biosystems use solar energy and photosynthesis to capture nutrients from polluted air, water and organic solids. Air pollution sources may be any exhaust stack such as power or cement plants, factories, breweries or restaurants. Wastewater may come from any source, including municipal, agricultural, industrial, rivers or aquifers. Solids organic wastes may need pre-treatment such as pulverizing into small particles. Waste nutrients from solids may also come from waste-to-energy sources such as gas plasma, gasification or anaerobic digestion.

Scarce nutrients – Phosphorus

The naturally occurring mineral nutrient P is critical for cellular metabolism. With the exception of water, P is the most critical limited resource for crops because P sustains all living cells. Phospholipids form and maintain cell membranes and serve as the key structural components of DNA and RNA. Available P creates the shape for DNA, and provides the blueprint of genetic information contained in every living cell. A sugar-phosphate backbone forms the helical structure of every DNA molecule. The element also regulates ATP (Adenosine-5'-triphosphate), which is the main energy storage and transfer molecule in cells.

Accessible P plays an essential role in photosynthesis and helps plants to mature properly. Massive global P consumption for food production depletes P stores rapidly. Fertilizers are made up of N-P-K, and the price of each of these components directly affects the prices of the other two. Only five countries control 90% of the world's phosphate, which creates an oligopoly pricing model. Each year P costs more to extract because mines are deeper. Many P mines are degrading as the easily mined, high quality upper layers deposited on the floor of an ancient ocean have been mined. The costlier extraction of lower quality rock necessitates extracting more phosphate rock to produce each ton of fertilizer.

Plants need more P than any other element, besides carbon, because P drives photosynthesis, sugar production, (stored energy), root growth, blooming, fruiting and seed production. The element also promotes N_2 fixation in legumes. Plants stop growth and die with insufficient P.

Plants cannot be fooled by substituting other elements for P. There are no synthetic substitutes. After mines of P, manganese, zinc, copper and other vital elements are depleted, the only available source will be recycled waste streams or ocean water. Neither option is used today because those sources are too salty for direct use on land and conventional extraction methods require far too much energy to make economic recovery possible.

Can Ana Save Modern Industrial Agriculture?

As world reserves of this critical natural resource diminish, prices will skyrocket. Scientists at Linköping University in Sweden and Arizona State University predict peak P will occur about 2031. ASU scientists recognized the strategic importance of P and created the Sustainable Phosphorus Initiative in the Global School of Sustainability. Peak P will pose a serious threat to agriculture as global reserves of high-quality phosphate rock go into terminal decline.

Eleven US states have passed laws that ban certain forms of P fertilizer for use or sale to home owners. No similar laws affect farmers – yet. Germany understands P so strategically that the Federal Ministry of Environment passed the sludge ordinance, (AbfKlärV). The law makes phosphorus recovery from sewage sludge obligatory for all large German sewage works. China has used "night soil," (human wastes) for centuries to cycle P back to fields. This strategy is not possible in the US, because Americans uses too many pharmaceuticals that pass out as waste.

Many algae cultivars are able to recover P and other nutrients and produce oils for biofuels at the same time. A research team at the Rochester Institute of Technology demonstrated that three types of microalgae, *Scenedesmus*, *Chlorella*, and *Chlamydomonas* can efficiently convert nutrients to fuel on a diet of municipal waste water in a harsh and salty environment. The algae adsorbed 99% of the ammonia and phosphates, and 88% of the nitrates.

This research used a two-staged model where algae produce lipids at their normal rate in the waste water until the N and P are depleted. Then, the algae respond to starvation by turning on their reserve nutrient stores to produce more lipids. The lipids are harvested for biofuel and the remaining biomass is fermented with an anaerobic digester to make biogas. The remaining nutrients in the residual digestate can then be recovered as mineralized fertilizer from the solid and liquid fraction. The bio-methane (CH_4) coming off the digester burns in a combustion chamber, making more energy. The CO and CO_2 gases from combustion are cycled back to provide additional carbon for algae production.

Surplus pollutive nutrients

Algae bioremediation can recover excess nutrients such as N, CO_2, and CH_4 efficiently. Nutrients from agriculture, industry and human lifestyles pollute and poison ecosystems and contribute to climate chaos.

Farmers put massive amounts of fertilizers on field crops, but only about half is absorbed by the plants. Chemical fertilizers are highly soluble and they percolate or drain out of fields quickly with rain or irrigation. The chemical runoff enters fragile water ecosystems, disrupting the delicate nutrient balance. The residual fertilizer erodes from the field polluting waterways and causing entrophication and dead zones.

Entrophication occurs first as algae bloom ignited by the surplus nutrients. Algae add huge amounts of oxygen to the water. Algae produce sugars, which attract swarms of bacteria that eat the algae and consume all of the dissolved oxygen. Bacterial consumption suffocates all plants and aquatic creatures, creating a dead zone.

A Smithsonian-led study of 410 dead zones found they have doubled in size every 10 years since the 1960s, largely due to increases in nutrient-filled agricultural runoff. The US has 265 dead zones, including several in the Great Lakes. Dead zones occur at smaller lakes and estuaries at the mouth of every river that flows from agricultural areas. The Gulf of Mexico Dead Zone at the mouth of the Mississippi River kills all aquatic life over 8,000 square miles, an area the size of New Jersey. Fisheries at the mouth of rivers are typically the most productive and diverse sources of fish. The US loses valuable fisheries to deadly fertilizer poisoning.

Pollutive nitrogen

Every organism including a single cell, plant, tree or human requires N for its physical structure, function and reproduction. Although the atmosphere is made up of 78% N, plants cannot use atmospheric N directly. The N must be converted into nitrates or ammonia, which is often accomplished by N fixing bacteria and algae.

Production of reactive N, nature's most promiscuous element, has increased 15 times since 1960, to 115 billion tons in 2017. Over 80% of this N is used in MIA. Synthetic N production is over double that of all natural processes on land combined. In the U.S., people consume only about 10% of the N farmers apply to their fields every year. The remainder volatizes into the atmosphere or runs off to waterways.

Building a food supply system dependent on industrially fixed N and mined inorganic chemicals, makes our ability to feed ourselves dependent upon nonrenewable fossil fuels, limited agricultural chemicals and the wisdom, benevolence and cooperation of a few corporate executives that head the world's chemical fertilizer plants, mines and petroleum companies. These executives share a very poor history.

Fertilized soils release more than two billion tons of greenhouse gases every year, especially CO_2, methane and NO_x, (N oxides). A recent scientific report of nine global environmental challenges that may make the Earth unfavorable for continued human development identified N pollution as one of only three problems – along with climate change and loss of biodiversity – that have already crossed a boundary that could result in disastrous consequences if not corrected.

The excess reactive fertilizer is mobile and rides on air and water from the field. Additional N in the form of nitrate seeps into drinking water, where it lurks as a poison that can damage internal organs. High levels of nitrates in drinking water have been linked to blue baby syndrome, when a baby's blood can't carry sufficient oxygen, as well as miscarriages. A review by the National Institutes of Health shows elevated nitrate concentrations in drinking water raise the risk of cancer, Alzheimer's, diabetes and heart disease and drives up mortality rates. In the heart of the corn belt, Iowa's largest sewage treatment plant spends millions on nitrate removal. A 2007 Iowa Natural Resources report indicated 274 Iowa waterways were seriously polluted. Studies in all the corn-belt states have produced similar results. A majority of waterways and well water contain fertilizer pollution.

Fertilizer run-off causes such a problem that Iowa was forced to install the largest and most expensive in the world. The Des Moines plant was forced to invest another $19 million in new equipment to reduce the P found in the state's waterways and well water. Rural families not connected to the city's water treatment plant must depend on well water, which puts their families at substantial health risk, because their water contains carcinogens and other deadly poisons.

A recent study estimated the cost of mitigating fertilizer pollution in the Mississippi River at $2.7 billion a year. The use of algae bioremediation in algae biosystems called smartcultures, could reduce that annual cost by a factor of at least 10. A wastewater bioremediation system uses algae raceways to allow algae to biosorb the nutrients from organic waste.

Large amounts of nitric oxide volatize into the atmosphere as ammonia, where it creates smog and causes respiratory disease. Agriculture releases the largest human caused source of nitrous oxide, a highly reactive form of N that contributes to global warming and reduces stratospheric ozone that protects from ultraviolet radiation. Ecological N pollution in waterways also enables the spread of invasive species such as ragweed that elevates pollen pollution and mosquitoes and snails that carry. Algae wastewater bioremediation can clean wastewater and recover nutrients using solar energy and photosynthesis.

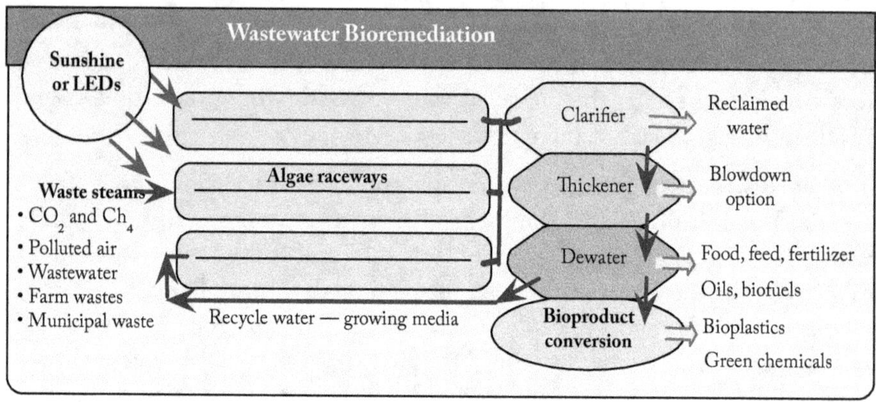

Algae nutrient recovery in wastewater

Algae biosystems can remove N from water. A study on closing nutrient cycles using algae at the Netherlands Institute of Ecology demonstrates that microalgae can effectively recover nearly all the P and N from anaerobically treated black water, (toilet wastewater). An algae biosystem captures the nutrients and generates algae biomass in one step. Screening experiments with green microalgae and cyanobacteria showed that all tested microalgae species successfully grew on anaerobically treated black water. A subsequent experiment in flat-panel photobioreactors, showed *chlorella* removed 100% of the P and N from the medium.

Frank Rogalla has developed a wastewater-to-biogas plant in Spain. The facility grows algae in saline wastewater and harvests the algae oil. His team worked out the metrics and concluded the process achieves a positive energy balance. This energy and cost efficiency makes algae-waste-to-energy a significant commercial viability.

Jordan Lind and a team at Clearas in Montana have developed a biological nutrient recovery system from wastewater that increases dissolved oxygen, and produces no chemical by-products, eliminating costly disposal fees. The patented process accelerates photosynthesis, consumption of CO_2 and excess nutrients. Advanced microfiltration filters out the activated algae, which can be used for a variety of bioproducts. The **Clearas** site shows their process video.

Frank Rogalla and his team at Aqualia produced the algae oil used for the first Volkswagen powered by algae biogas. The team produced All-gas, (algae in Spanish), from the waste water treatment plant located in El Torno, Chiclana, Spain. The vehicle's efficient hybrid engine generates zero emissions.

Pollutive carbon

Carbon, (often CO_2 or CH_4) garners the most press as the villain of global warming and the resulting climate chaos. Pollutive C contributes to life-threatening air pollution such as smog that triggers asthma attacks, heart attacks and reduces crop production. As the earth approaches a 1.5°C temperature raise, decarbonizing our economy has become paramount. Successful decarbonization requires a change the way carbon is used and a focus on preserving the carbon budget for essential uses. Pollutive carbon can be found in abundance in all the wrong places. Agriculture discharges carbon plumes, as do power plants that also release black smoke carbon particulates that pollute cities. Industry currently recycles metals, plastics and paper. The next logical step, recycling carbon, makes sense using the principles of the circular economy to convert it into useful bioproducts.

Algae have evolved to be the most important CO_2 fixers in aquatic ecosystems and the major biomass constituent in marine and freshwater environments. Scientists can achieve significant carbon capture by taking advantage of algae's unusual gift; to capture and fix CO_2.

Algae offer the most promising solution for industrial capture of emitted CO_2. Algae's ability to convert CO_2 into carbon-rich lipids and protein greatly exceeds food crops and does not compete for arable land or fresh water. Each ton of algae absorb 1.8 tons of CO_2. This exchange is possible because the atomic weight of C is 12, while the atomic weight of O is 16. Algae releases enormous amounts of O_2, 200 tons per hectare per year, while assimilating the C in its biomass.

Ana Feeds Our World

David Dah-Wei Tsai and team at the Feng Chia University in Taiwan published a study where they compared the efficiency of several algae cultivation systems with terrestrial plants for carbon uptake. Carbon capture in the algae biosystems were close to 100%. The scientists found that trees and shrubs tested in 16 countries captured less than 20% of the available carbon.

Carbon smart companies will capture waste emissions from power, cement plants and factories and repurpose the carbon into chemicals to make biofertilizer, biofeed and biofuel. Others will make bioplastic as fibers for running shoes, green chemicals or high value medicines.

Several power plant flue gas systems are under development. Michigan State University and $PHYCO_2$ has built a test carbon capture to algae process. The University of Kentucky project with Duke Energy offers a good video. Global Algae Innovations in Hawaii has also posted a video of their robust carbon capture to algae production system. Power Plant CCS provides a brief history on algae carbon capture and storage.

Toxic heavy metals

Heavy metals are natural constituents of the environment, but substantial use for human purposes has altered their geochemical cycles and biochemical balance. Human overuse allows release of heavy metal poisons such as arsenic, cadmium, copper, lead, nickel, mercury and zinc into the soil and aquatic environments. The cost of fertilizers to farmers and the environment is terrible, since less than half the nutrients are absorbed by the crop and the rest pollute ecosystems. The cost of pesticides to farmers and the environment is catastrophic because less than 1% of pesticides are absorbed by the crop, while the residue poisons air, water and soil.

Toxic metals	Industrial uses	Toxic effects	EPA limit (mg/l)
Arsenic	Pesticides, herbicides	Cancers, respiratory, neuro, cardio, immunological, and endocrine damage	0.02
Cadmium	Batteries, plastics, pigments, plating	Kidney, bone, neurological damage, and lung cancer	0.06

Chromium	Dyes, alloys, tanning	Respiratory, allergic dermatitis, kidney and liver damage	0.05
Lead	Batteries, pesticides wire and cable, alloys	Neurological, blood damage, and reproductive effects	0.1
Mercury	Caustic soda, thermometers, batteries, pesticides,	Neurological effects, kidney damage, lungs, heart, immune, skin	0.01
Manganese	Pesticides, batteries	Central nervous system effects	0.26
Zinc	Pharmaceuticals, dyes, batteries	Gastrointestinal, digestive, heart, anemia, pancreas.	15

Toxic effects of heavy metals in pesticide residue

The economic toll of pesticides residuals in fields, on food and food packaging is astonishing. Pesticides create an urgent public threat posed by endocrine disrupting chemicals, especially to our children. Pesticide residuals disrupt the body's hormones and are linked to a myriad of severe health problems, such as impaired brain development, lower IQs, behavior problems, infertility, birth defects, obesity and diabetes and all the follow-on diseases.

Toxic heavy metals attach to major organs and interrupt normal organ functions. Lead poisoning in Flint Michigan focused world attention on the effects of heavy metals poisoning. The Flint problem affected 100,000 people. Persistent pesticide residue exposure affects at least 10 times more people nationally and 100 times more people globally.

A recent study led by Pete Myers, founder of Environmental Health Sciences, calculates that pesticide costs the US more than $45 billion annually from health care costs and lost wages. Pesticide exposure causes an estimated 2 million lost IQ points and another 7,500 intellectual disability cases annually. The calculations are made from metrics developed by the Endocrine Society, WHO and the UN Environment Program. Additional illnesses will add to the pesticide drag due to the lag effect in heavy metals exposure. Many illnesses such as cancers, neurological, brain and respiratory diseases from toxic chemical exposure appear years after exposure.

Heavy metals are natural constituents of the environment, but indiscriminate use for human purposes has altered their geochemical cycles and biochemical balance. This results in excess release of heavy metals such as cadmium, copper, lead, nickel, zinc *etc.* into natural resources like the soil and aquatic environments. Prolonged exposure and higher accumulation of such heavy metals can have deleterious health effects on human life and aquatic biota.

The Geological Survey (USGS) and Fish and Wildlife Service (FWS) found that pesticide endocrine disruption cause sex changes among small and largemouth bass. Males had female eggs inside their testicles.

Algae are voracious pollutant scavengers for a broad category of chemicals released into the environment from the domestic, industrial and agricultural sectors. Besides the usual organic and inorganic fertilizer residue compounds present in the wastewater, algae cells can also assimilate and/or break down more persisting molecules such as hydrocarbons, antibiotics, PPCPs, EDCs and heavy metals.

Australia's James Cook University demonstrated algae are effective at bioremediation of CO_2 and heavy metals, (Al, As, Cd, Cr, Cu, Ni, and Zn), *in situ* at a coal-fired power station. Macroalgae were grown in shallow wastewater ponds containing CO_2 and fly ash and removed nearly all the metals.

Algae Reactors at James Cook Univ.

Bioremediation of excess nutrients in wastewater by microalgae has been prevalent in the US for the past 70 years. When algae bioaccumulates toxic wastes, the biomass may not be useful for normal bioproducts. The toxic biomass can be converted to biochar through pyrolysis or gasification. The biochar can be used as soil amendment with reduced risk of leaching of toxic material such as heavy metals, since the pyrolysis process integrates and binds up the metals in the solid matrix.

Bioremediation uses naturally occurring organisms as a treatment to break down hazardous substances such as waste or pollutants into less toxic or non-toxic substances. Bioremediation with nutrient recovery serves as the first step in nutrient cycling. Considerable bioremediation research focuses on the capture of nutrients harmful to the environment, animals or people, such as toxic heavy metals from pesticides.

The role of microorganisms in biotransformation of heavy metals into nontoxic forms is well-documented. Understanding the molecular mechanism of metal accumulation has numerous biotechnological implications for bioremediation of metal-contaminated sites. Cell wall components of various algae groups is closely related to the metal binding capacity of algae. These biotechnology layers are described in *Adsorption and Absorption of Heavy Metals by Microalgae*, by Li Li.

After bioremediation, algae has accumulated the toxic heavy metals so the biomass is not fit for anaerobic digestion or biofertilizer. Pyrolysis of the cultivated algae immobilized the accumulated metals in a recalcitrant C-rich biochar. While the algal biochar has 10 to 50 times higher metal concentrations than the algae feedstock, the biochar had very low leachable metals. The metals were bound up (chelated) into the biochar matrix, providing nutrients for crops but sequestering the toxic metals for decades.

Summary

Bioremediation lays the foundation for nutrient cycling. Nutrient capture in algae biosystems provides the feedstock for a wide variety of bioproducts. Since modern environments offer so many pollutive point sources for carbon and other nutrients, algapreneurs have many choices for nutrient collection. Carbon capture using current mechanical technologies cost \$40 to \$50 a ton, but those methods are not sustainable. Algae-based CO_2 capture and sequestration costs more than conventional methods currently, but are more sustainable. In addition, algae produce bioproducts that can be monetized. Algae-based CO_2 and nutrient capture will present a profitable business in the near future with rising oil prices, carbon trading and social policies directed at polluters.

Algae's three immediate bioremediation contributions to agriculture will be recovering phosphorus, reducing nitrogen and carbon wastes, and capturing and sequestering toxic heavy metals from pesticide residues. The strongest leverage to agriculture from algae bioremediation may be algae biofertilizers. Most importantly, algae-based CO_2 abatement enables monetizing carbon credit + nutrient value + biomass value for bioproducts. A coal power plant produces about 1 ton of CO_2 for every MWh of energy produced. Yield of algae biomass per hectare is about 0.3 to 1 ton per day. Algae biotechnology will offer a safe and sustainable solution to the problems associated with CO_2 emissions from coal power plants and other carbon sources.

Once algae performs the magic of carbon and nutrient capture, the next important step is to repurpose those precious nutrients into useful bioproducts. The ZooPoo project illustrates recovery, recycle and reuse process.

5. Algae Bioregeneration – Repurpose Nutrients

*Algae transform poo at the zoo to clean, green energy
while recovering nutrients for recycle and reuse to benefit
the animals and the zoo.*

Nature has used biological regeneration sustainably for eons because nature recycles and reuses nutrients many times. Bioremediation paired with bioregeneration operates on nature's basic principle that there is no such thing as waste.

"Your waste is my food."

Waste carbon and nutrients become the food energy that algae pair with solar energy to grow valuable bioproducts. The key to successfully following nature's path requires thoughtfully integrating carbon and other nutrient pollution sources and syncing them with algae biofactories designed to capture nutrients and to grow bioproducts.

Rather than positioning nutrient recovery and reuse on a farm, where only a few people can see it, why not create a world class demonstration project at the zoo, where millions can share and see the experience? If we can do ZooPoo at the zoo, we can recover and repurpose energy and nutrients anywhere.

Futurists have positioned algae bioremediation and bioregeneration for NASA and DARPA's 100-Year Starship project. Algae are proposed to provide food, life-support, waste cycling, green chemicals, bioenergy, and building materials. Algae are also recommended to make the medicines necessary for 100 years of life in space. ZooPoo provides a more down-to-earth opportunity for algae biosolutions.

The intriguing positioning of algae cycling and reuse in both a long-voyage spaceship and a zoo creates an important question. NASA calculated that six liters of algae water will produce 600 grams of food, (540 grams is 2500 calories, an average daily food requirement), 600 liters of oxygen, and consume 720 liters of CO_2. Is there any other organism on earth that can sustain both a starship and a zoo?

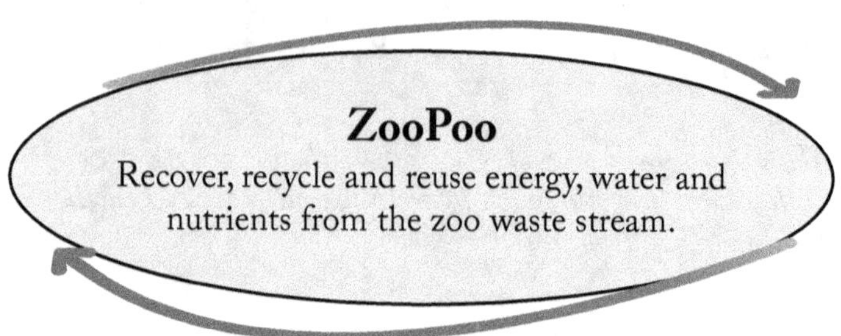

Imagine that your zoo becomes the world's first EcoZoo, and demonstrates nature's preferred mode of energy storage and harvest – green solar energy in rich algae biomass. Nature's first and simplest energy system, algae, uses only sunshine, wastewater and surplus CO_2 to recycle and reuse ZooPoo to produce clean, sustainable, carbon neutral food, feed, energy, fertilizer and freshwater.

ZooPoo enables the zoo to move towards a net zero:

- **Carbon footprint** – no net carbon dioxide emission.
- **Freshwater footprint** – no net freshwater consumption.
- **Fossil fuels footprint** – no net fossil fuels consumption.
- **Fossil nutrient footprint** – no net fossil nutrient consumption.

The ZooPoo exhibit shows visitors how farmers can grow healthy foods and bioproducts while protecting all the animals and plants on earth from the overconsumption, waste and pollution associated with industrial agriculture.

Zoo waste problems

Discussions with zoo directors and managers revealed that some zoos pay more to manage ZooPoo, botanical and animal wastes, than their animal feed. In the name of ecological safety, bureaucrats have levied layers of protections, e.g. inspectors from various bureaus, on zoos to monitor their waste management. California imposes no less than five agencies to monitor zoo waste streams.

Zoo waste management has become a major cost because the current process is extremely labor and energy intensive. Zoos must carefully gather their waste products and transport them to a holding facility where no discards can leach into the ground – even if it rains. Typically, the poo (animal manure) must be covered to avoid unpleasant odors. After inspection, the manure wastes are loaded into trucks and transported long distances to an approved waste dump. In addition to all these costs, some local or state governments add fees by weight to waste that go to dumps. Incredibly, the zoo must go to great expense to manage ZooPoo and then forfeits the entire poo value.

ZooPoo contains roughly 60% of the energy originally in the plants eaten by zoo animals. Elephant poo contains about 80% of the original plant energy because while elephants have the biggest appetites of all zoo animals, but they have the lowest energy and nutrient absorption. Elephants are enormous, rich poo factories. Zoos provide an excellent model for nutrient cycling because ZooPoo retains 80% of the nutrients originally in the plants eaten by zoo animals. Zoos currently lose both the energetic and nutritive value in animal and botanical wastes.

Each zoo dumps a gold mine of rich energy and recoverable nutrients into already overfilled waste dumps. ZooPoo bioremediation and bioregeneration can transform a huge zoo cost to a profit center. Even better, the process can create a superb destination for ecotourism and learning center.

Kill waste dumps

Eco-smart states, such as California, Massachusetts, Oregon, and Washington have passed disposal bans on certain products, including yard materials and botanical waste. Those wastes are removed by vehicles on a fee for service basis. Experience shows there is no effective practical way to enforce a recycling goal. However, public officials are able to enforce disposal bans. As a political strategy, pursuing disposal bans has a better chance of success with public acceptance than attempting to pass a comprehensive state or federal solid waste plan.

Many countries in Europe and central America have passed laws to completely prohibit dumping. The motivation for these dumping bans is simple; countries have run out of land acceptable for waste disposal. Spain, Denmark, Canada and other leading green countries are finding surprisingly profitable business in waste-to-energy technologies, including gasification and gas plasma.

Conventional waste-to-energy plants that use mass-burn incineration can convert one ton of MSW, (municipal solid waste) into about 550 kilowatt-hours of electricity. Gasification technology is about twice as efficient with feedstock and uses one ton of MSW to produce about 1,000 kilowatt-hours (kWh) of electricity. Plasma gasification offers similar efficiencies and can be used to convert carbon-containing materials to synthesis gas that can be used to generate power and other useful products. Gas plasma provides safe waste-to-energy solutions for hazardous, biomedical, hospital and chemical materials. Anaerobic digestion (see discussion below), of wet organic wastes can generate 300 to 1,000 kWh per ton while producing digestate as a valuable byproduct that can be composted as a soil amendment or further processed into solid and liquid fertilizer for growing beneficial crops.

Mass-burn waste-to-energy technologies create two pollutive emissions, incineration flue gasses and the biochar residual in the combustion chamber. The flue gasses can be remediated by algae to produce more biomass. The biochar serves to safely sequester potential pollutants in a slow release soil amendment to support field crops.

Goals

The ZooPoo exhibit architecture will demonstrate the value of nutrient cycling. Many zoo guests recycle their organic material at home and their grocery bags, so they are already aware of the recycle-reuse value proposition. The primary nutrient cycling takeaway is the ability to monetize waste and pollution. ZooPoo transforms costs into a profit center. Target market guests, those who currently pay to burn or bury their wastes, include:

- **Farmers,** who will be able to realize value from animal and plant wastes and moderate pollution and waste.

- **Municipal waste facilities,** that will be able to create value from human waste streams.

- **Community (food waste, garden and trash) waste facilities,** that will create value from recyclable trash and garden botanicals.

- **Power and cement plants** and manufacturers, that will create value from their surplus CO_2 while avoiding emissions.

- **Citizens** who desire to learn how to minimize their waste streams and ecological footprint.

- **Children** who wish to convey the message of conservation and renewal to their peers and parents.

- **Churches** that desire to convey green and sustainable lifestyles to their communities.

- **Schools** that want engage students in sustainable systems.

- **Green and environmental social networks** that want to see ecologically responsible production of food, feed, and freshwater.

- **Zoo visitors** interested in food and energy security by reclaiming and recycling surplus inputs that are affordable and, unlike fossil resources, will not run out.

- **Visitors committed to global stewardship** by moderating pollution while producing valuable bioproducts that cycle or store rather than release carbon. If only a fraction of people — 20% — made small, environmentally beneficial changes, such as switching furnace filters, using low energy light bulbs, or driving less aggressively, overall energy consumption would drop by up to 20%."

- **Educators** in sustainable and affordable food and energy (SAFE) production, that creates a positive ecological footprint.

ZooPoo will be designed to convey mission critical solutions for social, economic and environmental challenges.

Challenge

Many animals, plants and entire ecosystems are threatened with extinction due to global climate change, food costs, freshwater scarcity and the availability of fossil fuels and fossil nutrients (i.e. fertilizers). ZooPoo addresses each of these challenges and shows visitors how to change their own behaviors to save animals, plants and ecosystems as they enhance our communities. *"Sustainable You at the Zoo"* will provide a take-home checklist to support ecosmart lifestyles.

ZooPoo will show energy and nutrient recovery, recycle and reuse demonstration and learning facilities that enable guests of all ages to see, experience and learn how to adopt green behaviors and lifestyles.

ZooPoo uses the zoo waste stream, ZooPoo, and recovers and reuses energy and nutrients to produce electricity, freshwater, vitamins, minerals, health foods, animal feed, fertilizers and medicines for zoo animals and plants. Algae recover the hydrocarbons stored in ZooPoo, which can then be used for energy rather than burning fossil fuels. The facility will also include demonstrations of other renewable forms of energy such as solar, wind and possibly geothermal systems.

Elephants are among the smartest animals at the zoo. They may serve as the ZooPoo icon because each adult elephant contributes more than 300 pounds a day to the ZooPoo pile. Elephants have the most inefficient digestive systems, at 40% of their intake, even though they have 19 meters, (21 yards) of intestine.

ZooPoo will demonstrate how to transform ZooPoo from waste to valuable bioproducts that benefit plants, animals and people.

Cycling history

Mother Nature has been cycling nutrients successfully with algae for 3.5 billion years. ZooPoo builds on nature's first and most efficient food and energy production system. Many people are unaware of the potential for algae to provide carbon neutral food, feed and fuel. The few algae producers have worked under the public radar, distant from population centers. ZooPoo raises algae farming to a new level by enabling algae production and its many coproducts from the zoo's waste stream. After constructing the demonstration, production, and education centers, ZooPoo will be self-sustaining environmentally and economically.

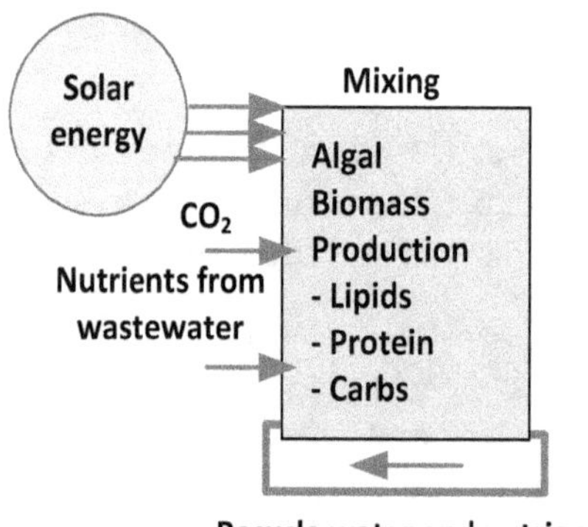

Recycle water and nutrients

Algae production (left), creates biomass with surplus inputs that are cheap and will not run out – sunshine, CO_2 and wastewater nutrients. Algae production systems get most their needed energy free from sunshine but require some additional energy for mixing and extraction.

The energy stored on earth comes from the sun. Nature transformed the algae biomass from ancient oceans into fossil fuels, but the process took tremendous pressure and heat over 400 million years. Fossil fuels offer a convenient form of concentrated energy, but pollutes the atmosphere with heat-trapping gases, as well as heavy metals and black soot particulates. Algae produces biofuel in weeks rather than eons.

Algae biofuels displace the use of fossil fuels gallon-for-gallon. Unlike fossil fuels, during production, algae release only pure oxygen to the atmosphere. Algae oil creates clean, renewable biofuels that burn with no black soot particulates because the algal oil has not fossilized. The ZooPoo facility will have a small motor running on algae oil. Guests can attest that the simple vegetable oil burns cleanly, but has a bit of an odor similar to French fries.

After recovery of algae oil for energy, other coproducts may be extracted from the remaining biomass. or can be processed into renewable natural gas or transportation fuels. Solid wastes are remediated through anaerobic digestion that provides both gasses and waste water that provide more algae feedstock.

Anaerobic digesters (left), use a series of biological tools and apply micro-organisms (anaerobes) to break down biodegradable material in the absence of oxygen. An end product, biogas, may be combusted to generate electricity. Flue gas from combustion can feed more algae.

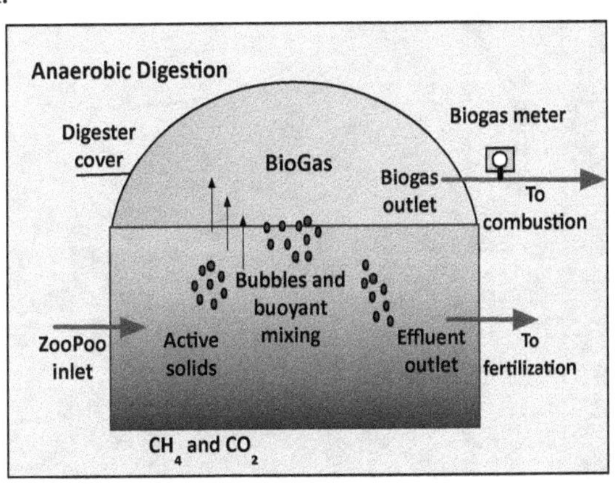

The water used to culture the algae may come from any source, but high-nutrient wastewater offers many advantages, especially free nutrients. Water may be recycled and the residual nutrients reused up to 10 times. Lipids may be pressed out of the biomass for use healthy oils for animal feed or converted to liquid transportation fuel. Algae protein provides food energy for animals, fowl and fish. The remaining carbohydrates can be refined into energy, biodegradable bioplastics, paper, fabrics, green chemicals and many other bioproducts. Algae can also provide vitamins, medicines and vaccines for the zoo animals.

The ZooPoo exhibit purpose is simple: show rather than tell visitors how to recover, recycle and reuse nutrients from zoo animals and botanical wastes. The message also includes how to practice abundance methods that use no or minimal fossil resources

ZooPoo process

ZooPoo includes the liquid and solid the wastes from animals, plants and zoo trash. The exhibits will use about 60% virtual – videos, and 40% interactive. Waste-to-energy videos will provide guests with sights of amazing processes using big screens that avoid the required footprint, odors and the noise. The interactive exhibits will entertain and engage target guests of all ages.

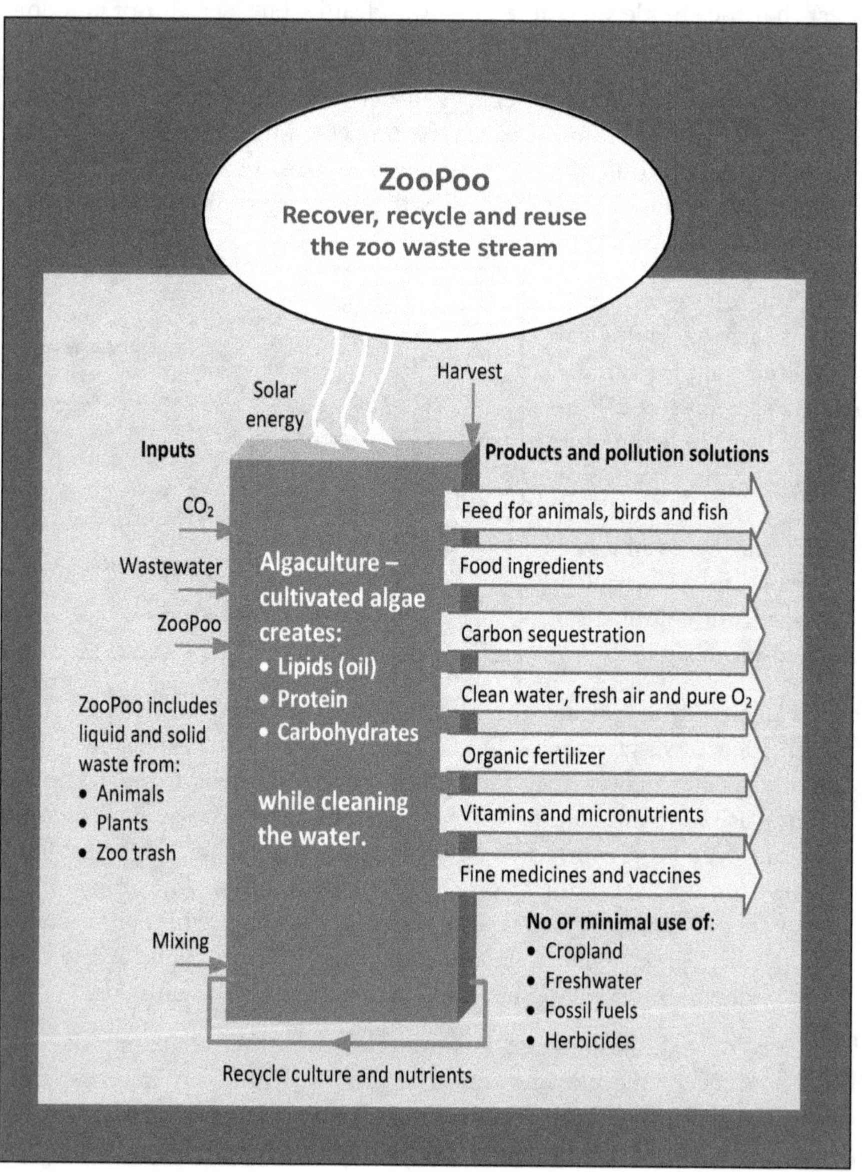

ZooPoo employs a clean and adaptable carbon-neutral production process that consumes large amounts of CO_2 and transforms the carbon into high-value products while releasing pure oxygen into the atmosphere. ZooPoo uses abundant, (renewable) or surplus inputs while producing valuable products and pollution solutions.

ZooPoo biosolids will be filtered, dried in the sun and then burned in a closed kiln in a process called pyrolysis. Burning the organic matter in the closed system releases no CO_2 to the atmosphere and creates three valuable components: H_2, CO gases and biochar.

The H_2 is piped to a generator to create more electricity for the ZooPoo exhibit. The carbon monoxide gas is piped to an algae pond where it provides the carbon for additional algae production. The biochar is sold to farmers as a slow release biofertilizer and soil conditioner.

The core carbon neutral technologies provide a showcase for abundance. Carbon neutral production means that no new carbon enters the atmosphere. Abundance production methods insure that no or minimal fossil resources are consumed in production.

- **Nutrient recovery** – algae bioaccumulate and store nutrients from the poo tea created from animal and plant waste streams.

- **Energy recovery** – burning animal and plant solid wastes in a closed system, gasification or pyrolysis, creates H_2 for energy production and more CO and CO_2 to feed algae.

- **Food and feed production** – algae are harvested and separated into component products with the protein going to produce feed for fish, birds and animals.

- **Clean water** – algae clean wastewater and make it suitable for irrigation, animal or human use. Wastewater treatment is the oldest algae application in the US and dates back 70 years.

- **Energy production** – algae are harvested and the oil is pressed out to create clean, green diesel that burns with no black smoke particulates. Additional energy is created by the H_2 produced from gasification of solid wastes.

- **Biofertilizer** – selected residual from algae production may be used as a fertilizer for the many plants at the zoo. Biochar, a byproduct from pyrolysis waste management, will provide additional fertilizer and soil amendment for Zoo plants. Some

> local algae will be grown as liquid biofertilizer for drip systems in greenhouses and in hydroponic production of vegetables.

- **Biofeeds** – high protein algae cultivars will be grown for animal feed. Most animals will receive a mix of algae and food grains, or in the case of carnivores, meat. The aquaponics exhibit will display fish eating repurposed nutrients in their algae diet.

- **Farmaceuticals and medicines** – algae compounds are harvested to make animal health foods, vitamins and minerals, including Omega-3 fatty acids, which improve the health of zoo animals.

The ZooPoo algal production system illustrates the steps in carbon neutral production where fuel, electricity, food, feed, fertilizer and other products are made using no or minimal fossil fuels or fossil carbon products such as fertilizers or agricultural chemicals. The algae may be harvested and processed to create biodiesel, high-protein feed, carbohydrates, biofertilizers and a host of other products. Carbohydrates may be converted to ethanol, paper or textiles.

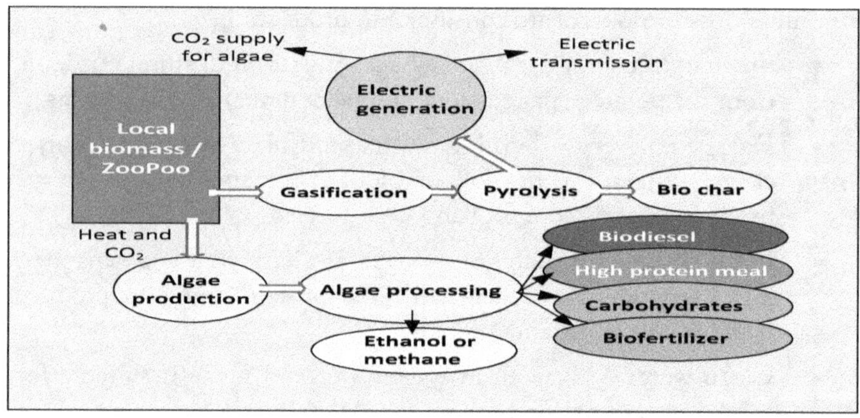

Carbon neutral production

Excrement

ZooPoo may not be pretty in a classic sense, because waste streams are dirty. The ZooPoo mantra will show in various ways how recycled nutrients can create bioproducts that are clean for people, animals, plants and our environment. Critically, the exhibit will smell good because released orders indicate a waste of valuable nutrients.

ZooPoo will turn poo upside down and celebrate poo as a treasure that transforms brown into gold; clean, green food and energy. Exhibits will demonstrate steps in the process to assure cleanliness, healthiness and nutrient value. There will be many examples of how poo is used globally, such as China's farmers that have used human poo on their fields successfully for thousands of years. Organic farmers use animal waste regularly on their fields to produce healthy crops. Students may not know that beer and wine comes from the excrement of yeast cells, or that the Plains Indians, as well as early settlers used buffalo poo regularly for their cooking fires. Poo retains high-value energy and nutrients, why waste it?

Beneficiaries

ZooPoo will benefit zoo visitors of every age. The learning facility will serve as a gathering point for environmental and socially conscious networks. ZooPoo provides engaging learning opportunities for people interested in carbon neutral production of food and energy, ecologically sensitive lifestyles as well as water, food and energy conservation. The facility will support extensive R&D plus visual, interactive exhibits for sustainable food and energy.

ZooPoo exhibit

The ZooPoo exhibit will cover several acres. Exhibits will include Peace Microfarms growing algae for several purposes, a microorganism interactive learning center as well as several satellite exhibits. A consortium of experts will design the exhibits. We will engage environmental design architectural students, as well as professional architects to develop ideas for the learning facility. We will also rely on the Zoo Board of Directors to align the project with the vision and values embedded at the zoo.

There will be interactive displays about the miracles algae has already created. Displays will show how algae were used by ancient cultures for food, feed, fertilizer and medicines. Of course, there will be plenty of nutritious, tasty and free algae-based foods to sample.

The microorganism interactive learning center will bring microbes to life on big screens. Guests will be able to see live microbe interactions including feeding, mating, birthing offspring and the many special things microbes do. Selectable videos will provide entertaining microorganism education. Some lucky guests will be able to perform algae bioprospecting right on site. If they find an organism not already named, they will be able to choose a name for the new organism.

Advanced sensors paired with big data and artificial intelligence will assist in the search for new microbes.

The algae biosystems may use bags, tubes or flat plastic rectangles as illustrated in the pictures available at *Imagine Our Algae Future*. The microorganism interactive learning center will collaborate with Micropia *in Amsterdam, the* Smithsonian, *the* Exploratorium *in San Francisco and imaginative STEAM, (science, technology, engineering, arts and math) learning sources such as the* Arizona Science Center.

The signature ZooPoo exhibit will display the benefits of Abundance farming methods and Freedom Foods, based on the power of single-celled organisms. The context will be a spaceship traveling for years to distant planets. The astronauts will have to grow their own sustainable food, feed and fertilizer. The interactive display will allow student astronauts to cultivate bioproducts they want for their journey to distant planets with algae.

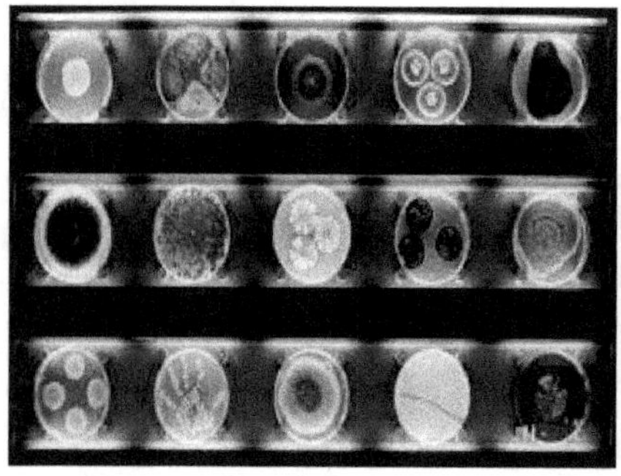

Images from Micropia in Amsterdam

After student astronauts understand how nano cells can produce sustainable food in a spaceship, their transition back to earth will seem quite simple. They will follow Ana's journey to create food justice by recycling nutrients and repurposing them for zoo animals, food crops and people. Students will be able to use 3D printers to print a variety of healthy algae-based foods. They will be able to design favored tastes, colors and textures into their food products.

Guests will learn how animal production over-consumes finite resources, uses them once and then pollutes ecosystems. Animal production consumes tremendous amounts of resources and adds substantially to greenhouse gases. For example, one cow-calf pair produces more CO_2 equivalent greenhouse gas than a car emits each year. Students will see cows happily growing in pole barns with peaked roofs. Fresh air comes in the sides of the barn while the cows' substantial methane emitted from both ends of the cow, rise to the peaked roof. When a sensor identifies a sufficient concentration of methane, a pump flows the gas to a combustion chamber, where it is burned for energy that powers the farm's microgrid. The combustion chamber gasses are piped to an algae raceway to provide carbon for the next algae generation.

ZooPoo summary

At the top level, ZooPoo will focus on the value of the zoo waste stream to demonstrate how energy and nutrients can be recovered, recycled and reused for a wide variety of products and solutions. ZooPoo will demonstrate human future lifestyles in terms of sustainability, conservation, pollution solutions and ecological preservation. ZooPoo will provide practical demonstrations of solutions desperately needed by current societies including how to produce sustainable and affordable carbon neutral food, feed and fuel without using fossil resources.

Several exhibits will demonstrate the substantial value proposition for algae biofertilizer, which is explored in the next chapter.

6. Ana Cultivates Algae Biofertilizer

We know more about the movement of celestial bodies than about the soil underfoot.　　　　　*- Leonardo da Vinci*

Leonardo was right, our modern society spends 100 times more on space, NASA has a $18.3 billion budget, than on soil research. Ancient, as well as current indigenous civilizations worshipped the soil as the foundry of life. Proof of soil veneration comes from Latin name for man, *homo*, which is derived from *humus*, the stuff of life in the soil.

Fertile soils are among the most beautiful resources on our planet. Soils hold more than twice as much carbon as the atmosphere and play a crucial role in carbon cycling, food production, and water and nutrient retention. Each acre houses many living creatures, including over 900 pounds of earthworms, 2,400 pounds of fungi, 1,500 pounds of bacteria, 133 pounds of protozoa, 890 pounds of arthropods and algae, and possibly some small mammals. An acre of soil may contain over 10,000 species of microorganisms, which contribute to soil and ecologic biodiversity.

Modern industrial agriculture, (MIA) systemically extracts, erodes and brutalizes soil, eventually killing it. About five million acres of fertile agricultural lands in the US are lost to production every year due to urban development or degradation. America loses one square mile of farmland every hour, or 9.5 acres per minute. When cropland becomes infertile, farmers may have to move their family and leave their farm. This chapter explores another algae miracle – restoring life, organics and fertility to worn out and abandoned cropland.

Algae biofertilizer

After nutrient cycling, biofertilizers provide the strongest tool single-celled organisms can provide to improve food production. The survival of our children depends on knowledge and respectful behaviors to soils, as well as actions that preserve and protect precious croplands.

Soil ecosystems provide the foundation of human life. Food production depends on fertile land to grow the produce that provides energy, health and vitality. The intensity and scale of modern cropland use and abuse suggest we have much yet to learn and implement to sustainably manage cropland. Soil remains possibly the least understood of nature's critical ecosystems, and are among the most degraded.

Biofertilizers grown and delivered though smartcultures recycle nutrients in a manner that enables farmers to leave each field better than they found it in terms of *in situ* nutrients, organic material, soil structure and erosion resistance. The smartcultures design engages farmers to transform food production from a systemically extractive and pollutive industry to regenerative and clean. Smartcultures also allow substantially more social equity in food production than industrial farming.

Smartcultures, (Sustainable Micro-Algae Regenerative Technologies), reengineer the food production system, beginning at its foundation – soil – with tiny microflora in plant roots that are ingeniously self-regulating and self-regenerative.

Soil ecology

In the 11,000 years humans have practiced agriculture, communities survived or starved based on their relationship with their soil. Preserving fertile soils enabled farmers to grow crops to feed their families, communities and societies. Some of the earliest written documents on record are agricultural manuals that organized, preserved and conveyed soil and crop production knowledge.

For the last 60 years, MIA has treated cropland as a disposable commodity. Systemic soil overuse, abuse and abandonment are foolish, wasteful and extremely pollutive. Much of the best cropland has been farmed for years, but millions of those fertile acres will be unavailable to our next generation because they are worn out. Cropland expansion requires more inputs because the new ground is less favorable, flat and fertile. Not only will our next generation be short of fertile cropland, but they will also find some of the critical inputs for fossil food production have become extinct. If a foreign country inflicted the current level of soil degradation and pollution of US ecosystems that we impose on ourselves, our nation would declare war on that country. As we deplete, degrade and discard our soil, we silently erode the foundation of our society.

Cropland loss

When our soils and natural resources are no longer able to support food production, our society as we know it will end. Failing sufficient resources for food production, we will have no economy, no viable society and no national security. President Franklin Delano Roosevelt saw the ravages of the soil degradation that led to the US Dust Bowl and said:

"The nation that destroys its soil, destroys itself."

The FAO reports that 33% of the world's cropland has become so degraded, it has been abandoned in the last 40 years, and continues at 29 million acres a year. The U.S. net cropland losses from 1982 to 1992 covered an area the size of New Jersey. Farmers should be stewards of their land, but a recent USDA report shows that about 40% of US cropland is leased. Even worse, 80% of the lessees are non-farming landlords, who show little concern for sustainable practices.

Cropland degradation occurs from several MIA practices. Farmers plant monocultures repeatedly that wear out the soil by extracting the essential nutrients and humus. Genetically modified seeds need more cultivation, water, fertilizer and pesticides – all of which damage soil fertility. Both chemical fertilizers and irrigation increase soil salinity, which builds and eventually becomes fatal for crops.

When fields become unfertile, they must be abandoned because the soil does not support crops. Half the remaining cropland globally is so degraded it takes twice as much fertilizer and three times more irrigation water to achieve normal crop yields. Several Central American countries had to abandon over 75% of their cropland due to erosion. Farmers clear-cut rainforests, then their topsoil vanished.

Nature requires about 500 years to replace 25 millimeters, (1 inch) of lost topsoil. The minimal soil depth for agricultural production is 150 millimeters, (about 6 inches), but most crops need deeper soils. Fertile soil is a nonrenewable, endangered ecosystem that with degradation, systemically diminishes crop yields until the soil become unfertile and sterile. Restoration of degraded cropland using current technology may cost $40,000 and acre, making the process non-economic.

The Environmental Working Group collaborating with the USDA found that the rich, dark soil in America's Heartland is being swept away at rates many times higher than official estimates. In some places in Iowa, storms have triggered soil losses that were 12 times greater than the USDA average for the state, which is 6 tons per acre. A single storm can strip 100 tons of soil per acre from cropland, according to researchers using the new measurement techniques.

Organic farming

In spite of the numerous advantages associated with organic food production, less than 1% of the world's croplands are farmed organically. About 4% of European Union's farms, where farmers receive subsidies to use organic methods, practice organic farming. The US has only 0.8% of cropland and 0.5% of pasture certified for organic production. Organic farms are smaller than industrial farms. Nearly all the research on organic production has been conducted on small farms.

Animal manure creates several problems; nutrient pollution, pharmaceutical disposal and inefficiency as a fertilizer. Over 70% of pharmaceuticals sold in the US go into animals and 80% of antibiotics. Both flow out in the animal waste.

Animal waste polluting watershed

While the actions taken by organic farmers are commendable and less pollutive, most industrial farms in the US are unlikely to convert to organic production any time soon. The US would need at least 10 times more farmland than currently exists to create enough organic compost to transition all farms to organic production.

Organic famers run the risk of animal pharmaceuticals re-emerging in their produce. The USDA and FDA organic regulations limit raw manure use to no more than 120 days before harvest, to limit the possibility of foodborne illness being present on the crops. Many crops have less than a 120 growth cycle, which makes organic farming difficult. Manure animals are often raised thousands of miles from field crops – which makes transporting heavy manure impractical. Even if meat and dairy animals were raised close to grain fields, there are far too few animals to supply sufficient manure for the vast Corn Belt croplands.

Organic fertilizers are highly variable in nutrient composition. Synchronizing nutrient availability with plant growth and development needs represents a major challenge for organic farmers. For many farms, organic fertilizers simply may not be available or affordable, or the transportation costs are prohibitive.

Organic and industrial farming are equally consumptive of fossil resources, including fertile cropland, fresh water and fossil fuels. Organic compost and manure as fertilizer consume huge amounts of fuel, time and physical labor. Organics must be collected, loaded, stored, transported, and then applied to fields. Compost must be plowed into soils in order to avoid N volitazation. Organic farming saves on agricultural chemicals, but organic farmers must pay more for fertilizer and often experience lower crop productivity.

The Root of the Problem

Land plants made a major compromise when they evolved from algae 500 million years ago – the development of roots. Roots were necessary to hold land plants in place, as well as to create a plumbing system to extract water and nutrients from the soil. Unfortunately, roots created a heavy production drag for plants because growing and maintaining root structures consumes about 30% of a plant's energy. Roots also anchor the plant in place, creating a dependence on the soil moisture and bioavailable nutrients present in the plant's root zone or rhizosphere. The rhizosphere constitutes the narrow region directly influenced by soil microorganisms where roots can absorb them.

Communities of nano-sized algae have lived symbiotically with plants for millennia. As land plants moved inland from ancient shorelines, they needed a foundation and food but they had no roots. Algae formed soil crusts that provided the foundation that enabled plants to withstand wind and weather. Algae also supplied food energy in bioavailable nutrients before plants had roots. Thus, algae provided the bridge that enabled water-based plants to adapt to terrestrial ecosystems. Today, terrestrial algae continue to live symbiotically with land plants. Algae, and the microflora they attract, provide plants with a full set of macro- and micronutrients, while they continuously improve soil structure.

Roots significantly limit plant growth because these delicate appendages can take up nutrients when they are in a bioavailable form, usually after they have been broken down by soil microbes in a process called mineralization. Therefore, even though a nutrient such as P may be present in rhizosphere, a plant cannot use that nutrient until it has been processed and mineralized by microorganisms into a digestible form, called reactive or bioavailable P. When a plant experiences a growth phase without a needed macro- or micronutrients in bioavailable form, growth may continue, but with a dilution of nutrient density.

Erosion of Nutrient Density

The post–World War II, Green Agricultural Revolution increased crop yields, but half our global population currently suffers from caloric and micronutrient deficiencies. Many people consume thousands of empty calories, yet remain malnourished and obese because their diet is deficient in essential vitamins, minerals and micronutrients.

Calories are empty in the sense that the foods have high levels of sugar and starch while delivering few other nutrients per calorie consumed. Consumers want to consume foods that deliver more nutrients per calorie rather than less. In *The End of Food*, Paul Roberts describes how and why nutrient erosion degrades the sensory qualities of food, especially color, texture and taste.

MIA's focus on increasing yields has caused slow, yet systemic erosion in the nutritional quality of our food. The levels of essential nutrients in the food supply has declined in each of the last few decades, with double-digit percentage declines in iron, zinc, calcium, selenium and other nutrients essential for human health. Farmers grow produce with higher yields by weight, but with more starch and sugar but fewer total nutrients and lower nutrient density.

Consequently, each calorie delivers more sugar and starch with fewer vitamins, minerals and other micronutrients. The erosion of the nutritional value of food diminishes human health and contributes to a litany of diseases, especially obesity, diabetes and heart problems. Higher yields make farmers more money but create the hidden costs of lower nutritional quality with amplified health risks.

Genetically engineering seeds to grow bigger produce causes the plants to devote energy in head or seed production at the expense of deep roots. Industrial agriculture causes roots to atrophy because plentiful chemical macronutrients, (but not micronutrients) are readily available in the topsoil. Modern fertilizers act like Twinkies, junk food for plants.

Aggressive use of chemical fertilizer and tillage increases soil erosion, degrades local ecosystems, increases water demand, and dilutes nutrient density. Lack of micronutrients makes crops weak and vulnerable to pest and disease vectors.

Ana Cultivates Algae Biofeed

Microflora

Microflora serve plants and animals at the bottom of the food pyramid and remain the most undeveloped biological system on earth. Nature places millions of microorganisms in the roots of every plant, similar to their placement in the human gut, to support natural processes that improve digestion. Smartcultures simply **cultivate** and **amplify** nature's nanocultures to improve crop production and produce quality.

Microalgae and their microorganism symbionts form the foundation for the soil food web and provide bioavailable nutrients for higher-level plants and animals. These nano-communities work as a team to improve soil structure and fertility. Algae represent nature's oldest energy production and storage system and they attract vibrant communities of microflora that are beneficial to plants in many ways. Algae communities grow quickly and can restore soils that have been diminished, depleted or destroyed by industrial agriculture.

Algae provide an efficient organic nutrient-delivery system for crops. Algae biofertilizer delivers the full spectrum of nutrients plants need, including micronutrients, vitamins and minerals, which moderates or eliminates hidden hunger. Smartculture algae biosystems permit microfarmers to cycle nutrients for biofertilizer.

Smartcultures

Smartcultures, Sustainable Micro-Algae Regenerative Technologies, are SMART, in the sense that they follow nature's path. They reduce farmers' costs while they improve produce yield and quality.

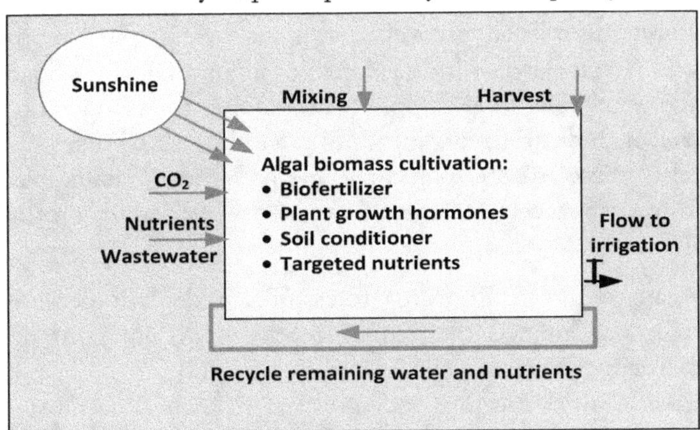

Smartcultures algae biosystem

Rather than paying high prices for chemical fertilizers, and using them once, farmers can continuously recycle and reuse nutrients from the farm's waste stream. Rather than systemically extracting soil nutrients and organics, farmers can cultivate algae and microflora to add nutrients and organics to their cropland. Rather than using chemicals that destroy soil microbes and soil structure, smartcultures cultivate microbial communities that improve soil structure. MIA degrades soil, promotes erosion and creates severe pollution, while smartcultures improve soil structure and reduce nutrient waste, erosion and pollution.

Smartcultures represent a set of biotechnologies that mimic nature to provide enhanced soil structure and nutrients to plants. Every farmer and gardener knows plants thrive in amended soils; they grow faster, stronger, and larger, and they have better color, taste and texture. Smartcultures enable farmers to minimize the high cost of fertilizers by recovering nutrients from the farm waste stream.

Smartcultures leverage the power of nature's tiny biofertilizer biofactories. These microbial communities rebuild stronger soils by gathering and delivering nutrients and growing rich organic material that produces heavier, healthier and hardier plants. Target nutrients carried in algae biofertilizers can be delivered in precise amounts at specific times during a crop's growing cycle.

Algae biofertilizer stimulates natural plant growth hormones and acts biologically to condition soils. Plants germinate earlier and grow faster, larger and hardier with smartcultures. Stronger plants are better able to withstand the stressors of heat, drought and pests.

Smartcultures add nutrient recovery and microalgae biofertilizer delivery to the actions associated with sustainable organic farming. Success in developing a reliable food supply will require the cooperation and integration of industrial, organic and abundance farming methods. Fortunately, these diverse farming methods are compatible, and smartcultures can accelerate the adoption of ecofriendly practices by industrial farmers.

Farmers may use smartcultures regardless of altitude, latitude, longitude or geography, as long as their farms receive sufficient light to grow crops. Smartcultures are easy to use and require only a few hours a week of a farmer's time during the growing season. In most cases, smartculture technologies require no heavy lifting, operation of large equipment or exposure to agricultural chemicals or poisons.

Nature provides very little for free, and smartcultures are no exception. Smartcultures leverage nano biofactories that can capture N_2 from the atmosphere and solubilize P and other nutrients locked in the soils. These biofactories can bioaccumulate nutrients from waste, brine or ocean water. While these actions are not free, they create only a modest expense and can be accomplished with minimal or no consumption of fossil resources.

This portable smartculture unit (left), grows algae in vertical tubes, using the farm's waste stream nutrients. The algae may be harvested for a host of bioproducts, or metered into irrigation water to carry nutrients to crops. Special nutrients may be added to the culture at various stages of crop growth to improve yield.

The nutrients needed to support crops must come from an organic or inorganic source. Smartcultures favor organic sources from waste streams. However, in circumstances where insufficient organic material is available, farmers may resort to inorganic chemicals to grow algae biofertilizers. Farmers may choose to operate one or both nutrient recovery and/or delivery systems. A nutrient recovery biosystem with an accessible irrigation system may service a large area of cropland. Farms without irrigation can leave the algae in liquid concentrate and spread the biofertilizer on the fields.

Large farms may site their recovery biosystem on one part of the farm and place several delivery systems near the fields. Another model uses one large smartculture for biofertilizer production. Tanks on trailers take the biofertilizer to various locations where it is metered into irrigation water or, without irrigation, sprayed on fields.

The configuration for nutrient recovery operations is site specific depending on the type of farm. An animal production facility may set up nutrient recovery near the manure source. Crop-based farms may site nutrient recovery at a location where water tends to run-off the farm. Smaller farms may operate as cooperatives for community nutrient recovery.

Nature's path

Smartcultures addresses food production challenges with sustainable solutions. The core concept comes from Aristotle, who suggested using nature's way.

> *"If one way be better than another, that you may be sure is nature's way."*
> — *Aristotle*

Smartcultures mimic nature by employing nature's original nutrient-delivery system for plants – algae – to deliver targeted organic nutrients precisely when plants need them.

Crop yields increase significantly because the plants receive targeted nutrients in a form immediately bioavailable to them, at each step of growth, development and fruiting. Field tests demonstrate that crops grown with algae biofertilizer have larger, stronger and deeper root systems, enabling them to absorb the micronutrients that give produce enhanced nutritional profile, size, color, taste and texture.

Bioavailable nutrients are nano-sized and are quickly absorbed by plants, minimizing or eliminating nutrient waste, erosion and pollution. Algae continue to grow in the field, building stored energy in humus that plants can tap at a later time. Algae attract symbiant communities of microflora that, together, create a rich soil crust that stores nutrients and minerals while minimizing wind and water erosion. The additional humus improves soil organics, fertility and water holding capacity. Smartcultures typically uses local algae that has evolved through eons to thrive in situ, in the local soil and microclimate.

Algae biofertilizer

Microalgae and macroalgae, (seaweed) are different in nutritional value but both act as excellent biofertilizers. Farmers along coastlines have used seaweed as biofeed both crops and animals for millennia.

Algae biofertilizer and soil conditioners are made up of an array of water soluble minerals. While chemical fertilizers typically contain only NPK nutrients, algae biofertilizers may deliver over 80 minerals, growth hormones, amino acids, fatty acids, cytokinins, auxins, vitamins and enzymes. Biofertilizers stimulate organic activity in the soil and lower toxic residues from various salts and chlorinated hydrocarbons. Toxins from harmful organisms such as nematodes, molds and fungus infestations are also reduced by activated plant growth hormones that are stimulated from algae bioactive compounds.

Algae kindle production of natural plant growth hormones that accelerate cell division and elongation, producing taller, greener and lusher plants that produce higher yields. Algae also stimulate plants to secrete compounds that repress harmful bacteria, fungi and other pests. In some cases, algae operate as a catalyst that helps plants manufacture natural insect repellent on their leaves.

Biofertilizers decrease the need for insecticides by activating the plants' natural self-defense to stressors. Biofertilizers enable plants to produce a distasteful waxy film on their surfaces to repel insect attacks. Insects bypass treated fields in favor of untreated plants. Algae biofertilizer improves the health and density of beneficial soil microbes which suppresses the proliferation of pathogenic microbes. Hardier plants build stronger cell walls due to the presence of silica, which provides resistance to temperature spikes.

Algae biofertilizer creates positive effects on the growth of vegetables, fruits, nuts and other crops. Algae biofertilizer is used for conditioning seeds and as biofertilizer for soil or foliar application during the growing season. Biofertilizer stimulates seed germination, growth and yield for many different crops.

Fish emulsion is well-known among farmers and gardeners to provide hearty nutrients for excellent produce. Fish are what they eat, which is algae. Fish emulsion provides a liquid form similar to algae biofertilizer. Macroalgae products make up over half of the biofertilizers and growth enhancement products sold for home hydroponics. Crop enhancement results published on macroalgae biofertilizers are similar to microalgae.

Algae Bioamplification

Smartcultures cycle nutrients to amplify the indigenous terrestrial algae present in local soil. A two-year field study with Del Monte Fresh Foods in Yuma, Arizona provided metrics that demonstrate the benefits of biofertilizers compared with chemical fertilizers. The algae bioamplification worked as the metrics obtained over several crop cycles exceeded the values shown in the following table.

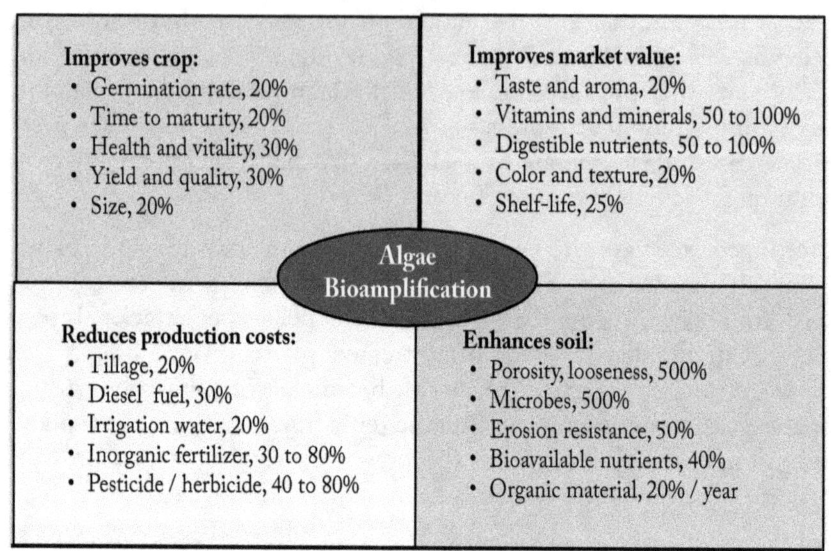

Algae biofertilizer value proposition

This project cultivated algae biofertilizer next to a melon field and flowed the biofertilizer into the 200-acre field. The field, bordered on three sides by raw desert, had been abandoned because the soil was worn out from years of production. The desert soil had high pH, 9.4, and extreme salinity and compaction. A drip irrigation system 18 inches underground delivered the biofertilizer in the irrigation water. A section of good adjacent cropland was fertilized with standard chemical fertilizers as the control.

Algae physioactivators strengthen and accelerate plant growth and development and improve crop quality. Physioactivators contain active algae ingredients that stimulate plant nitrate reductase, phosphatase and other plant enzymes that are responsible for absorbing minerals and their uptake in the plant. Algae physioactivators stimulate root development, which improves nutrient absorption. The mechanism improves photosynthesis by increasing the activity of chlorophyll and its contents in the stem and leaves. Physioactivators increase plant biomass, both above ground and the root system.

Algae biofertilizer improved germination rates, speeded time to maturity and increased plant flowers, leaf and fruit size. Earlier melon maturity created a 20% market price premium. Melon yield increased over 30%, and size increased over 20%.

Algae physioactivators support flowering and fruit setting by stimulating the synthesis of polyamines – compounds responsible for flowering, pollination efficiency and fruit set. Higher levels of polyamines stimulate the intensity of cell division, which leads to faster growth. Physioactivators make plants more stress tolerant to extreme weather conditions, pests and diseases.

The biofertilized melons had better color, aroma and texture. Nutrient analysis performed by an independent lab found the melons had 300% more sugar and 60% more vitamin C. Blind taste tests at Arizona State University preferred the biofertilized melon 17:1. The farmer was most delighted with tests that showed three extra days of shelf life, since the melons were shipped from Yuma to New York City.

The field soil structure improved substantially. The pH dropped to from 9.3 to 7.8, while soil porosity, or looseness, improved 500%. The looser soil allowed irrigation water to percolate below the root zone, taking with it the excess salt. The melons were grown on six-foot berms covered with black plastic to diminish weed competition. When, after four crops cycles over two years, the black plastic was removed, the red desert soil had turned green. The algae cells that were not bioabsorbed by the plants had continued to grow using the sugars given off by the melon roots. The algae had provided substantial new organic materials to the soil, which led to a 20% improvement in moisture retention. Improved soil structure reduced tillage and diesel fuel cost, as well as water for irrigation.

The increase soil organic carbon increased as the algae grew in the soil. The organic matter improved moisture retention as it slowed the loss of water and nutrients below the rhizosphere, netting 25% less irrigation. Algae produced sugars that attracted a host of beneficial microorganisms. All the microbes worked symbiotically to bring the dead soil back to life.

The farm manager was able to reduce N fertilizer by 70%, due to the N_2 fixing cyanobacteria. Both P and K fertilizers were reduced about 50%. Algae solubilized considerable P fixed in the soil, which substantially reduced fertilizer cost. Algae biofertilizer also delivered micronutrients, vitamins and trace elements, which improved yields and quality. A nearby field was destroyed by a whitefly invasion. Some whiteflies visited the biofertilized field, but the plants were able to produce a natural pesticide that seem to ward-off the whiteflies. The whiteflies fled the field without pesticides.

Algae biofertilizer review articles align with these results for both micro and macroalgae biofertilizer. Macroalgae biofertilizer typically uses dead seaweed material, which does not add soil organics or humus benefits. Macroalgae fertilizer, like commercial chemical fertilizer works fine in the near term, but damages the soil over time, due to residual salt.

Summary

Smartcultures can increase farmers' income by improving crop quality and quantity. Farmers can save money and energy by lowering their consumption of fossil fuels by and reducing the need to apply chemical fertilizers. Smartcultures benefit the local ecology and can decrease air, soil and water pollution by 80%. Crop productivity, resource consumption and cost savings vary substantially based on soil fertility and structure. Smartcultures provide the highest added value for abandoned cropland, compacted soils depleted of nutrients or soil structures prone to erosion. Smartcultures provides the unusual value proposition that every farmer can leave each field stronger and more fertile after every crop.

Algae's nano package of nutrients stimulates plant metabolism and improves yields and quality. Animal cellular metabolism overlaps with plants in many ways. Animals need the same essential nutrients for successful metabolism, in different proportions. Algae biofeeds deliver these essential nutrients that improve yields and quality for animal farmers.

7. Ana Cultivates Algae Biofeed

"If anyone wants to save the planet, all they have to do is just stop eating meat. That's the single most important thing you can do. It's staggering when you think about it. Vegetarianism takes care of so many things in one shot: ecology, famine, animal cruelty".   *- Sir Paul McCartney*

Ana's quest to resolve world hunger cannot ignore the billons of committed carnivores that eat millions of tons of meat and dairy products. Increased consumption of animal proteins creates a towering demand for animal feed to grow animal protein for people.

In 30 years, algae meat substitutes will replace animal products as the primary source of protein for most sensible people. Consumers will hit a tipping point when algae meat substitutes clearly deliver a superior combination of health, taste, cost and ecological benefits.

Until consumers have a healthier choice, algae can improve animal products in a fashion similar to algae biofertilizer. Algae biofeed will improve animal products by delivering better nutrition than conventional animal feed. Healthier nutrition will result in healthier animal products, with enhanced nutralence, fats, color and taste.

A fascinating irony will occur with algae biofeeds. Staunch Texas meat producers will begin producing algae biofeeds for their animals. They will see excellent results in their animal's heath due to the algae biofeed foundational work from Texas A&M University's AgriLife.

After several years, a light bulb will flash in each farmer's brain. Farmers are smart, and they will think: "It's my mission to grow the best protein for human consumption, at the least cost. Why should I go to all the trouble to grow animals for protein when my algae biofeed delivers twice the protein of beef – and the protein is healthier?" Farmers will decide to grow protein for direct human consumption and skip wasting resources, time and money on animals. Farmers, or their children, will lead the charge to "save our animals."

Until algae meat substitutes are available, algae can lift farmers by reducing the cost of animal feed and substantially cutting the ecological footprint required for feed production. Comprehensive nutritional and toxicological studies have demonstrated that algae biofeed as supplements or substitutes for food grains, support healthier animals that grow faster, enjoy higher survivability and create less waste.

Meat consumers

Today, two out of three world citizens subsist on local or imported grains and local plants because they cannot afford meat. Livestock are the single largest user of land as meat production accounts for 70% of all agricultural land and 40% of the land surface of the planet. In order to produce meat, roughly one-third of the world's food grains go to feed livestock. Livestock are responsible for nearly 20% of all GHGs.

Meat is dramatically underpriced relative to plant foods because meat production benefits from huge crop and Big Oil subsidies. Meat prices reflect no environmental accounting, even though meat producers extract trillions of gallons of fossil water, billions of gallons of fuels and millions of tons of chemicals. Agricultural waste streams are the primary polluters of surface and groundwater, yet the public costs and resource losses are not reflected in meat prices.

Many new consumers have become carnivores and demand animal-based foods, which create an ecological cost of multiple pounds of grain for each pound of meat or dairy. People around the world desire to emulate the consumption patterns of the rich, especially in China, India and Indonesia. Animal production is neither ecologically cheap nor efficient. Feed conversion ratios, grain to meat, are:

- Farm raised tilapia or catfish   2:1
  (most weight gain in fish is water trapped in tissues)
- Poultry – chicken or turkey   3:1
- Salmon and trout   5:1
- Beef, pork or lamb   8:1

Algae biofeed does not change feed conversion ratios, but algae biofeed will provide an eco-smart alternative to consumptive food grains.

Meat production consumes one-third of the world's fresh water. A fast-food half-pounder costs $6 and requires 2,600 gallons of water to feed the steer. *Scientific American* published an excellent case about the alarming ecological cost of beef. Algae biofeed can cut the water cost of beef by 70%.

Ana Cultivates Algae Biofeed

Squeeze on animal producers

Social actions and medical research have put meat producers in a bind. Animal activists criticize farmers' cruelty to animals. Social justice voices shout that 760 million tons of food grains are fed to farmed animals so that people can eat meat. Environmentalist are backed by the UN's *Livestock's Long Shadow*, which concludes that eating meat is "one of the top two or three most significant contributors to the most serious environmental problems, at every scale from local to global." Eating meat causes 40% of greenhouse-gas emissions, more than all the cars, trucks, ships and planes in the world combined. Health advocates point out that vegetarians live six to 10 years longer than meat-eaters. A healthy vegetarian diet supports a lifetime of good health and provides protection against numerous diseases and the biggest killers – heart disease, cancer and strokes.

Composition

Algae biomass provides excellent nutritional value for biofeed. **Lipids** are long carbon chain molecules. Lipids store energy for the plant and serve as the structural components of cell. **Proteins** are large organic compounds made of amino acids arranged in a linear chain connected by peptide bonds. The plant's genetic code determines the sequence of the amino acids, but nutrient limitations may cause changes to the production of amino acids. Most proteins are enzymes that catalyze biochemical reactions and plant metabolism. Other proteins maintain cell shape and provide signaling functions. **Starches** are complex carbohydrates which are insoluble in water. Plants use starches to store glucose as plant sugar.

The composition variation among species varies tremendously. Some algae hold 80% lipids while others are 60% protein, and still others are 92% carbohydrates. Species selection is critical, not just for the desired composition, but for a host of micronutrients and growth biostimulants that vary widely across species and strains.

Algae varieties offer almost infinite combinations of features and useful bioactive compounds. Special attributes such as omega-3 oil production are being enhanced through selection screens for naturally occurring organisms and mutagenesis, which is similar to a rapid hybridization process. Some companies are modifying algae to express more, (or less) of certain compounds. Algae biofeeds will become far more desirable as specialty compounds that help animals with digestion, biosorption, and protection against pathogens are discovered and used.

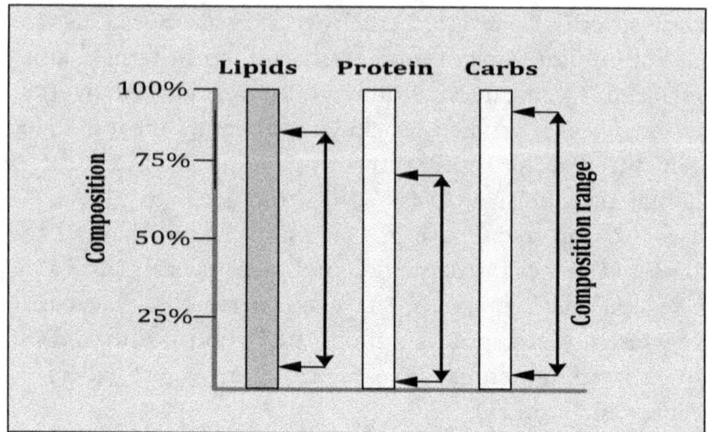

Various algae species display wide composition variation

Algae biofeed provides the full set of essential nutrients for animals. Considerable research focuses on protein quality, which varies across various species of terrestrial plants and algae. Unsurprisingly, different types of animals grow faster and better with different proteins and micronutrients.

Algae composition displays some variation by season. Therefore algae biofeed formulation requires continuous monitoring, which is similar to field grains. Traditional crops such as corn are often mixed with antibiotics to improve digestion. Other supplements such as omega-3s may also be added. Algae biofeed can eliminate pharmaceuticals and feed additives. Various algae species provide different amounts of each specialty oils.

- **Linoleic acid, LA,** a non-essential unsaturated omega-6 fatty acid used for soaps, emulsifiers, quick-drying oils and a wide variety of beauty aids.

- **Arachidonic acid, AA,** is an omega-6 fatty acid but is not essential. It may moderate inflammation and plays a role in the operation of the central nervous system.

- **Eicosapentaenoic acid, EPA,** an omega-3 fatty acid that gives the same benefits as fish oil.

- **Docasahexaenoic acid, DHA,** an omega-3 fatty acid is the most abundant fatty acid found in the brain and retina. DHA deficiency causes cognitive decline and increases neural cell death.

- **Gamma-linolenic acid, GLA** an omega-6 fatty acid that fights inflammation.

Many species are tolerant of wide variations in growing conditions. Some species are nearly blind to geography.

The following table displays compositional ranges for popular cultivars shown as a percentage of dry weight, (dw).

Algae	Lipids	Protein	Carbohydrates
Anabaena cylindrica	4–7	43–56	25–30
Aphanizomenon flosaqua	3	62	23
Arthrospira maxima	6–7	60–71	13–16
Botryococcus braunii	86	4	20
Chlamydomonas rheinhar.	21	48	17
Chlorella ellipsoidea	84	5	16
Chlorella pyrenoidosa	2	57	26
Chlorella vulgaris	14–22	51–58	12–17
Dunaliella salina	6	57	32
Euglena gracilis	14–20	39–61	14–18
Prymnesium parvum	22-38	30-45	25-33
Porphyridium cruentum	9-14	28–39	40–57
Scenedesmus obliquus	12–14	50–56	10–17
Spirulina platensis	4-6	46-630	8-14
Spirulina maxima	6-7	60-71	13-16
Spirogyra sp.	11–21	6–20	33–64
Spirulina platensis	4–9	46–63	8–14
Synechococcus sp.	11	63	15

Algae protein

Algae provide a sustainable protein source for animal feed, but is it good enough protein? Comprehensive medical and nutritional studies have demonstrated that many different types of algae produce high quality proteins that are comparable to alternative protein sources.

All proteins are not created equal. Proteins are composed of different amino acids. The nutritional quality of a protein is determined by the content, proportion and availability of its amino acids. A good measure, the protein efficiency ratio (PER), is expressed in terms of weight gain per unit of protein consumed by test animals in feeding trials. Another metric, the biological value, (BV), is a measure of nitrogen retained in an animal's tissues for growth or maintenance.

Digestibility also reflects the quality of a protein, which is measured by the digestibility coefficient (DC). Finally, the net protein utilization (NPU) – equivalent to the calculation $BV \times DC$ – is a measure both of the digestibility of the protein and the biological value of the amino acids absorbed from the food.

E.W. Becker's review article presents these values for popular algae species. E.W. Becker concluded that the average quality of the algae protein was equal, and in many cases superior to conventional plant proteins, including soy.

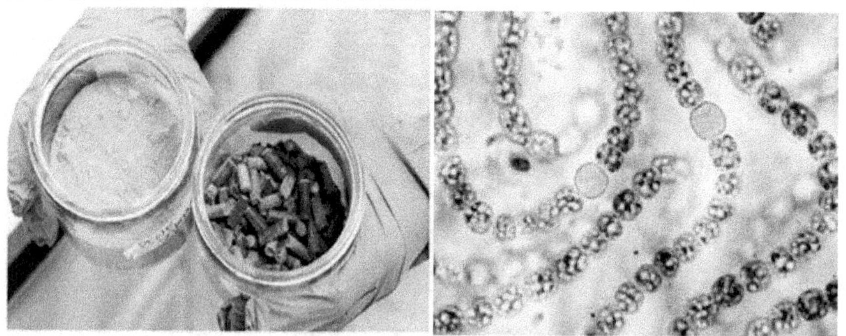

Algae biofeed process in powder, pellets and growing

Algae provide far more than just good protein. Algae deliver a superior breadth of high quality nutritional compounds, including peptides, carbohydrates, lipids, vitamins, pigments, minerals and trace elements.

Algae regulations

Before a new food item is declared safe for human consumption, it must undergo a series of detailed toxicological tests to prove the harmlessness of the product. No serious anomalies have been reported in short-term or long-term feeding experiments, or in studies on acute or chronic toxicity.

Many algae producers in the US have acquired GRAS status, the FDA recognition that the material is Generally Regarded as Safe. The list of food authorized under the provisions of the European Union includes algae as feed material. No GMO algae biofeeds are available today. GMO's foods or feeds are not allowed in the European Union.

Algae biofeed nutrition

The nutritional contents of algae are rapidly gaining traction as valuable components in animal feed. Algae biofeeds provide a renewable source to substitute the conventional ingredients in animal feed for meat, dairy, poultry and fish.

Algae contain all the vitamins, minerals and micronutrients needed for healthy biofeeds, including Vitamins A, B1, B2, B6, B complex, C, D, and E. Algae are rich in niacin, iodine, potassium, iron, magnesium and calcium. Each cell contains polysaccharides, sugar and starch, as well as iron, sodium, phosphorus, magnesium, copper and calcium. Algae biofeeds deliver nutritional benefits not available from land plants, strong antioxidants such as omega-3 fatty acids. Productivity metrics for algae are extraordinary.

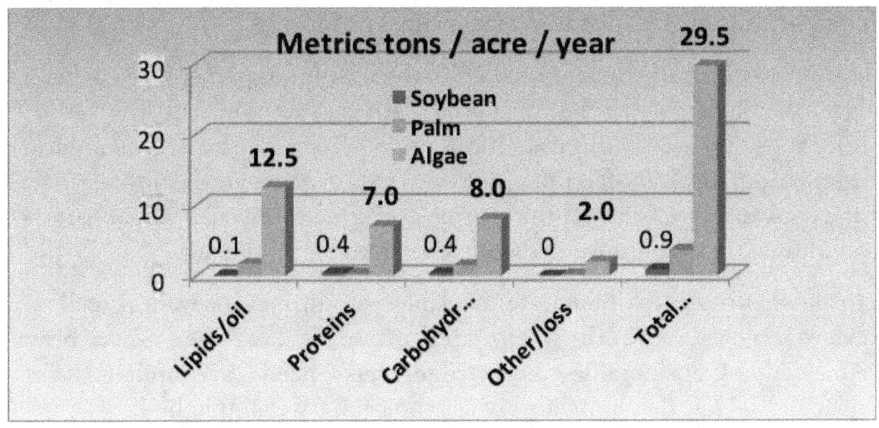

Productivity of algae biofeed compared with palm and soybean

Algae biofeed grows with substantially more productivity per acre or hectare today. Biofeed productivity will probably increase 10x in the next ten years due to innovations in biotechnologies.

Algae biofeeds provide a rich source of high quality protein, vitamins, micronutrients (trace elements), and carotenoids. Algae also deliver polyunsaturated fatty acids (PUFAs), especially of n-3 and n-6 series such as eicosapentaenoic (EPA), docosahexaenoic (DHA), and arachidonic (AA), which are considered pharmacologically important for animal and human dietetics and therapeutics. Algae produce valuable biomolecules including astaxanthin, lutein, beta carotene, chlorophyll, phycobiliprotein, and beta-1,3-glucan. Several studies explain how each biomolecule enhances animal health.

Most these valuable algae biomolecules are not synthesized in the animal, (or human) body, but are considered essential for healthy body and brain growth and development. Therefore, animals must get them through their diet. Algae provide both an ideal nutrient package and the delivery system. The algae package is so small it becomes immediately bioavailable to the animal. The algae delivery system provides higher nutralence than conventional animal feed, with significantly higher nutrient quality, density, diversity and bioavailability.

Limitations

A few limitations are key to understanding why algae biofeeds do not yet dominate the feed market, except in aquaculture. Most of the investment in algae production has gone into biofuel. This has helped algae as nutrition indirectly, because the non-lipid portion of the algae biomass is often considered as biofertilizer or biofeed.

The current cost of conventional animal feeds, food grains, is lower than algae, thanks largely to the substantial subsidies to crops and Big Oil. If those subsidies were removed, and a price put on carbon and ecological degradation, algae biofeed production would be substantially lower cost than conventional feeds. If the true cost of irrigation water were charged to farmers, they would immediately switch to algae biofeed.

No books on algae biofeed are available yet, although several excellent review articles on both micro and macroalgae as feed have been published. Considerable knowledge has been accumulated for aquaculture, and fish biofeed serve as the primary example here.

Cellular metabolism across animal species enjoys more similarities than differences. However, as with any discipline, the devil is in the details. Different animal life stages, herbivore or carnivore, type of mouth, number of stomachs, gut microbes, digestive and excrement systems, make each animal species idiosyncratic.

Demand limits algae production today. Without demand for algae biofeeds yet, there are simply no commercial producers. Algae scientists are making substantial progress on producing more and higher quality biomass at lower cost. Demand for algae bioproducts will expand quickly as production costs fall. Feed formulations also limit algae biofeeds. Considerable research suggests algae may provide the best nutritional solution as a supplement rather than replacement to conventional feeds. Certain animals may need time to adapt their digestive system microbes by starting with a partial algae diet. Feed formulations will advance quickly as more food scientists explore the largely unexplored, but rich nutritive value of algae biofeed.

Algae biofeeds will make the biggest impact with omega-3 fatty acids. Algae are the "whole foods" of the ocean, serve as a natural nutritional source for most fish. Salmon are carnivores, but also eat lots of algae. Their beautiful pink color comes from the astaxanthin that they cannot synthesize themselves, but get from their algae diet. Algae provide similar color and fish oil for krill, shrimp, crabs and lobsters.

Algae biofeeds have already penetrated the aquaculture market. About one-third of the algae produced in 2017 goes to feed fish. Fish farming needs algae biofeed solutions because fish farming puts tremendous strain on wild fish.

Aquaculture's dilemma

Due to vast overfishing, nearly 90% of global fish stocks are either fully fished out or overfished. Humans have managed to wipe out 92% of the ocean's largest fish. These animals: sharks, Bluefin tuna, swordfish, marlin, and king mackerel, are at the top of the marine food chain. Fishermen now overfish further down the food chain, depleting the oceans of prey fish. Scientific studies predict that aquaculture will outgrow the supply of fishmeal as soon as 2020. Farmed fish production outstripped beef production for the first time in 2015.

The FAO report, *The State of World Fisheries and Aquaculture 2016*, demonstrates that global fish consumption per capita has reached record-high levels due to aquaculture and consumer demand. An average person now eats roughly 44 pounds of fish per year, which doubles the 1960s sea food consumption.

While fish stocks are plummeting, consumers accurately view fish as healthier protein than other meats, which creates an exploding demand for fish protein. Increased demand for fish follows the compelling health benefits research on fish oil, omega-3 fatty acids.

Omega-3 fatty acids

Omega-3 fats are essential polyunsaturated fatty acids (PUFAs) for digestion, muscle activity, blood clotting, visual acuity, memory and many other body functions. They are particularly important for proper cell division and function of cell receptors.

About 8% of the human brain's weight is comprised of omega-3s—the building block for an estimated 100 billion brain neurons. DHA and EPA play pivotal roles in neural structure and function, protecting them from oxidative damage, inflammation, and cumulative destruction inflicted by other chronic insults.

Strong evidence shows how fish consumption, and in particular oily fish or omega-3 supplements, lowers the risk of death from coronary heart disease (CHD) by 36% as well as cancers and inflammatory diseases like arthritis. The research shows that daily intake of only 250 mg of EPA+DHA per adult gives optimal protection against CHD. Children need only 150 mg for optimal brain development. A recent FAO/WHO report concluded that fish in the diet of women giving birth to children lowers the risk of suboptimal development of the brain and neural system in newborns.

Omega-3 fatty acids advertisement for stronger brain

Other research suggests that DHA+EPA prevent several types of mental illness, including depression, bipolar disorder, schizophrenia and substance dependency. Brain disorders are dramatically increasing globally in the cost of mental disorders is not greater than the cost of CHD and cancer combined. Fish or fish oil supplements boosts the effectiveness of antidepressants and improves attention both in those with ADHD and those without attention deficit hyperactivity disorder. In the young and cognitively healthy, fish oil supplementation improves memory performance.

Omega-3s have been shown to possess antidepressant and neuro-protective properties. Julius Goepp found that aging humans who consumed more omega-3s had increased gray matter. Most new tissue development was observed in the part of the brain associated with happiness and intelligence. Other studies indicate omega-3s may slow the progression of brain impairments, including dementia. Similar studies showing the cognitive benefits of omega-3s for newborns appeared in the prestigious journal *Lancet*. In one of the largest studies of its kind, scientists analyzing the diets of 12,000 pregnant women found that children of those who consumed the least omega-3s were 48% more likely to score in the lowest quartile on IQ tests.

To meet consumer demand, fish farming tripled from 1995 to 2007. By 2009 aquaculture, culturing fish in a controlled environment, accounted for 50% of the fish consumed globally. A World Bank and FAO study, *Fish to 2030: Prospects for Fisheries and Aquaculture*, predicts that 62% of food fish will come from aquaculture by 2030. This may seem like good news for wild fish, but it is not.

Sourcing problem

Wild fish are being slaughtered by the billions for oil their bodies do not synthesize, omega-3s. No animals self-manufacture omega-3s. Wild fish obtain their oil through their diet, which is algae or algae feeders. Farmed fish fed only food grains are not marketable because they have no omega-3s. Farmed salmon not supported by omega-3 dietary supplements grow white meat that is not marketable. Consequently, 88% of global fish oil consumption goes to aquaculture.

Farmed salmon are carnivorous and eat about five pounds of wild fish to produce each pound of salmon. Today 60% of the world's salmon production is farmed. In 2015, more than 2.2 million tons of farmed salmon were produced, which cost the lives of 11 million wild fish.

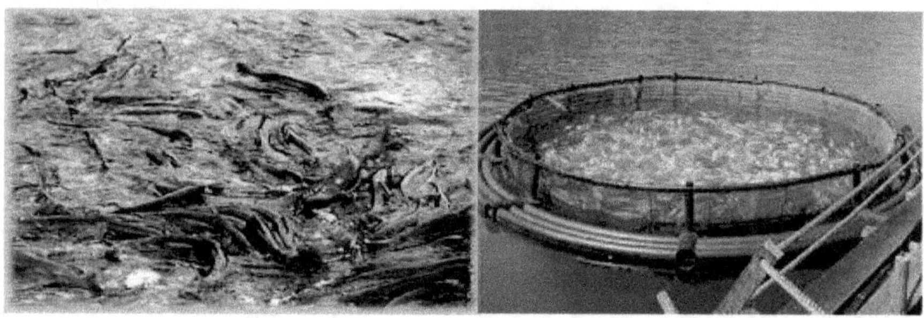

Salmon farming

Actually, farmed salmon are responsible for the consumption of even more prey fish, which are used for providing better color, flavor and omega-3s. A FAO report estimates that salmon retain only about 43% of the essential EPA+DHA from their diet in their flesh. Additional millions of prey fish are sacrificed to make salmon and trout marketable to consumers that expect good color, flavor and fish oil.

Pet food market

Pet foods add to the demand for wild fish. Fish protein has emerged as a major portion of the $24 billion US pet food market. Many companies such as Merrick, BioOregon Protein and Purina One market pet foods with whole fish as the main product, followed by fish meal. These pet foods advertise pure proteins in the form of fish protein concentrate, fish bone meal, dehydrated shrimp and crab, as well as fish oil.

Orijen promotes wild caught fish extensively with the package promise that each 6kg package of Six Fish contains 5kg of fresh, raw or dried wild-caught fish. The promise continues saying that 2/3 of Orijen's fish are fresh, or raw (flash-frozen), including the top 6 fish ingredients.

Pet food producers are adding substantial demand to the wild fish catch, but they are also building market intelligence that will help algae biofeeds. Hill's Science Diet, among many others, promote specific feed formulations for each life stage and emphasize healthy aging. Pet food companies are educating consumers on the value proposition for natural antioxidants and preservatives, colorants, emulsifiers and thickeners, functional ingredients and vitamins and minerals. Nearly every pet food company now offers pet probiotics to improve the health of each animals' microbiome or ecosystem.

Pet food producers know that many people feed their pets with even more care than they give to their family. Educating consumers through their animals about food ingredients will accelerate the transition to algae biofeeds for animals and algae foods for people.

Pet foods consume massive amounts of wild fish

The plight of krill

Krill are the tiniest prey fish harvested, but their premium fish oil makes them valuable. They are also a favorite meal for penguins, albatross and fur seals. About 4 million tons of krill are harvested from the Southern Ocean each year, primarily for their omega-3 oil.

Fish are what they eat. When tiny, translucent krill move, the algae inside their thin shell quivers. Prey fish like krill are algae concentrators. Their eating habits benefit predator fish by collecting algae nutrients in a higher density package. Billions of krill are harvested annually for the omega-3 oils they compressed from their algae diet.

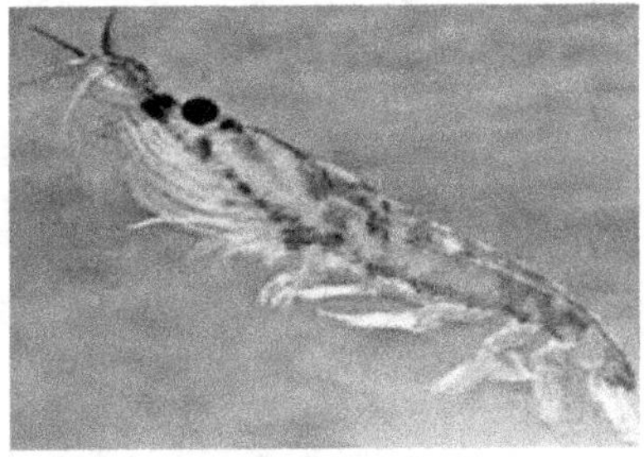

An adult krill

Krill are threatened by climate change and overfishing. Young krill need deep water with low acidity and a narrow range of temperature for their eggs to hatch and develop successfully. Krill larvae feed on algae on the underside of sea ice. Adults require temperatures below freezing to digest their food. Each of these critical features for krill survival are threatened by climate change. Oceanographic scientists calculated krill populations have declined 80% since 1970, due to overfishing and warmer ocean temperatures and the loss of the krill nursery, sea ice.

Algae biofeeds can reduce the pressure on krill and other prey animals by delivering healthy fish oil and protein – without killing fish.

Algae biofeed

The major difference between feed sources is that algae biofeeds can be produced using abundance methods. They can be grown year-round with no or minimal fossil resource consumption. Algae do not require fertile cropland, so the biofeed does not compete with other food or feed crops. They can be grown without using fresh water or fossil fuels.

Cycling nutrients allows farmers to produce biofeeds without the high cost of chemical fertilizer and the time and energy required to apply those fertilizers. Algae biofertilizer permit farmers to minimize pesticides and poisons because the plants produce their own defensive shield. Farmers also benefit from avoiding erosion and pollution of their fields and local ecosystems. Algae biofeed offers many benefits for animal farmers, compared with terrestrial field crops.

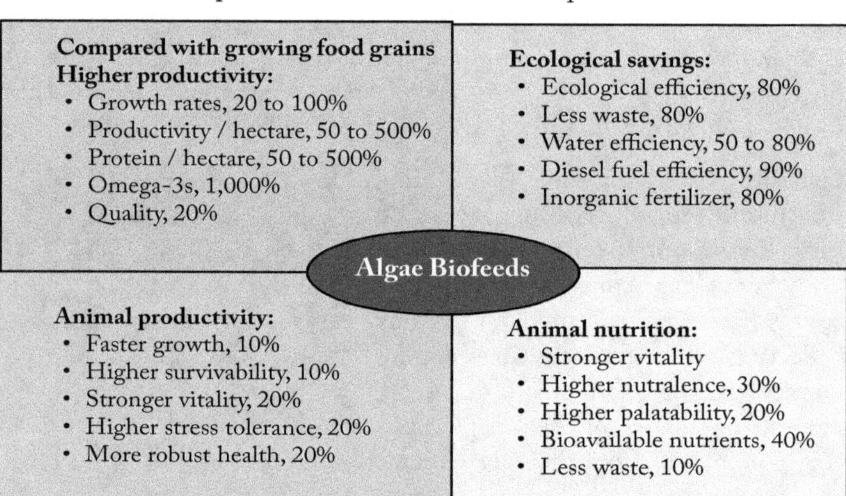

Algae biofeed advantages compared to conventional feed

Rick Barrows leads the USDA animal nutrition and productivity studies focused on aquaculture. The USDA Trout Grains research website has both an ingredient evaluation program and a digestibility database. Similar algae biofeed results have been created for chickens, but there have not been as many biofeed trials for other animals.

Higher feed productivity

Growth rates for algae biofeed may be 20 to 70 times faster than food grains. Grain crops grow only during the growing season, but algae production continues year-round. This is great for animals, because they are hungry year-round. Productivity per hectare can be a high multiple compared to field crops. Omega-3 fatty acids DHA and EPA are not available from food grains, but are abundant in certain algae cultivars. Plant-based omega-3 are found in a few sources; flaxseed, chia seeds, walnuts and leafy greens. These plants contain alpha-linolenic acid, (ALA), a shorter-chained PUFA built with 18 carbons bonds. Plant sources are completely devoid of DHA and EPA, that are built on 22 and 20 carbon structures, respectively.

Advertisers falsely promise that plant-based ALA is a precursor to EPA and DHA, so they can cash in on the omega-3 value proposition. However, the enzyme required to convert the shorter 18 carbon ALA into long-chained omega-3 does not work effectively in most people. Typically, less than 1% of the ALA is converted to EPA, which is too small to provide a positive health impact. Conversion rates are dependent on a person's genetic origin and adequate levels of vitamins and minerals.

Consumers bought more than 26 million gallons of Horizon milk supplemented with DHA oil in 2016, from plant-based ALA. The milk is promoted as a nutritional enhancement. The omega-3s allow Horizon to advertise health benefits and charge a higher price, with the claim: "DHA Omega-3 Supports Brain Health," Sales of the DHA supplemented milk topped $250 million, representing 14% of all organic milk sold in 2016.

Many modern products, such as omega-3 eggs and milk are mislabeled. They are enriched with plant-based 18-carbon-chain ALA omega-3. No ALA studies provide proof of any positive biological effects. Meta-studies have concluded that plant-based omerga-3 do no harm, but neither do they benefit the body, like their longer chained cousins, DHA and EPA.

Ecological savings

Algae biofeed production creates a positive ecological footprint. Food grains are horrendously consumptive and wasteful of nonrenewable resources. Algae biofeed can reduce waste and pollution by more than 80%. While algae biofeed production captures waste carbon and other nutrients, the only thing emitted is pure oxygen.

Algae biofeed can grow using no freshwater. Algae thrive on waste, brine and even seawater. Half of the water stored in the earth is brine water, with a salinity in between fresh and seawater. The modest energy required to produce algae can come from green renewable sources such as solar, wind or geothermal. The use of non-potable water sources saves substantial amounts of freshwater for other purposes.

Algae Biosciences in Holbrook Arizona produced algae for EPA and DHA using the pristine brine water under the Painted Desert. The team found that they could produce nine successive algae crops with the nutrients from the ancient ocean before the essential nutrients for algae growth were depleted.

Animal nutrition

Animal growth and development is dependent on the quality, density, diversity and bioavailability of nutrients. Algae deliver extraordinary nutralence in their nano-cell package. Every bite the animal takes contains 30 to 100% more essential nutrients than food grains. Food grains often disguise their hidden hunger, due to lack of vital micronutrients, vitamins and minerals. The algae package brings the full set of micronutrients, around 70, that improve animal growth and vitality. The nano cells are so tiny day are easily absorbed by the animal digestive system.

Proof of high bioavailability displays at the other end of the animal. Animals fed algae biofeed typically produce 10 to 20% less waste. The California Farm Bureau reported that cost of waste management per cow on dairies was $0.45 an animal per day. Since some California farms milk herds of over 10,000 animals, a 20% reduction on waste would save a dairy farmer $27,000 a month.

Faster growth

Field studies show algae biofeeds can improve growth rates in fish up to 20%. Time is money for farmers, and faster growth and maturity improves cycle times and profitability. Animals display more stress tolerance to temperature spikes and pathogens. Animals with stronger vitality enjoy higher survivability, which improves yields. Robust health means farmers can save on farmaceuticals, which are very costly.

Algae-based bioactive peptides add significant value to animal feed. Natural algae peptides can reduce the total cost of growing animals by improving nutrient uptake, which reduces total food intake, and animal waste. Peptides can add sensory appeal to foods, including color, aroma, mouth appeal and taste. Peptides can reduce animal stress, enhance digestibility and improve growth and development.

Peptides activate the immune system, which increases growth and survival rates in meat and dairy animals. These tiny segments of protein increase the number, size and weight of eggs in fowl and increase hatch rate. Peptides counter bacterial and endotoxin anorexic effects, which improves health and vitality.

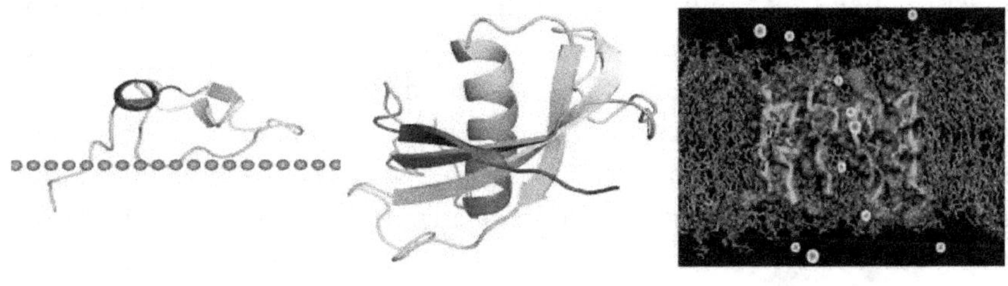

Antimicrobial peptides   *Defensins*   *Protegrins*

Immunostimulants

Antimicrobial peptides make up a part of the innate immunity of most organisms and are often involved in the immune system's first line of defense when faced with an invader. Defensins peptides consist of 18-45 amino acids attached to small cysteine-rich cationic proteins. Defensins function as host defense peptides and are active against bacteria, fungi and many viruses. The immune system uses these antimicrobial peptides to assist in killing bacteria, by binding to the microbial cell membrane. Once embedded, they form pore-like membrane defects that allow cells to pump out unwanted toxic substances, or allow entry of essential ions and nutrients. Protegrins are small peptides containing 16-18 amino acid residues. Protegrins are also highly microbicidal and also create membrane disruption, similar to other antibiotic peptides.

Polysaccharides, consisting of long chains of repeating sugar units, make up one of the most important classes of biopolymers. They provide biological activities such as enhancing immunity, antitumor, antibacterial, antiviral, and wound healing activities. These immunostimulants derived from algae and fungi have been used as dietary additives to improve fish health, weight gain, feed efficiency, and/or disease resistance. Immunostimulants can improve the innate defense of animals providing resistance to pathogens during periods of high stress, such as grading, reproduction, sea transfer and vaccination. The immunostimulants in fish larvae can improve larval survival by increasing the innate responses of the developing animals until its adaptive immune response is sufficiently developed to mount an effective response to the pathogen.

A review of β-glucan in aquaculture concluded that beta-glucans enhance growth, survival, and protection against infectious pathogens that threaten fin and shell fish. β-glucan is composed of a glucose molecule linked by the glycoside bond. It forms the major constituents of cell wall of some plants, fungi, bacteria, mushroom, yeast, and seaweeds. β-glucan has been studied to build knowledge on its receptors and the mechanism of action. The receptor present inside the animal body recognizes and binds to β-glucan, which in turn renders the animal with high resistance and enhanced immune response. Scientists have more questions than answers about β-glucan and immunostimulants.

Other animals

The premier world expert on algae-based biofeed, E.W. Becker, published a review article of macro and microalgae as biofeed inputs to the diets of poultry, pigs, cattle, sheep, and rabbits. Considerable research on algae biofeed has been carried out with poultry, probably due to their promising prospects for improved productivity. Supplementing poultry feed with microalgae as a protein source can improve their health, productivity, and value.

Chickens fed with algae biofeed were reported to have increased viability, improved overall health and reduced plasma concentrations of cholesterol, triglycerides, and fatty acids. These birds benefited from improved immune system as demonstrated by a significant increase in white blood cell count, improved fertility rates, and enhanced macrophage phagocytic activity. Spirulina intensifies the color of egg yolks, that makes eggs more esthetically pleasing for consumers. The intensified yolk coloration is due to increased levels of beta-carotene.

Of all the animals evaluated for algae biofeed or supplements, ruminants are the most promising because their stomachs best digest the high fiber content with the most extraction efficiency. Cattle will preferentially drink water containing 20% suspended Spirulina, increasing their daily water intake by 24.8 g/kg. This study also reported that 20% of the consumed Spirulina bypasses degradation within the rumen, allowing for increased digestion and biosorption of protein and nutrients within the abomasum. Incorporation of 200 g/day Spirulina with cattle feed was reported to be an economically effective method of increasing animal body weight, (8.5%–11%) and daily milk production, (21%). As well as increasing milk quantity, Spirulina supplementation has also been demonstrated to increase milk quality by decreasing saturated fatty acids, while increasing monounsaturated fatty acids and PUFA.

Tryon Wickersham and team at Texas A&M University's AgriLife division, has performed a series of feeding trials with algae biofeeds. Their conclusion is that the biofeeds performed well nutritionally and cows liked the taste. Wickersham noted that the algae biomass used did not have enough fiber or roughage, which cows need to keep their stomachs from becoming too acidic. Flax has the most fiber of all land plants, an is sometimes added to feeds. Some algae species have 10x the fiber of flax, so roughage should not be a serious issue.

Australian Premier Annastacia Palaszczuk announced plans for an algae biofeed farm in Queensland. She said: "Woods Grain will establish a new algae farm in Goondiwindi and trial new technology for the extraction of omega-3 oil from the algae. This could produce a high-protein feedstock for animals and open up the possibility of a brand new agricultural industry in the state."

Algae biofeed farm in Queensland, Australia

Acadian Seaplants in Nova Scotia, Canada developed Tasco[®], a proprietary algae meal derived from *A. nodosum*. Tasco has demonstrated beneficial properties when included in animal feed. Tasco has identified their algae biofeed offers enhanced feed for animal production.

Benefits include resistance to stressors, improved immune system, increased productivity/quality, and a reduction in pathogenic microorganisms in the final meat product. Higher animal productivity and health has been observed in several species, including both monogastric and ruminant species.

Summary

Algae promise to provide farmers with a higher quality protein that can be grown sustainably, year-round. Farmer do not have a choice today because there are no producers yet. As algae production becomes more productive, algae biofeeds will make farmers happy by lowering production cost and saving the substantial time, energy and ecological cost of growing animal feed on cropland. Algae biofeeds will make animals happy because they will be healthier, more stress tolerant and more animals will survive to maturity.

Algae will make consumers happy by delivering enhanced ingredients in food products, which we explore in the next chapter.

8. Algae Snacks, Condiments and Food Ingredients

The doctor of the future will give no medication, but will interest patients in the care of the human frame, diet and in the cause and prevention of disease. — *Thomas Edison*

Thomas Edison was right. Modern consumers and their doctors want food ingredients to protect the human frame. Microalgae such as Spirulina provide an excellent source of snacks, condiments and food ingredients such as lipids, proteins, polysaccharides, phenolics, carotenoids. Spirulina offers rich protein, about 60% by weight, which is 2-½ times more protein per kilogram than red meat. Spirulina contains the highest nutralence found in any food, offers more beta-carotene than carrots, more iron than raw spinach, and more calcium than milk on a gram per gram basis.

The tasty plant contains all of the essential amino acids, and 10 of the 12 non-essential amino acids, along with a potent array of other nutrients. The initial focus here is Spirulina, but other algae cultivars also offer a wide range of nutritional and health benefits.

Spirulina contains the highest concentration of protein for any plant, herb or animal on a gram per gram basis. The amino acid content of its protein is very close to the WHO standard. Spirulina also contains several essential vitamins, including vitamin A, (beta-carotene) and vitamin B12. It is also a very rare source of GLA (Gamma Linolenic Acid), an essential fatty acid. Spirulina also provides bioavailable iron.

Spirulina's protein efficiency ratio is very high, meaning the body efficiently uses the amino acids. Medical research has proven that Spirulina's biosorption by the body is among the highest of any foods. Field studies show that children who received a Spirulina supplement daily five days a week for two months had better nutritional status and improved intellectual status compared to those who did not. Web MD posts ratings on vitamins and supplements. Spirulina received 5 star ratings on effectiveness, ease of use, and satisfaction.

Shelf life and nutritional retention are critical for foods. Most plant and animal foods deteriorate very quickly at high temperatures. Shrimp, for example, offer a highly dense nutrient food package, largely because they are what they eat: algae. Both the shrimp meat and nutrients sour within minutes in the sun. Spirulina's adaption to heat allows the cells to go dormant when heat stress occurs so it can regenerate and begin quickly propagating again when good growing conditions return. Spirulina biomass retains its nutritional value when subject to high temperatures during growing, harvest, processing and storage.

Digestible protein (82-90% digestible), no cellulose cell walls.	B complex vitamins exceptionally high B-12), vitamin K, and other vitamins.	Phytopigments (phycocyanin, chlorophyll, carotenoids).	Minerals, including Ca, Fe, Mg, Se, Mn, K and Zn.
Vitamin E, comparable to wheat germ. Four times as much vitamin B12 as raw liver.	Best natural source of gamma-linolenic acid (GLA); important fatty acid for heart and joint health.	Essential fatty acids, e.g. sulfolipids may protect against HIV infection, T-helper cells.	Metallo-thionine compounds bind with radioactive isotopes.
Naturally rich in iodine.	Low carbs, 5-20%.	P, Ca and Mg > cow's milk.	Eighteen amino acids.

Spirulina's impressive nutralence package

The plant's prolific cellular reproductive capacity and their proclivity of cells to adhere and form spiral colonies makes Spirulina a large and easily harvested green biomass. Indigenous people harvested Spirulina using baskets to sweep the biomass off the surface of the water. Today, microfarmers typically use a fine mesh sieve to filter the spirals out of the water. Spirulina is a "nuclear plant," on the developmental crossroad between plants and animals. It is considered above plants because it does not have the hard-cellulose membranes characteristic of plant cells. Spirulina does not have a well-defined nucleus, hence its classification as a cyanobacteria.

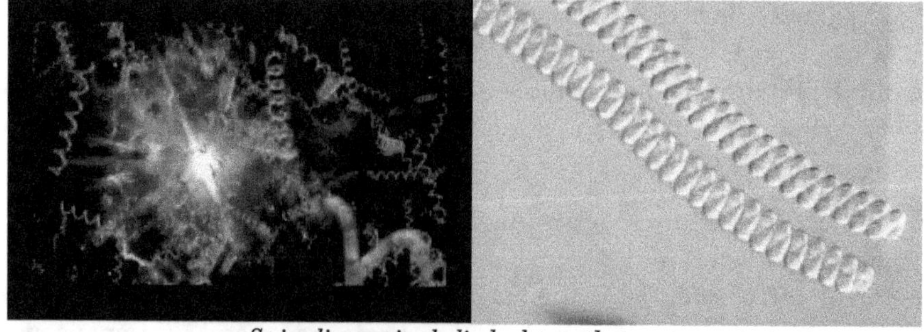

Spirulina spirals linked together

Spirulina produces direct food energy similar to other photosynthetic plants utilizing sunlight and chlorophyll. Spirulina embodies the simplest form of life. In contrast, other algae such as chlorella have developed the hard, largely indigestible walls characteristic of plants. The cells are extremely large for a single-celled organism, 0.5 millimeters in length. This is about 100 times the size of most other algae.

Spirulina grows naturally in mineral-rich alkaline lakes, which can be found on every continent, often near volcanoes. The largest natural stands of Spirulina today can be found at Lake Texcoco in Mexico, around Lake Chad in Central Africa and along the Great Rift Valley in east Africa. Many species have been found globally, but two that are indigenous to California, Mexico and Mesoamerica are *Spirulina platensis* and *Spirulina maxima*. Each has been widely cultivated and studied extensively due to their high nutritional and therapeutic values.

In Mexico and Central America, Spirulina grows spontaneously in ponds and lakes. It thrives in fresh, brine and salt water. Many climates in Mexico and Central America can grow Spirulina year-round. Spirulina is typically eaten locally fresh or dried. Solar drying it into a powder creates a flour similar to food grains that can be made into bread, tortillas, crepes or cakes. Fresh Spirulina can be eaten directly without any processing or cooking, eliminating costly energy consumption.

Spirulina has a colorful history as a nutritional food source for the Aztecs in Mexico. One of Cortés' soldiers described how local Aztec women harvested green biomass from Lake Texcoco and sold cakes called Tecuitlatl in the local market. French researchers rediscovered Spirulina in the lake during the 1960s, and the industry has flourished since. Spirulina served as a food in Chad, as far back as the 9th century Kanem Empire. Chad women make Dihé, (below), which adds protein, taste and nutrients to soups, stews, breads, snacks and cookies.

Today Spirulina is consumed by millions of people all over the world due to strong health benefits and nutritive value. Spirulina became popular again when both the Soviet Space Program and NASA proposed that it could be grown in space and used by astronauts for food, nutritional supplements and for reclaiming wastewater. The Great Algae Space Race in the 1950s and 60s reignited demand for Spirulina. Recent NASA and European Space Agency research on travel to Mars has rekindled interest in Spirulina for space flights.

The UN FAO recommends both national governments and inter-governmental organizations to re-evaluate the potential of Spirulina to fulfill both their own food security needs as well as a tool for their overseas development emergency response efforts. WHO calls Spirulina "An interesting food for multiple reasons, it is rich in iron and protein, and can be administered to children without any risk. We at WHO consider it a very suitable food." WHO currently sponsors small microfarms in Kenya, Iraq, Republic of the Congo, Dominican Republic/Haiti, Peru and Columbia. Spirulina was declared by the UN World Food Conference of 1974 as the "best food for the future."

Spirulina grows in microscopic spirals, which tend to stick together, making it easy to harvest. It has an intense blue-green color, but a relatively mild taste. The FDA allows manufacturers to use Spirulina as a color additive in candy and other packaged foods. Spirulina may be marketed in the U.S. as a food supplement and has GRAS status, (Generally Accepted as Safe) from the FDA.

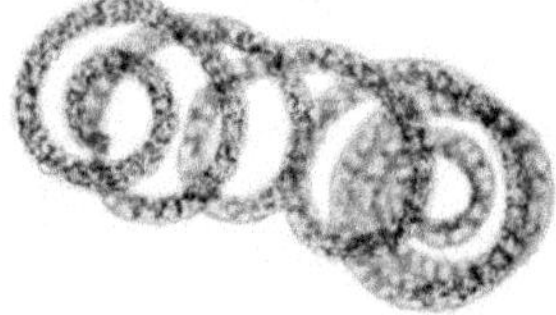

Spirulina's spirals and valuable blue and green pigments

A single tablespoon, (7 grams), of Spirulina powder contains 4 grams of protein, the B vitamins, copper and iron. It also contains magnesium, potassium and manganese, and small amounts of almost every other micronutrient humans need. A tablespoon delivers only 20 calories and 1.7 grams of digestible carbohydrate. A tablespoon of Spirulina contains a small amount of fat, (around 1 gram), including both omega-6 and omega-3 fatty acids in about a 1.5:1 ratio.

The quality of the protein in Spirulina is considered excellent, comparable to eggs and contains all the essential amino acids. A quarter pound Spirulina vegie burger delivers 2.5 times the protein of beef and twice the protein of soy bean.

Health benefits

Spirulina contains strong phytonutrients like phycocyanin and polysaccharides that offer substantial health benefits. Scientific studies that show that Spirulina benefits in the areas of is modulation or regulatory adjustment of the immune system, antioxidant and anti-inflammatory protection, cardiovascular health, cellular protection, detoxification from heavy metals and drugs and probiotic effects. The bulk of the scientific evidence supports the immunomodulation and antioxidant effects and most of the other benefits are also indirectly related to these two effects.

Animal and human studies have shown that Spirulina promotes innate, (inborn) immunity, the body's first line of defense. Spirulina promotes macrophage and T-cell proliferation, natural killers of pathogenic cell activity. Macrophage cells are responsible for detecting, engulfing and destroying pathogens and apoptotic cells. Macrophages signal the immune system to the presence of invaders.

Spirulina increases production of antibodies, infection-fighting proteins, and other cells that improve immunity and help ward off infection and chronic illnesses, such as heart disease and cancer. The immune response is vital to the regulation of antibody production, (acquired immunity). Spirulina stimulates the production of IgE, (immunoglobulin E antibodies) that modulate inflammation. Studies also show that Spirulina promotes IgA production in the saliva, thereby inactivating foreign bodies and toxins found in food. Spirulina contains phytonutrients that have strong antioxidant and anti-inflammatory activities. Antioxidants support cellular health by protect-ting cells from the damaging effects of reactive oxygen radicals. Both normal or abnormal metabolism result in oxidative stress, which damages cell membranes and DNA. Reactive oxygen radicals result in premature aging. The bioactive compounds in Spirulina have stronger antioxidant and anti-inflammatory effects to those obtained from eating fruits and vegetables.

Spirulina has been used as a protein and a nutritional supplement, as protein composed of amino acids make up 62% of Spirulina. Allergic reaction studies suggest that Spirulina protects against allergic reactions by stopping the release of histamines, substances that contribute to allergy symptoms, such as a runny nose, watery eyes, hives and soft-tissue swelling. Spirulina help with antibiotic-related illnesses. Although antibiotics destroy unwanted organisms in the body, they may also kill "good" bacteria called probiotics, such as *Lactobacillus acidophilus*. This can cause diarrhea. Spirulina boosts the growth of *L. acidophilus* and other probiotics.

Infection studies suggest that Spirulina offers both preventive and therapeutic activity against herpes, influenza, and HIV. Several recent publications reported that HIV/AIDS patients recovered faster with Spirulina. Spirulina helps with cancer too. In a placebo-controlled study, taking Spirulina reduced precancerous lesions known as leukoplasia in people who chewed tobacco. Lesions were more likely to go away in the Spirulina group than in the placebo group.

Preliminary evidence suggests that Spirulina may help protect against liver damage and cirrhosis (liver failure) in people with chronic hepatitis. Spirulina contains a high concentration of zeaxanthin, an important nutrient linked to eye health. Spirulina may help reduce the risk of cataracts and age-related macular degeneration.

Excellent books on Spirulina: Robert Henrikson and Gershwin / Belay.

Robert Henrikson's *Spirulina World Food* makes the case for this food's place in the global food chain. Gershwin and Belay's book not only describes the medical research supporting extensive therapeutic value, but also explains the various mechanisms that Spirulina nutrients use to enhance human health. Almha Belay, who has dedicated his scientific life to Spirulina, notes in the book that decades of Spirulina research have found no harmful effects from Spirulina as a food ingredient or human or animal food. "No harm" creates the opportunity for doctors to try Spirulina therapeutic solutions safely, instead of prescribing drugs that have serious side effects.

Algae vitamins

Algae absorb a wealth of mineral elements that concentrate about one third of its dry biomass. The mineral macronutrients include sodium, calcium, magnesium, potassium, chlorine, sulfur, and phosphorus, while the micronutrients include iodine, iron, zinc, copper, selenium, molybdenum, fluoride, manganese, boron, nickel, and cobalt. On average, one tablespoon of dry algae provides the same amount of calcium as ½ cup of milk, 1½-cups of soybeans, 8 carrots, or 22 tomatoes. A tablespoon provides the same amount of magnesium as 2½ cups of milk, ½-cup of soybeans, 9 carrots, or 6 tomatoes and the same amount of iron as 32 cups of milk, ⅓ cup of soybeans, 11 carrots, or 5 tomatoes.

Algae are also rich in iodine and selenium, critical trace elements that are highly variable in food supplies by geographic region. These minerals have been associated with endemic deficiency disorders throughout history. Algae concentrate these trace minerals and only small amounts of algae (one tablespoon) provide sufficient levels of these nutrients. Starship nutrition will benefit from algae nutrients integrated in natural and functional foods, which makes nutrient supplements superfluous.

Algae snacks and food ingredients

Beta-carotene, (provitamin A) is particularly high in algae, and algae powder is a common source of beta-carotene in dietary supplements and functional foods. Algae produce antioxidant vitamins (C and E) in concentrations several times higher than land plants. Vitamin E helps avoid neurological problems due to poor nerve conduction and anemia due to oxidative damage to red blood cells. Algae are a good source of all seven B vitamins including vitamin B12. Algae are unique as a plant source of vitamin B12 and algae, (particularly nori) is currently recommended as a dietary supplement for vegetarians who desire to obtain vitamin B12 from a natural, non-animal source.

Algae provide a mineral profile superior to that of land plants and even milk or soybeans. Mineral availability from land plants, particularly legumes and grain, is often compromised by phytic acid, which binds the minerals rendering them unavailable for absorption into the blood stream. In one investigation, phytic acid was undetectable in four species of algae, and iron absorption was 3.5-fold greater for algae compared to rice. Algae iron is easily absorbed by the human body because its blue pigment, phycocyanin, forms soluble complexes with iron and other minerals during digestion, making iron more bioavailable. Unlike iron derived from terrestrial plants, the bioavailability of algae iron is comparable to that of heme iron in meats.

Sea vegetables

The *National Geographic* Genographic Project shows human migration out of Africa 60,000 years ago. Our distant ancestors followed coastlines, probably because high nutralence sea vegetables were usually abundant. Over 200 sea vegetable varieties are eaten regularly along the Asian Pacific Rim today. Soups and broths are excellent ways to extract the bulk of the useful minerals and nutrients from sea vegetables. The texture and color of sea vegetables is incredible and unique.

Sea vegetables have historically been used as food ingredients, garnishes, flavorants, stock bases, and side dishes. Kelp supplements but does not replace spinach or lettuce in salads in Japanese households. Sea vegetables have such high nutralence, especially minerals such as iodine, that they are best used as a supplement. The RDA of 150 micrograms for iodine can be reached with a single serving of sea vegetables. Japanese consumers typically ingest 5-10 mg iodine daily, and experience lower rates of most Western diseases.

Sea vegetables dried in airtight packaging are an ideal pantry staple as they hold their nutrients for several years when stored in a cool dry place. They are found at Whole Foods, Trader Joe's, Costco, Fry's, Safeway, and Asian markets. Sea Vegetables can be found in the Asian foods section at mainstream markets.

Popular sea vegetables contain a broad array of health-promoting compounds compared to terrestrial plant and animal-based foods. Many offer high protein and most have very low fat. They are is a rich source of essential minerals such as potassium, iodine, magnesium, calcium, copper, selenium, zinc, and iron. They contain a trove of antioxidants, phytonutrients and rich fiber content that is required by the body. Sea vegetables are high in vitamins A, B, C, E and K. Many also contain omega-3 fatty acids and all the vital amino acids necessary for the body as per the WHO and FAO guidelines.

The Nielsen Global Snack Food report indicates algae snacks are among the fastest growing vertical market in the snack food category. Sea vegetables packaged as chips, dips, bits, bars, shakes and powders, enjoy both the best history and present positioning among algae snacks.

Credit: Dan Saelinger

Sea vegetables available in the West are typically dried. Soaking the leaves for several minutes makes them pliable. When rehydrated, the plant typically returns to its original rich color, which improves palatability. Sea vegetables can be added to soups or stews to add flavor, color, and texture, and to recover the nutrients. The cooking forum Epicurious.com offers superb sea vegetable recipes.

Some sea vegetables contain cancer-fighting agents that are useful in fighting or slowing tumors and other cancer conditions, such as colon cancer and leukemia. Brown sea vegetables such as kelp, wakame, and kombu contain glycoprotein and sulphated polysaccharides called fucoidans that possess immuno-stimulant, anti-viral, and anti-cancer properties. Research studies on the effectiveness of dietary sea vegetables on breast cancer have shown promising results in reducing the production of cancer-promoting hormones, including estrogen. They inhibit the proliferation of malignant cancer cells.

Fucoidans stimulate the immune system in several ways. The numerous important biological effects of fucoidans are related to their ability to modify cell surface properties. Consumption of algae that contain fucoidans offers protective effects through direct inhibition of viral replication and stimulation of the immune system, (innate and adaptive) functions. Fucoidan has been found to restore the immune functions of immune-suppressed mice, act as an immunomodulatory directly on macrophage, T lymphocyte, B cell, natural killer cells.

Sea vegetables offer a rich source of iodine, which is a vital nutrient required for the normal regulation of thyroid function, which also involves the brain and pituitary gland. A deficiency of iodine in the body can result in abnormalities such as thyroid enlargement or goiter, hypothyroidism, and mental retardation. Iodine is extremely crucial in pregnancy and breastfeeding for the normal development of the brain cells of the baby. Deficiency during these periods or early childhood can lead to weak intellectual growth and abnormal brain development.

Many sea vegetables have antiviral properties, which is why they are often used as a base for contraceptives. Some have the ability to help cells block penetration from viruses, including HIV, herpes, and human papilloma virus. Other species produce anti-bacterial compounds, adding to their protective properties.

Kelps produce alginates that specifically bind to toxins, including heavy metals and radioactive isotopes in the intestines, which allow the poison to flush from the body. They also assist in removing cholesterol from the liver and alleviating fatty liver conditions, which is a rising epidemic among obese people. Fucoxanthin keeps the body from absorbing up to 75% of ingested fat, making it a complimentary addition to fatty meals.

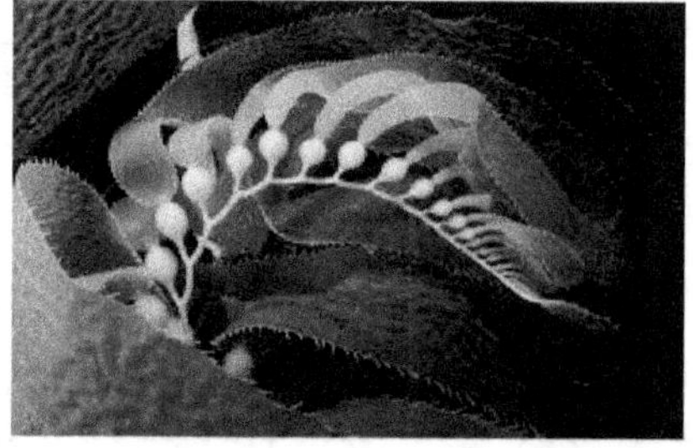

Kelp is the most readily available type of edible seaweed. In Asian countries, kombu and wakame are popular forms of edible kelp. Kelp products may come in granulated form, to be used in place of salt or as a mineral supplement in any food.

Kelp contains the highest natural concentration of calcium of any food – 10 times more than milk. Recent studies have explored the role of sea vegetables and kelp in particular in estrogen-related and colon cancers, osteoarthritis, and other conditions. Researchers found that kelp can slow the spread of colon and breast cancers.

A study found that a compound in the chloroplasts of brown seaweed called fucoxanthin may promote weight loss in obese patients. When combined with pomegranate oil. Other studies suggest that brown seaweed may influence glycemic control and reduce blood glucose levels, benefitting people with type 2 diabetes.

Wakame, (Undaria pinnatifida), is a leafy kelp with a salty-sweet zest. It provides calcium and magnesium, which protects against osteoporosis. It also acts as a diuretic, which helps reduce bloating. The wakame pigment, fucoxanthin, improves insulin resistance and burns fatty tissue.

Wakame provides abundant omega-3s and contains zinc and selenium. The calcium is bound in an organic chelated form, making it easily absorbable by the body. Wakame is a very popular menu item in Japan and Korea where it is served fresh or reconstituted, tossed with a bit of sesame oil over a bed of lettuce. Wakame adds spice and texture to miso soups or simple broths, floating thin strips. To prepare wakame, soak the leaves until tender. Add them to a cucumber salad, dressed with rice vinegar, sesame oil, and soy sauce.

Nori, (Porphyra), comes in paper-thin sheets with a mild earthy taste. Nori is the mildest form of sea vegetable generally available roasted in sheets. Nori has rich protein, (50% dw). One sheet has as much protein and three eggs.

Each sheet has as much fiber as a cup of raw spinach and more omega-3 fatty acids than a cup of avocado. Nori contains several antioxidants, especially vitamins C, and B12, which support cognitive function, as well as taurine, which helps control cholesterol. For a snack, toast strips of nori in the oven at low heat. A nori sheet may be covered with cooked brown rice layered with vegetables and wasabi. Roll up the assemblage and dip in a sauce of tamari, toasted-sesame oil, ginger, and rice vinegar. Nori makes a good wrapper for tuna salad tossed in olive oil and balsamic vinegar. Nori also comes as granules, which can be, sprinkled over salads or any food for a quick, healthy snack.

Kombu, (Laminaria japonica) is a leafy kelp with a full-bodied, savory flavor. Some kombu species are so high in sugar, they are called sugar wrack, containing mannitol, which is blood sugar balancing. Some chai teas are made from sugar wrack. Kombu provides iodine, which is needed to produce the two key thyroid hormones that control metabolism. The kelp is also rich in fucoidan, a phytochemical that acts as an anticoagulant.

Kombu has an almost magical ability to render beans more digestible and less gas-producing. Kombu contains enzymes that help break down the raffinose sugars in beans, which are the gas-producing culprits. Once they are broken down, the body can able to absorb more of the nutrients, and people can enjoy legumes without intestinal distress.

Kombu, sea cabbage, enhances flavor and offers huge health benefits for its tiny size. Kombu is reduces blood cholesterol and hypertension. The plant absorbs high amounts of iodine, which is essential for thyroid functioning.

Kombu also absorbs iron, which helps carry oxygen to the cells; calcium, which builds bones and teeth; as well as vitamins A and C, which support eyes and immunity. Kombu's triglyceride absorption has won praise for its effect on diabetes. Research found the antidiabetic effect can be attributed to the presence of alginic acid, which is abundant in kombu. Dashi soup stock is made by simmering dried kombu in water for five minutes. Kombu cooked with beans improves digestion as the glutamic acid renders the beans more easily digestible and less gassy.

Arame, (*Eisenia bicyclis*) displays long, thin, sweet-tasting strands that have a nice chewy texture. Arame provides lots of potassium, a mineral known among athletes for preventing muscle cramps. Arame has antiviral properties and an antiobesity effect, (at least in mice).

Arame　　　　　　　　　　　*Dulse*

Arame has a sweet, mild flavor. To make a summer salad, toss arame with pasta, sautéed mushrooms, tomatoes, basil, and olive oil. Dress up any cooked grain or potatoes with chopped arame. Add to stir-fried vegetables such as greens, turnip and squash with a dash of chili pepper.

Dulse is a red seaweed that attaches itself to rocks in the North Atlantic and Northwest Pacific oceans. Fresh dulse sautéed with butter and garlic makes a great starter. It may be rubbed with olive oil and salt and roasted in the oven to make chips. It is often shredded, dried, and sprinkled on soups.

The wealth of minerals found in dulse, including calcium, magnesium, and iron, contribute to bone mineral density. Dulse reduces the probability of developing osteoporosis protects joints and tissues. Dulse contains high levels of potassium, well-known vasodilator, that helps reduce the strain and damage to blood vessels and arteries caused by high blood pressure. Helping to lower blood pressure also protects against atherosclerosis, coronary heart disease, strokes, and heart attacks. Potassium can also help increase blood flow to the brain and capillaries.

The high levels of vitamin A found in dulse make dulse an ideal solution for vision problems. Vitamin A acts as an antioxidant and prevents free radicals from damaging the tissues of the eye and causing macular degeneration. Vitamin A can also slow the development of cataracts. The high iodine content in dulse keeps the thyroid gland behaving normally, and regulating many different hormonal interactions in the body.

Dulse is very high in dietary fiber, which helps regulate digestive processes, particularly for people suffering from constipation or diarrhea. The dietary fiber bulks up the stool and stimulates peristaltic motion, while also reducing inflammation and symptoms like bloating and cramping. The iron found in dulse regulates the production of hemoglobin, and aids in circulation. Having an appropriate level of iron in the blood staves off anemia, with its unpleasant symptoms of stomach and headaches, cognitive issues, and overall weakness. Dulse is rather chewy. It has only 20% of the iodine found in kombu, with high amounts of magnesium and calcium. Dulse also comes in shakable flakes, which are used for flavoring food.

Alaria is commonly used as a health supplement in avoiding or treating goiter. Bladderwrack was the first source of iodine discovered for treatment of thyroid disorders. The high levels of beta-carotene found in bladderwrack make it an ideal solution for someone trying to improve their vision. Beta-carotene is a strong antioxidant that can directly neutralize free radicals in the eyes and cornea. Bladderwrack can slow macular degeneration and prevent the development of cataracts.

Alaria, a winged kelp, is found in the North Atlantic Ocean, Greenland, Scotland, Iceland and Ireland. All count it among their traditional foods. The mature fronds can be used as a sunscreen, or to help heal burns. It suppresses nosh signals to the brain and accelerates metabolism, which also supports weight loss. Alaria can neutralize the inflammation, reduce swelling, and relieve pain for people suffering from gout, arthritis, hemorrhoids, or skin irritation. Eating alaria or rubbing it on sore muscles and joints relieves inflammation and pain.

Kombu and alaria contain the highest fucoidan content of all the sea vegetables. Fucoidan is a unique type of fiber that is found in high quantities within alaria. Research has connected fucoidan with many health benefits; lowering cholesterol, reducing blood sugar levels, and anti-tumor effects. Alaria fucoidan regulates a pathway-mediated TGFbeta receptor necessary for cell reproduction and growth. The compound degrades and inhibits cell growth and mobility *in vitro* and *in vivo* in breast and lung cancer. Slowing cell growth reduces cancer proliferation.

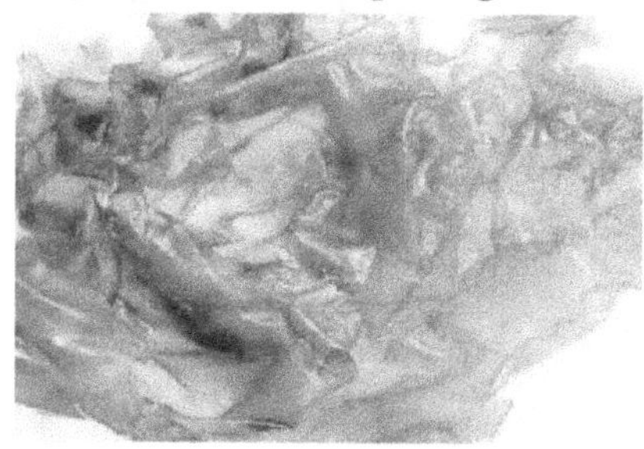

Sea lettuce, (*Ulva lactuca*) has a high mineral and trace element content because it thrives in nutrient-rich environments. When used topically, it tones the skin, and promotes the formation of collagen and elastin. Cats and dogs enjoy eating fresh sea lettuce.

The protein and iron in sea lettuce is higher than egg yolks or spinach. It also has loads of calcium, silica, manganese, potassium, and vitamins A, B, and C. Sea lettuce has proven to be strong antiviral against influenza/ antibacterial. Indigenous people carried dried sea lettuce to cover wounds and treat burns. All people had to do was soak the leaves in water to make a band aid for cuts, abrasion and bruises.

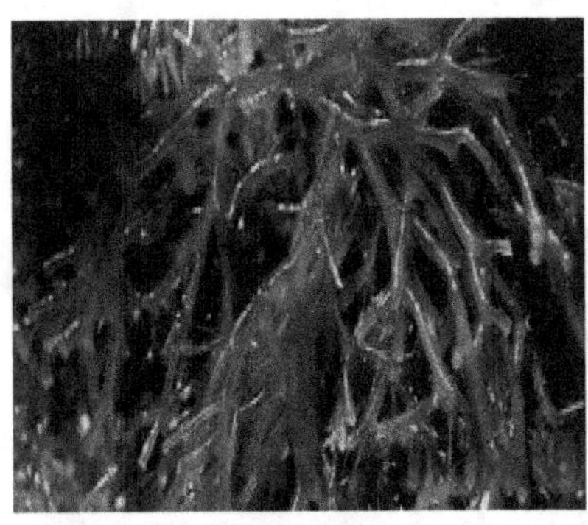

Irish Moss, or carrageen moss grows along the rocky Atlantic coasts of Europe and North America. It is a source of potassium chloride, a nutrient which helps dissolve catarrhs, inflammation and phlegm in the mucous membranes. Catarrhs cause congestion. It also contains antimicrobial and antiviral agents, helping to get rid of infections.

Irish Moss contains about 15% mineral and 10% protein. It softens into a jelly-like substance when heated in liquid. Caribbean natives boil Irish moss until it turns to jelly, add flavoring like vanilla or cinnamon, and top it off with rum and milk.

Natives claim the drink fights impotence and confers aphrodisiac qualities. The Irish and Scottish boil it to make a tapioca-like pudding dessert. Foods and drinks made with Irish moss provide good nutrition and are high in iodine, magnesium, calcium, manganese, zinc, bromine, and other minerals.

Caution, the consumption of excess sea vegetables may increase the quantity of iodine above acceptable levels. This can raise the concentrations of thyroid-stimulating hormone, which can cause serious conditions like thyroid and goiter. The guidelines of the Food and Nutrition Board set the daily level of iodine for adults at 150 mcg per day, and the tolerable upper limit is 1100 mcg/day.

Algae ingredients

Algae ingredients have added color, flavor and texture to foods for millennia. Most ingredients today come from sea vegetables because they have the longest history in foods because they are highly visible and accessible. People were not even aware of microalgae, except for Spirulina that grows in long strands, until the invention of the microscope.

Algae components are already intensely integrated in the food system. An Arizona State University study performed a market basket test across seven grocery stores. They found that 72% of processed foods included algae compounds. These included beer, sodas, soups, dairy products, bakery goods and canned vegetables.

Example algae food ingredients include:

- **Beer and diet sodas** — clarifier to remove haze-causing proteins.
- **Frozen foods** – pies and pastries fillings and ice cream.
- **Dairy** – whipped toppings, milkshakes, skim milk, evaporated milk, chocolate milk, ice cream, cheeses, cottage cheese, infant formulas, flans, custards, yogurt and instant breakfasts.
- **High protein drinks** – protein, vitamins and minerals.
- **Fruits** – fruit juices, syrups, jams and jellies.
- **Sauces, gravies and soy milk** – thickeners, emulates whole milk.
- **Pâtés and processed meat** — substitute fat with low calories.

Marine sea vegetables are exposed to extreme mechanical shear stress from waves and currents. They evolved unique substances that provided flexibility and toughness – carrageenans and agar. Land plants use stiff cellulose and lignin, which would shatter in pounding surf.

The **carrageenan** colloid cell-wall material finds many uses in foods. It acts as a stabilizer or emulsifier in many dairy and bakery products. Carrageenans have large, highly flexible molecules which curl, forming helical structures. After harvest, the sea vegetable dry in the sun, are baled and sent to a manufacturer where the biomass is ground and sifted to remove impurities. After treatment with a hot alkali solution, the cellulose is removed from the carrageenan by centrifuge or filtration. The carrageenan solution gets concentrated by evaporation.

Carrageenan – Red algae harvesting – Alginates

Carrageenans have no nutritional value on their own but have the ability to form a variety of different gels at room temperature. Food processors use carrageenan as thickening and stabilizing agents. Carrageenan exhibit pseudoplastic properties and thin under shear stress. Thinning makes food products easy to pump up in a food processing or packaging plant. The material recovers its viscosity and stiffens once the stress is removed.

The three main commercial classes of carrageenans are: **Kappa** that supply strong, rigid gels; **Lota** for soft gels; and **Lambda**, which forms gels when mixed with proteins rather than water. Lambda is used to thicken dairy and soy products. Example products include: Aqua fresh Tooth Paste™ – carrageenans keep the stripe from mixing – candy bars, chocolate milk, ice cream, sour cream, puddings and pie fillings.

Alginates provide alginic acid from brown algae which are used to thicken liquid products and make them creamier and more stable over wide differences in temperature, acidity and time. Kelp, fucus and sargassum produce alginic acid. Sargassum is fascinating sea vegetable. It begins its life growing in the tropics near coral reefs. Then, it breaks off and begins to drift, while continuing to grow at both ends. Ocean currents, such as the Gulfstream, carry the biomass across oceans.

Alginic acid is extracted from the cell walls. Alginate is a colloidal product used for thickening, suspending, stabilizing, emulsifying, gel-forming or film-forming. About half of the alginate produced is used for making ice cream and other dairy products, to make them smoother and to prevent ice crystals from forming. The remainder is used in products such as shaving cream, lotions, rubber and paint.

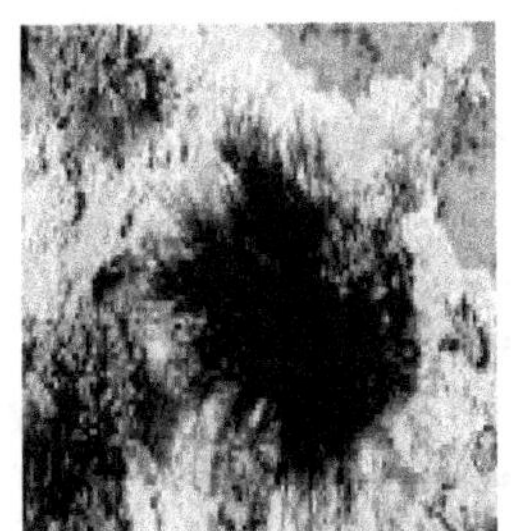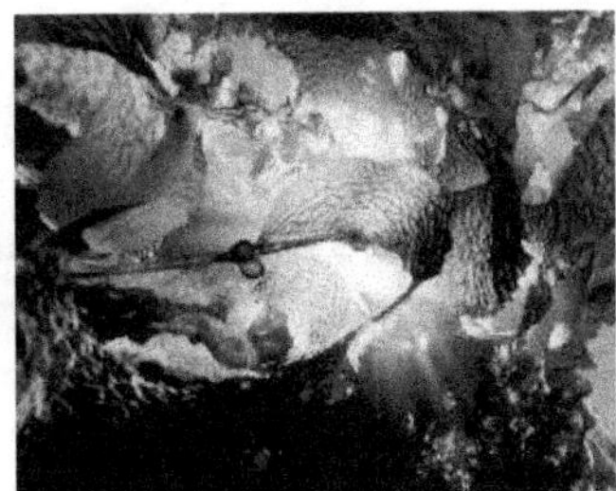

Alginic acid and Kelp

Alginates are used to thicken fiber-reactive dye pastes in textiles, which facilitate sharpness in printed lines, while conserving dye. Dentists use alginates for teeth impressions. Other products include: kelp shampoo, antacids, salad dressings, syrups, and Top Ramen Noodles.

Pigments form a large group of algae products because algae grow a spectrum of pigments to absorb sun light. Green algae absorb all colors of light but reflects one wavelength; green. Consequently, the pigments algae use to absorb all the other colors are available in the plant for photosynthesis. Three major classes of photosynthetic pigments occur among the algae: chlorophylls, carotenoids (carotenes and xanthophylls) and phycobilins.

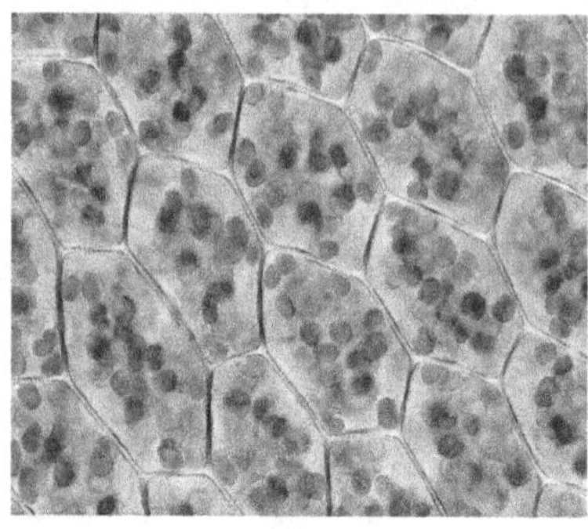

Chlorophylls (left) and carotenes are generally fat-soluble molecules that can be extracted from thylakoid membranes with organic solvents such as acetone, methanol or DMSO. **Chlorophylls** are the beautiful green pigments which algae use to capture energy from sunlight. Carotenoids are usually red, orange or yellow pigments and include carotene, which gives carrots their color. These compounds do not dissolve in water and are attached to membranes within the cell.

The phycobilins and peridinin, in contrast, are water soluble and may be extracted from algae tissues after solvent extraction of chlorophyll from those tissues. Carotenoids are called accessory pigments because they cannot transfer sunlight energy directly to the photosynthetic pathway, but must pass their absorbed energy to chlorophyll. Fucoxanthin, also a visible accessory pigment, gives the brown color to kelps and diatoms.

Agar. This substance, a polysaccharide, solidifies almost anything that is liquid. Agar is a colloidal agent used for thickening, suspending, and stabilizing. However, it is best noted for its unique ability to form thermally reversible gels at low temperatures. Agar has been used in China since the 17th century and is currently produced in Japan, Korea, Australia, New Zealand, and Morocco. Agar is important as a gelatin-like medium for growing organisms in scientific and medical studies.

Agar is used extensively in the pharmaceutical industry as a laxative or as an inert carrier for drug products, where slow release of the drug is required. Agar is a good source of calcium and iron, and is very high in fiber. It contains no sugar, no fat and no carbohydrates. It aids digestion and assists with weight loss. Agar carries toxic waste out of the body. Agar absorbs glucose in the stomach, passes through digestive system quickly and inhibits the body from retaining and storing excess fat. Its water absorbing properties also aids in waste elimination.

Examples of high-value algae ingredients are shown in the table:

Algae Snacks, Condiments and Food Ingredients

Ingredient	Algae source	Applications
β-carotene	Dunaliella salina	Pigmenter (food)
Astaxanthin	Haematococcus pluvialis, Chlorella zofingiensis	Pigmenter (aquaculture), anti-oxidant
Canthaxanthin	*Chlorella* spp., other green algae	Pigmenter (aquaculture, poultry and food)
Zeaxanthin	Chlorella ellipsoidea; Dunalielle salina	Anti-oxidant, food pigmenter
Lutein	Scenedesmus spp., Muriellopsis, others	Anti-oxidant
Phytoene	Dunaliella	Anti-oxidant, cosmetics
Echinenone	Botryococcus braunii, cyanobacteria	Anti-oxidant
Fucoxanthin	Phaeodactylum tricornutum	Anti-oxidant
Phycobilins, phycocyanin, phycoerythrin, allophycocyanin	Cyanobacteria, Rhodophyta, Cryptophyta, Glaucophyta	Natural pigment (e.g. cosmetics and food products), fluorescent conjugates, anti-oxidant
Arachidonic acid	Parietochloris incisa	Nutritional supplement
Eicosapentaenoic acid	Nannochloropsis spp., Phaeodactylum tricornutum, Monodus	Nutritional supplement
Docosahexaenoic acid	Crypthecodinium cohnii, Schizochytrium spp	Nutritional supplement
Sterols	Many species	Nutraceutical
Polyhydroxyalkonates	*Nostoc* spp, *Synechocystis* and other cyanobacteria	Biodegradable plastics

Polysaccharides	*Porphyridium* spp., *Rhodella* spp., various cyanobacteria	Thickeners, gelling agents etc., cosmeceuticals
Mycosporine amino acids	Cyanobacteria, Dinophyta and others	Sunscreens

High-value ingredients from microalgae – Michael Borowitzka

Summary

Algae offer a rich set of useful food ingredients. Food technology scientists leverage the valuable compounds to improve the function of foods beyond the obvious nutrients.

Algae functional foods are the explored in the next section.

9. Ana Cultivates Functional Foods

Let food be thy medicine and medicine be thy food.
– Hippocrates

Most modern consumers embrace the advice from Hippocrates, 2,500 years ago. People prefer getting their essential nutrients in natural food products rather than in pills, drinks or power bar supplements. This strong health movement has paved the way for functional foods.

Functional foods affect beneficially one or more target functions in the body, beyond adequate nutritional effects, in a way that is relevant to either an improved state of health and well-being and/or a reduction of disease risk. Considerable market research shows consumers want to eat enriched foods close to the food's natural state. Functional foods take many forms, including cereals, breads, bars, soups, stews or beverages that are fortified with specific nutrients, vitamins, herbs, and nutraceuticals. Common additions to functional foods today are long chain omega-3 fatty acids-DHA/EPA, flavones, beta-carotene, lutein lycopene, fiber, catechins, and anthocyanins.

Functional foods have gained substantial interest in food marketing. This new food category has become so important, two new scientific journals were born covering functional ingredients in the last few years. The *Journal of Functional Foods* serves as the official scientific journal of the International Society for Nutraceuticals and Functional Foods. The *Functional Foods in Health and Disease* is a peer-reviewed, open access journal. A library search for "algae and functional foods" returned over 400 articles. Market studies estimate the global sales for functional foods will eclipse $255 billion by 2024. When consumers realize the value of functional foods, that estimate is likely to double.

The XTC World of innovation, the most qualitative worldwide database of FMCG, (Fast Moving Consumer Goods), published a global database indexing innovative food products on the market. XTC reported several new food products containing algae launched in 2015–2016. These include sea vegetable crisps, enriched milk-based powder, sea vegetable biscuits, algae instant mashed potatoes, tagliatelle and *Wakame* salad.

The first comprehensive text on functional ingredients from algae was recently published. Herminia Dominguez, edited the comprehensive *Functional Ingredients from Algae for Foods and Nutraceuticals*, in 2013. The International Food Navigator launched an algae special edition newsletter in August 2016, highlighting new algae products and their derivatives.

Why the excitement?

The *Functional Foods: Key Trends & Developments in Ingredients* 2015 report predicted "Microalgae to be the most exciting functional food ingredients, showing great promise." The report projected algae protein, omega-3 fatty acids, vitamin D, magnesium and whole food microalgae would be the key algae ingredients incorporated in functional foods. The ingredients have driven the health-food market for years. Now they are entering the mainstream consumer food market.

Many food marketers target Millennials. These consumers, ages 14 to 33, view their food choices as healthier, more expensive, more natural/organic, less processed, better tasting and fresh. Millennials are also the most likely to believe that functional foods and beverages can be used in place of some medicines to relieve tiredness and lack of energy, retain mental sharpness with aging, and manage stress and eye health.

The *Journal of International Food Technology* reported that 80% of consumers believe that functional foods can help prevent or delay the onset of heart disease, hypertension, osteoporosis and Type 2 diabetes. Six in 10 associate functional foods with benefits linked to age-related memory loss, cancer and Alzheimer's disease. In 2014, 56% of consumers bought foods or beverages that targeted a specific condition, especially fat and cholesterol-lowering foods and drinks.

What are the functions?

Algae act as a natural biofactory of valuable compounds that can be extracted to serve as ingredients in functional foods. Algae contain carbohydrates, proteins, minerals, oil, fats and polyunsaturated fatty acids. Izabela Michalak created a table of useful algae compounds that serve multiple functions.

Function	Algae compounds
Antibacterial	Proteins, polyphenols, PUFAs polysaccharides, pigments: chlorophyll, carotenoids.
Antifungal	PUFAs, Pigments: chlorophyll, carotenoids, terpens, phenols.
Antioxidative	Proteins, mycospoine-like amino acids, PUFAs, carotenoids, tocopherol, ascobaate.
Anti-inflammatory	Proteins, PUFAs, carotenoids, polysaccharides, sterols – fucosterol, polyphenols – phlorotannins, porphyrin derivati, hoephorbide a and pheophytin a.
Anti-tumor	Polyphenols, carotenoids, polysaccharides.
Antiviral	Proteins, diterpens, polyphenols, polysaccharides, carotenoids.

Properties of bioactive compounds in algae extracts – Izabela Michalak

Scientific articles on each of these functions describe the mechanism for action. For example, algae antivirals use several ingenious strategies to attack or defeat viruses. Some compounds make cell walls like Teflon, so the viruses cannot stick and do their damage. Others guard the DNA and RNA, protecting the cell signaling from infection. Some block viruses from releasing its genetic material or disrupt their functions.

Another strategy inhibits the virus from reproduction. Algae can biostimulate the cell to produce macrophages that engulf the virus. The body senses the surrounded virus as a waste material and sluffs it off naturally from the body. A final strategy targets the virus indirectly, by increasing the efficiency with which the host's immune system can fight the viral infection.

The regulatory and product quality issues for functional foods and food ingredients have been reviewed by the FDA, USDA, multiple other countries and the European Union. Unsurprisingly, regulations vary substantially among different countries and cultures. Most the regulations focus on the type of food or nutrients, not nutrient levels.

What are the nutrient levels?

A good way to understand algae nutrient levels is by direct comparison with traditional terrestrial plant and animal foods.

Algae nutrient levels vs plants per kg	
Nutrient	**Algae is _ times higher than**
Proteins function as building blocks for bones, muscles, cartilage, skin, and blood. They are also building blocks for enzymes, hormones, and vitamins.	2x > than soy 3x > than beef, fish, pork 6x > than eggs
Iron carries oxygen in the blood. Many women in childbearing years have iron-deficiency anemia.	30x > than beef, fish, pork 65x > than spinach
B12 vitamin helps the body release energy, regulates the nervous system, aids in the formation of red blood cells, and help build tissues.	3 to 4x > than animal liver
Magnesium heart rhythm, build bones, maintains the immune system and normalizes blood pressure.	2x > than spinach 5x > than tomatoes
Calcium regulates nerve transmission, blood clotting, hormone secretion and muscle contraction.	10x > than milk
β-carotene, pro-vitamin A, boosts immune system, helps skin, eyes, protects against CHD and cancer.	5x > than carrots 40x > than spinach
Chlorophyll helps fight cancer, speeds wound healing, cleanses liver of toxins, improves skin, digestion and weight control.	30x > than spinach 20x > than wheatgrass
EPA and DHA, omega-3 fatty acids improve eyesight, brain function and protect from CHD.	1,000x > than any land plant 1,000x > than beef, poultry

Example nutrients available for functional foods

For consumers interested in maximizing health with valuable nutrients per bite, algae offer far better nutrition that terrestrial foods.

Bioavailability

Bioavailability represents the fraction of ingested food components available at the target for use in physiological functions. Bioavailability entails the entire process following food element consumption including: digestibility and solubility of the food element in the gastrointestinal tract; absorption or assimilation of the food element across the intestinal epithelial cells and into the circulatory system; and finally, incorporation into the target site of utilization. Studies examining the bioavailability of food elements are required to incorporate in vivo experiments that take place in living organisms.

Thousands of animal studies have been published on the nutritional bioavailability algae foods and biofeed. The results are mixed, for many reasons. Food scientists have learned how to process algae cells so that people and animals can gain high uptake from the algae nutrient package.

Algae bioactive compounds

Both macro and microalgae, are rich in bioactive antioxidants, soluble dietary fibers, proteins, minerals, vitamins, phytochemicals, and polyunsaturated fatty acids. Many algae species have therapeutic properties that improve health and prevent or treat disease.

Active compounds include sulphated polysaccharides, phlorotannins, carotenoids, minerals, peptides and sulfolipids, with proven benefits against degenerative metabolic disorders. A wide array of valuable micronutrients are also plentiful in algae. These bioactive compounds use different strategies to protect cells or block invasive pathogens. These compounds stimulate cellular metabolism in a fashion that causes the body's natural immune system to produce enzymes, hormones, peptides or other compounds that disrupt the sequence of the malady's onset.

Algae antioxidant extracts can prolong shelf life for food products. The antioxidants retard the oxidation and peroxidation processes. Algae compounds can improve the sensory perception of foods. In food sensory perception, taste dominates the assessment. Algae offer the umami taste that adds a savory flavor to any food product containing algae, such as soups, stews or salads. Algae also deliver significantly more nutralence, nutrients per bite, than terrestrial plants.

Algae bioactive compounds are displayed in the following table. Different algae types – sea vegetables, green and blue green microalgae – provide similar bioactive compounds, but in different proportions.

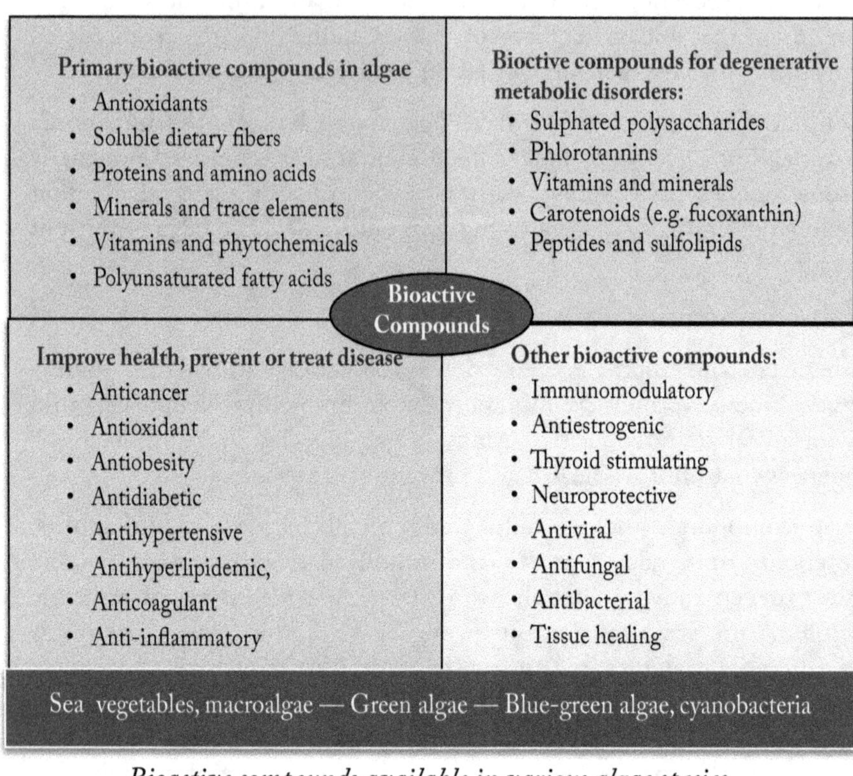

Bioactive compounds available in various algae species

Taste

Functional food consumers are clear – taste rules! Their primary concerns about algae foods are taste, texture, color, aroma and mouth feel. Considerable market research shows consumers are unwilling to sacrifice taste for health benefits. Wim Verbeke, from Belgium, did a series of studies that concluded the health benefit beliefs from functional foods emerged as the strongest positive determinant of willingness to compromise on taste. However, both the level of perceived benefits and its predictive power on willingness to compromise on taste decreased over time. Related research has shown that when people create high expectations for health or other attribute, their satisfaction diminishes quickly if they do not see or feel immediate health benefits.

Algae provide of all the essential nutrients, vitamins, minerals, and trace elements essential for health and vitality. Algae can satisfy any appetite with a broad spectrum of aromas, colors, tastes, and textures. Algae have a high content of glutamic acid that stimulate taste receptors, amplify taste differentiation and the desire to consume algae for its good taste. Most functional food studies try to develop new practical properties of algae nutrient extracts that enhance food palatability. For example, beef patty texture was improved by the addition of 3% *Wakame* powder.

Addition of algae in pasta reduces cooking loss without alteration of the sensory attributes. In the beer industry, sugar kelp found a place in beer, enhancing the malty taste. Other algae components improve liquid clarity. Laurie-Eve Rioux with the Canadian Institute on Nutrition and Functional Foods as done excellent work on the value of functional foods. She provides a comprehensive table with the algae species used, and a link to the producing company's website.

Some sea vegetables are rich in the sugar alcohol, about 30% mannitol. When the plant fronds are soaked in hot water, mannitol releases in the broth. Mannitol provides a sweet taste without the calories from sugar. Kombu, mannitol and glutamate, (in the form of monosodium glutamate) builds layers of the umami and sweet flavor in broth. The combination of mannitol with glutamate may open up to different flavoring profiles. Taste tests made by chefs shows that the palatability of low fat food is improved by umami flavors. Umami taste improves not only the food with the umami flavor, but also the rest of the meal.

Sea vegetable extracts have been successfully incorporated as nutrient and flavor enhancers. Wakame, when integrated in pasta provides antioxidant activity and good sensory attributes at levels up to 10%. Bread containing 4% *A. nodosum* can significantly reduce energy intake in overweight individuals in a meal following enriched bread consumption. Addition of only 4% of renin-inhibitory peptides from *P. palmata* hydrolysates produced positive sensory attributes, and the bioactive properties of the antioxidants survived the baking process.

Appetite suppression

More than two in three in the US are overweight or obese. Biomedical and clinical evidence suggest that chronic overconsumption of a Western diet – processed foods consisting high levels of sugars, fats and salt – is a major cause of this epidemic.

The research shows that chronic overeating and obesity are due to elevations in endocannabinoid signaling. The endocannabinoid system connects the brain to all peripheral organs. It orchestrates food intake, energy balance, and reward. It is comprised of lipid signaling molecules called endocannabinoids, which bind to cannabinoid receptors located on cells throughout the body.

A brain drug, Rimonabant, successfully blocks endocannabinoid signaling at cannabinoid receptors, which allows patients to reduce body weight. The drug has limited availability in Europe. Trials have shown it causes such severe psychiatric side effects, it was not given FDA approval. Algae bioactive compounds in functional foods can provide a natural solution to endocannabinoid signaling, without having to use synthetic drugs that try to fool the brain.

Nosh refers to eating greedily. Nosh has the connotation of eating on the sly, between meals, or possibly sweets in secret. Eating foods with empty calories leaves brain with no satiety, the feeling of fullness. The old Cracker Jack box expressed nosh perfectly, "The more you eat, the more you want!" This was a successful tagline when most people were skinny. Borden's and then Frito-Lay had to change their advertising for modern fat children.

The problem with obesity in children is that children listen to their nosh signal and eat more food, more often. If the food contains empty calories, their little brains continue to signal: "More, more, more."

Rimonabant or possibly other drugs could help children, but the brain signal side effects are far too dangerous, except for morbid obesity. Algae food may provide a safe therapeutic solution. Algae compounds provide an array of medical benefits for children plagued with nosh signals that lead to obesity and diabetes. Two unique strategies may be called fill-gut and gut-full signaling.

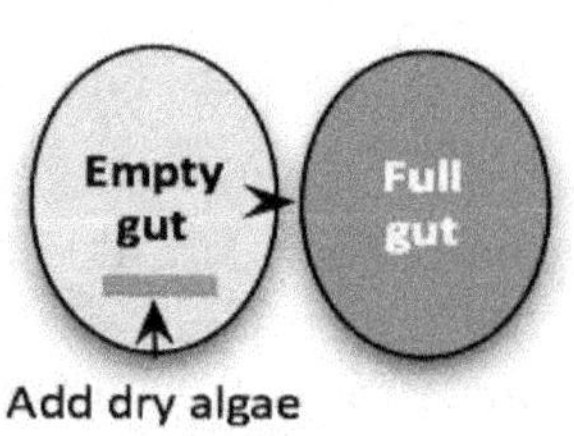

The **fill-gut** strategy adds a few grams of dried algae eaten early in a normal meal, possibly as sprinkles on a salad. The algae expand and fills the stomach. Alginates can absorb 300 times their weight in water, which quickly fill the gut and suppresses appetite by sending the gut full signal to the brain.

The **gut-full** signals work because algae compounds activate the stomach's natural **satiety** signals. Satiety signals an immediate feeling of fullness, which tells the eater to stop eating naturally. Algae satiety signals to the brain and quashes the nosh feeling.

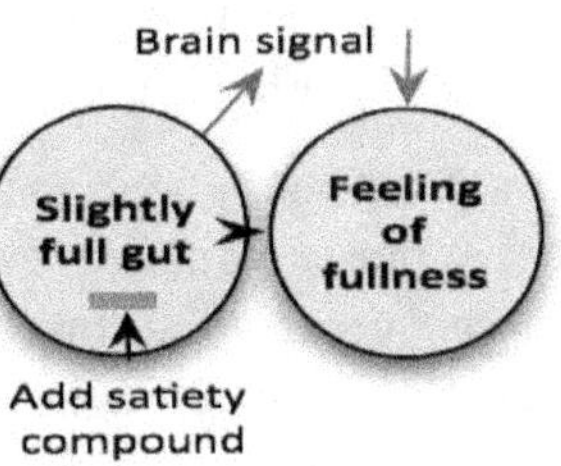

The nosh feeling hits children especially hard, which is why so many children are overweight. Many types of algae can quash the nosh directive, and help young people stay at healthy weight.

Strategies to prevent overeating

Sodium alginate reduces plasma glucose and protects the antioxidant system in diabetics. Alginic acid and other compounds in sea vegetables and microalgae exert a protective effect against diabetes. Alginic acid improves cell sensitivity to the action of insulin, thereby improving glucose tolerance and normalizing blood sugar.

Sodium alginate induces significantly lower postprandial rises in blood glucose, serum insulin and plasma C-peptides. The addition of sodium alginate in the diet leads to a delayed gastric emptying rate induced by the fiber, which moderates glucose response. Algae polyphenol extracts have anti-diabetic effects through the modulation of glucose-induced oxidative stress. These extracts slow starch-digestive enzymes such as alpha-amylase and alpha-glucosidase, which modulates the release of plasma glucose.

Autism

Omega-3 fatty acid supplements have been shown in several studies to moderate the symptoms of autism spectrum disorder, ADHD and related brain maladies. While algae compounds do not reverse autism, they essentially moderate the thunderstorm of disturbances in the neurological synapses and brain. This allows the patient to find calm.

Andrew Stoll at McLean Hospital studied omega-3 fatty acids in bipolar disorder. Dr. Stoll found that patients who took omega-3 supplements had longer remissions between episodes of mood dysregulation. Joseph Hibbeln at the NIH has published several research studies and notes that "In the last century, Western diets have radically changed. He notes that people eat substantially fewer omega-3 fatty acids now and that rates of depression have radically increased by perhaps a hundred-fold."

Captain Hibbeln and team were the first to establish a link among military personnel between low omega-3 levels and suicide risk. Suicide risk was greatest among service members with the lowest levels of DHA, the major omega-3 fatty acid concentrated in the brain. A recent review shows omega-3s are useful as add-on therapy in bipolar depression too. Since there is an increased prevalence of bipolar disorder in the extended families of autism patients, omega-3 has been proposed as a treatment for mood stabilization in patients with autism. Other studies have shown that omega-3 supplements can decrease hyperactivity children with ADHD.

Do no harm

Another thoughtful reminder from Hippocrates applies to algae therapeutics.

> *Make a habit of two things: to help; or at least to do no harm.*
>
> **– Hippocrates**

Algae compounds such as omega-3s are natural products and induce no side effects. This natural "no harm" advantage makes them a first choice for autism spectrum disorder treatment over pharmaceutical drugs that impose significant side effects.

Soluble fibers

Doctors recommend a high fiber diet for weight loss because fiber assists in shedding pounds, helps lower cholesterol, and reduces the risk of developing heart disease and diabetes. Consumers need to be cautious with fibers because some fibers may cause an upset stomach. Many protein, fiber bars and drinks that are marketed as health foods are loaded with artificial sweeteners to improve taste, but they leave out essential vitamins, minerals and antioxidants. Instead of helping with weight loss, the added sugars contribute to weight gain. These bars and drinks are often packed with synthetic fiber from artificial sources. Artificial fibers create indigestion and stomach pain for many people.

All natural fibers are not created equal. Soluble fiber dissolves in water and insoluble fiber does not. Soluble fiber, found in algae, oatmeal, lentils, fruits, nuts and many beans helps lower cholesterol. Foods containing soluble fiber benefit from water or other liquids. Consumers need to drink lots of water in order to reap the nutritional benefits. Soluble fiber also slows digestion, giving a feeling of fullness.

Insoluble fiber, found in whole grains, wheat bran, seeds, nuts, barley, and dark leafy vegetables, speeds up the digestion process and helps control irritable bowel syndrome symptoms. This kind of fiber is not absorbed by water and passes through the body quickly. Both soluble and insoluble fibers are useful for a healthy diet. The plentiful soluble dietary fibers in algae help avoid obesity and diabetes. The total fiber content of several algae species, (6 g/100g), is more than double the of fruits and vegetables promoted for their fiber content: prunes (2.4 g), cabbage (2.9 g), apples (2.0 g), and brown rice (3.8 g).

Macroalgae, sea vegetables, are particularly rich in dietary fibers. Seaweeds evolved with strong fibers so they could withstand the pounding of the surf where they grow in the intertidal zone. Sea vegetables have a total dietary fiber content varying between 30% and 72% on a dry weight basis. The majority of algae fibers are water-soluble, but some species have 15% to 50% insoluble fibers.

Processed foods do not yet contain algae fibers but several companies are experimenting with new high-fiber food products. Algae fibers such as alginates are used to make foods more attractive and more palatable. Algae offer an excellent source of fibers presenting chemical, physic-chemical, and rheological diversities that are beneficial in nutrition. Rheological characteristics define the stability and appearance of foods, *e.g.*, creaminess, juiciness, smoothness, brittleness, tenderness, and hardness. Algae components such as alginates are used the change rheological characteristics with emulsions, spreads and pastes.

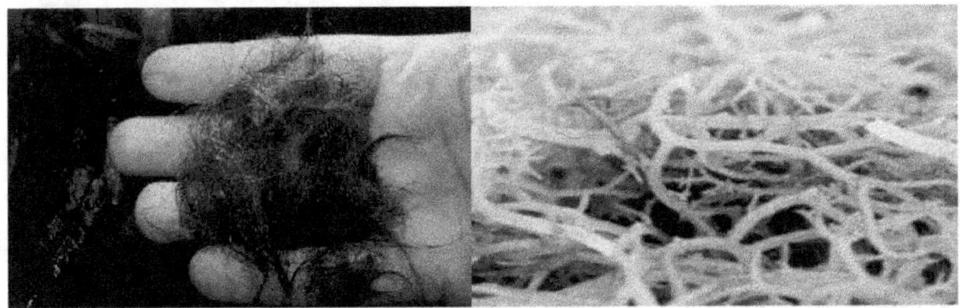

Algae fibers

Other research shows that viscous dietary fiber moderates insulin resistance syndrome and other diabetes and coronary heart disease risk factors. The properties of alginate solutions and gels suggest a suite of biomedical and pharmaceutical uses. No alginate food or medical products are yet on the market, but many foods and medical products contain alginates.

Obesity and diabetes

The Centers for Disease Control (CDC) reported that one out of three American children born after the year 2000 will contract diabetes – predominantly due to a poor diet of nutrient-deficient calories. Over 40% of women are likely to contract diabetes. The plague of obesity and diabetes creates havoc on our educational system and creates immense drag on our health system.

The cost of diabetes in the U.S. exceeds $245 billion annually. Neither the costs of obesity nor diabetes include the drag on education, social systems, businesses and the military. Our society will fail if we do not find solutions to obesity and diabetes – quickly. Diabetes is a serious disease because it is associated with an increased risk of life threatening complications such as a heart attack, stroke, or kidney disease. Overall, the risk for death among people with diabetes for these catastrophic complications is about four times that of people without diabetes. In addition to an earlier death, diabetes carries with it significant risks for serious complications such as blindness, the need for dialysis, and limb amputation. The cost of dialysis in the US is $42 billion, with $34 billion currently paid by Medicare.

Algae diabetes therapeutics

Diabetes mellitus occurs when blood sugar levels become elevated. Type 1 diabetes is associated with the destruction of the cells in the pancreas that manufacture insulin. Individuals with Type 1 diabetes require lifelong insulin for the control of blood sugar levels. In Type 2 diabetes insulin levels are typically elevated, indicating a loss of sensitivity to insulin by the cells of the body.

Kelp compounds moderate inflammatory diseases

Research on humans and animals shows algae components offer significant utility in the prevention and control of diabetes. Aligned studies have demonstrated algae's therapeutic value for the diseases common with diabetics; cholesterol management, blood pressure, heart disease and cancers. Algae can moderate chronic inflammation that often precedes and accompany degenerative diseases. Algae compounds provide therapeutic value for diabetes and fat metabolism.

Kelp contain up to 13 times more calcium than milk and powerful antioxidants that are not found in land plants; fucoxanthin and fucoidan. Kelps are macroalgae rich in B vitamins, vitamin C and vitamin K1 with high mineral content in magnesium, potassium and iron. The plentiful soluble dietary fibers in algae help avoid obesity and diabetes.

Benefits for athletes

Omega-3 supplements are popular for athletes and non-athletes for their ability to improve endothelial (i.e. blood vessel) function, reduce inflammation, and increase the provision of energy from fat. Protein is an essential nutritional component in the required to repair and build muscle tissue broken down during exercise. The FDA recommends between 1.2 and 1.7 g protein per kg body weight.

Algae are rich sources of protein and contain all of the essential amino acids at various concentrations. Algae provide a valuable resource for athletes requiring high levels of protein, especially for vegan athletes for whom eggs and dairy whey protein may not be suitable. The Cleveland Clinic's Katherine Patton notes omega-3 battles inflammation. Exercise is a form of good stress on the body but results in the production of inflammatory free radicals that cause oxidative stress and can damage cells. Omega-3s assist by counteracting inflammation and reducing joint pain and tenderness associated exercise-induced inflammation.

Omega-3s decrease delayed-onset muscle soreness, increases the rate of recovery, and reduces the risk for infection due to immunodeficiency. They coat and protect cell membranes. When incorporated in the membranes of red blood cells, they increase the deformability of the red blood cells. This allows the cells to move swiftly through capillary beds and efficiently deliver oxygen and remove carbon dioxide.

Whole algae

The microalgae Spirulina and Chlorella are sold as functional foods due to their extraordinarily high nutralence. They are generally regarded as safe (GRAS), by the European Food Safety Authority (EFSA) and by the FDA. *Arthrospira platensis* spirulina is a filamentous cyanobacterium that has the highest recorded protein content of any whole food.

Chlorella enjoys global sales exceeding $38B. The main substance found in Chlorella that is beneficial for human health is β-1,3-glucan, which is an active immunostimulant, free-radical scavenger and reducer of blood lipids. Chlorella is also rich in protein, (48% dw), polyunsaturated fatty acids, (39% of total lipids), and phosphorus. The nano cells also include vitamins, (B-complex and ascorbic acid), minerals (potassium, sodium, magnesium, iron, and calcium), beta-carotene, chlorophyll, and Chlorella growth factor (CGF). *Chlorella's* antitumor polypeptide, (CPAP) has immunosuppressive, anti-inflammatory, anti-hypertensive, anti-atherosclerosis and antioxidant capacities.

Algae ingredients have been incorporated into a number of functional foods, including noodles, bread, biscuits, drinks, sweets, and beer. Several businesses have been set up for the sale of algal products, such as AlgaVia®, (left), which produces protein and lipid-rich Chlorella flour.

AlgaVia® lipid-rich whole algae powder delivers a unique set of sensory and nutritional benefits to bakery products. The powder reduces overall fat, saturated fat, cholesterol and calories. The whole food ingredient adds fiber and protein, is non-GMO, vegan, and gluten-free.

Cell walls

Blue-green algae, cyanobacteria such as Spirulina have no cell walls, which makes the protein and nutrients readily bioavailable to the consumer. Many algae species evolved strong fibrous cell walls made of anionic polysaccharides to manage osmotic pressure within the cell. The cell wall makes digestion and protein extraction difficult for people. Food scientists have developed a wide array of treatments to disrupt the cellulosic cell wall with heat, ultrasound or other techniques that make algae proteins and other cell components more bioaccessible and easier to digest. Ongoing research on the best pretreatment of algae cell material includes fermentation and various approaches to drying.

Lectins and phycobiliproteins

Lectins and phycobiliproteins are two families of bioactive algae proteins that have many food and medical applications. Lectins are most commonly extracted from macroalgae, while phycobiliproteins are typically isolated from microalgae.

Lectins that bind with carbohydrates without causing modification with enzymatic activity. Lectins are involved in several biological processes, including host-pathogen interactions, cell–cell communication, induction of apoptosis, cancer metastasis and antiviral activities. Due to their carbohydrate binding capacity with high specificity, lectins are used in blood grouping, anti-viral (including human immunodeficiency virus type 1(HIV-1)), cancer biomarkers, and targets for drug delivery.

Phycobilins are water-soluble pigments found in the cytoplasm or in the stroma of the chloroplast. They occur only in cyanobacteria and rhodophyta. Green algae's pigment, beta-carotene, also is used as a natural food colorant. Other pigments include lutein, zeaxanthin, astaxanthin and phycobiliproteins. Unlike modern synthetic pigments, algae pigments add nutrients and health benefits to foods.

Phycobiliproteins play an important role in algae photosynthesis. They are components of phycobilins, which are large light energy-capturing complexes anchored to thylakoid membranes. The four main phycobiliproteins groups, based on their color and absorption, are phycoerythrin, phycocyanin, allophycocyanin, and phyco-erythrocyanin.

Phycobiliproteins are used be as natural dyes. Phycocyanin provides a blue pigment used in chewing gum, popsicles, confectionary, soft drinks, dairy products, and wasabi. The pigment gets wide use in cosmetic products, such as lipstick and eyeliner. They are used in fluorescent labeling, flow cytometry, fluorescent microscopy, and fluorescent immunohistochemistry. Credible sources explain beneficial bioactivities of phycobiliproteins for nutraceuticals, with anti-oxidative, anti-viral, antitumor, neuroprotective, and hepatoprotective activities.

Phycocyanin is known to support healthy inflammatory response and has many antioxidant effects. Studies have shown that phycocyanin can reduce oxidative stress and inhibit free radicals. Phycocyanin may reduce negative effects from the body's normal inflammatory response.

Phycocyanin pigments – Source: *Earthrise.com*

Inflammation is the body's first line of defense against foreign attack, but when it goes unchecked, it leads to conditions that promote premature aging. The antioxidants in phycocyanin have the ability to inhibit the key enzyme that is responsible for causing inflammation, pain, and discomfort. Studies show that consuming phycocyanin has been proven to reduce all types of free radicals including hydroxyl, alkoxyl, peroxyl and superoxides. Oxidative stress causes fatigue and pain and is associated with degenerative diseases.

Bioactive peptides

Peptides are molecules formed by joining two to 50 amino acids. Longer amino acid sequences are called proteins. Peptides and proteins are present in every living cell and possess a variety of biochemical activities. They appear as enzymes, hormones, antibiotics, receptors, carriers and signal enhancers. Peptides may be harvested from a number of sources, but algae are convenient because algae present simple cells.

A theory by a Harvard Medical School faculty team proposes that poorly presented peptides are more likely to cause diabetes and other autoimmune diseases, because they allow autoimmune T-cells to escape deletion in the thymus. Once they begin circulating in the body, T-cells are stimulated when they encounter high concentrations of the peptide that have been processed differently outside the thymus.

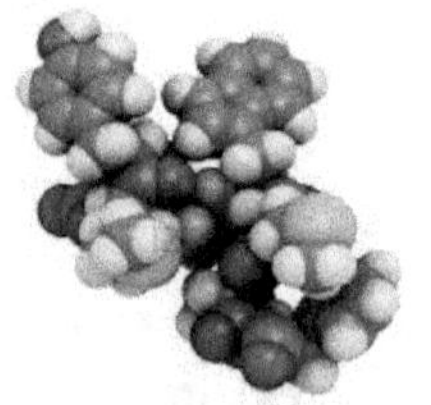

Connecting peptide

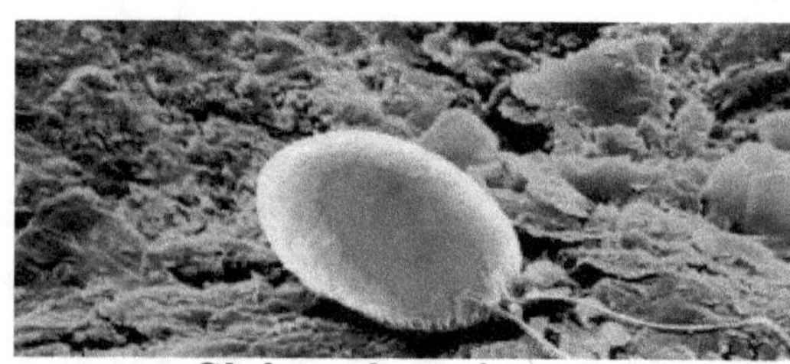

Cholecystokinin from algae

The connecting peptide, or C-peptide, is a short 31-amino-acid protein that connects insulin's A-chain to its B-chain in the proinsulin molecule. A C-peptide test measures the level of the peptide in the blood, which provides a valuable metric for diabetes diagnostics. Insulin helps the body use and control the amount of glucose in the blood. The level of C-peptide blood test shows how much insulin the pancreas makes because C-peptide is found in amounts equal to insulin. The C-peptide does not affect the blood sugar level in the body.

Peptides are released into circulation at the onset of eating or shortly thereafter. Some act as satiety peptides. They provide feedback that tells the brain the stomach is full and to stop eating. Among these are the intestinal peptide, cholecystokinin (CCK), and the pancreatic peptides, glucagon and amylin. CCK was the first gut peptide discovered to play a role in the control of eating. CCK peptides can create a feeling of fullness that inhibits food intake beyond individual meals and can do so over multiple days.

Peptides offer a therapeutic strategy to both mimic and enhance the body's own satiety signals. The gut hormone peptide tyrosine (PYY), which is released postprandially from the gastrointestinal tract, has recently been shown to be a physiological regulator of food intake. In humans, a single 90-minute infusion of PYY markedly reduced subsequent 24-hour caloric intake in lean, normal-weight as well as obese subjects. Obese subjects have been found to have low levels of fasting and postprandial PYY, suggesting a role for this hormone in the pathogenesis of obesity.

Research at Indiana University offers hope for peptides that reduce obesity. Obese rodents were injected with a synthetic peptide that simultaneously mimicked two naturally occurring hormones. The synthetic molecule possessed key features of two natural peptide hormones, glucagon and glucagon-like peptide-1 (GLP-1), which are involved in regulating glucose metabolism and appetite control. When injected into obese mice, after one week the animals' body weights had dropped 25%. Repeated treatment resulted in an even greater effect.

Biological differences between rodents and primates are a major hurdle for translation of anti-obesity and anti-diabetic strategies either discovered or developed in rodents to effective human therapeutics. Monkeys are closer relatives to humans and provide higher validity in medical research than rodents. Obese monkeys were given an algae peptide compound called adipotide. They lost 7% to 15% of their body weight and 14% off their waist. Adipotide resulted in rapid weight loss and improved insulin resistance in the obese monkeys.

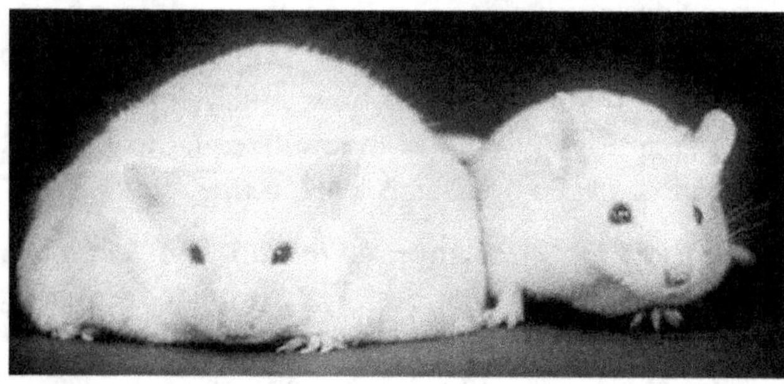

Mice lost 20% of their weight in 1 week after injection of an algae peptide

UCLA researchers demonstrated that an algae-based dietary supplement, GABA may inhibit development of insulin resistance and glucose intolerance. Both conditions are precursors to the development of Type 2 diabetes and metabolic syndrome. A naturally produced amino acid-like molecule called GABA was given orally to mice that were obese, insulin resistant and in the early stages of Type 2 diabetes.

GABA suppressed the inflammatory immune responses that are involved in the development of this condition. GABA helped prevent disease progression and improved glucose tolerance and insulin sensitivity, even after onset of Type 2 diabetes in mice. Researchers also identified the regulatory immune cells that likely direct GABA's activity in inhibiting inflammation. GABA taken as a supplement or related medications may provide new therapeutic agents for the treatment of obesity-related Type 2 diabetes and metabolic syndrome.

Bioactive peptides are inactive within the parent proteins, but can be released through fermentation or hydrolysis. Milk proteins remain the most common source for bioactive peptides today, but algae are the likely source in the future. Bioactive peptides offer a multitude of beneficial effects, including antihypertensive, antimicrobial antioxidative, antithrombotic, hypocholesterolemic, opioid, mineral binding, appetite suppression, immunomodulatory, and cytomodulatory properties. Algae peptides are likely to find homes in a variety of functional foods to make them healthier, safer and taste better.

Algae evolved the capability over eons tolerate extremely high levels of oxidative stress and free radicals in their environment. Algae developed many defensive systems that they pass on to their consumers that stimulate antioxidant activity. Peptides displaying antioxidant and anticancer bioactivity have been discovered in multiple algae species. These antioxidant peptides promise free radical scavenging and anticancer bioactivity.

Other algae peptides display several other bioactivities, including hepatoprotective, immunomodulatory, ultraviolet (UV), radiation-protective, anti-osteoporosis, and anti-coagulant. Several studies have reported that short algae-derived peptides are capable of resisting gastrointestinal digestion from enzymes such as trypsin, pepsin, and chymotrypsin. Avoiding digestion is an essential trait for bioactive peptides that is critical in order to achieve their physiological effect at their site of action.

Anti-Hypertensive Peptides

Hypertension is the single largest risk factor attributed to deaths worldwide, making it an ideal target for bioactive peptides. Angiotensin-I-converting enzyme, (ACE-I), is a proteolytic enzyme that affects vasoconstriction in two major blood pressure regulatory systems, the renin-angiotensin–aldosterone system and kinin–kallikrein system. These lead to the development of hypertension. ACE-I inhibitors have become one of the most commonly studied targets, and with global annual sales exceeding \$6 billion. Synthetic drugs such as captopril, enalapril, and alacepril, often bring very nasty side effects, including hypotension, dry cough, and impaired renal function. Functional foods with anti-hypertensive bioactivities have therefore become a popular alternative to synthetic drugs, especially for individuals who are borderline hypertensive, and do not warrant the dangers of prescription of pharmaceutical drugs.

Algae nutraceuticals

The algae nutraceutical market includes the elements discussed, plus nutraceuticals, probiotics, and cosmeceuticals. Cosmeceuticals are typically represented by different companies than nutraceutical suppliers. Many health product start-ups now offer both a line of healthy nutraceuticals and cosmeceuticals. Both are forms of foods, drinks, lotions and supplements that provide bioactive value.

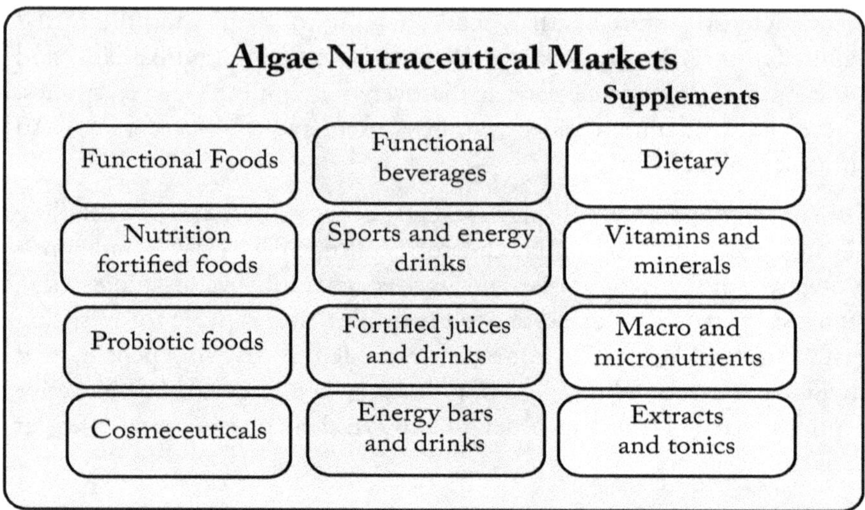

Nutraceuticals are food products that provide health and medical benefits, including the prevention and treatment of disease. Nutraceuticals, or 'food supplements' as they are defined by the FDA, are more highly regulated than cosmeceuticals. The nutraceutical market includes significant markets in biofeed and pet food and companion animal health. Physiologically-active nutraceuticals from algae include food supplements, dietary supplements, value-added functional foods as well as dietary supplements. Algae nutraceuticals are identical to those used for functional foods – omega-3s, carotenoids, astaxanthin, γ-linolenic acid, arachidonic acid, and β-carotene.

Carotenoids

Carotenoids are organic pigments found in the chloroplasts and chromoplasts of photosynthetic organisms including both land plants and algae. Chromoplasts are the organelle responsible for a plant's distinctive color, which comes from the accumulation of carotenoid pigments. Carotenoids cannot be synthesized by animals, but are essential as they serve as building blocks for cellular metabolism. Animals obtain carotenoids from their diets.

Over 600 carotenoids are found in nature, but only six are essential in the human bloodstream and only three – lutein, zeaxanthin and meson-zeaxanthin – are found in the human eye's macula. These three carotenoids accumulate in the macula at a concentration 10,000 times that found in the blood stream. The biochemical characteristics of lutein provide important structural components in cell membranes and act as a short-wave-length filter. Two carotenoids classes include xanthophylls that contain oxygen, and carotenes, which are purely hydrocarbons that do not contain oxygen.

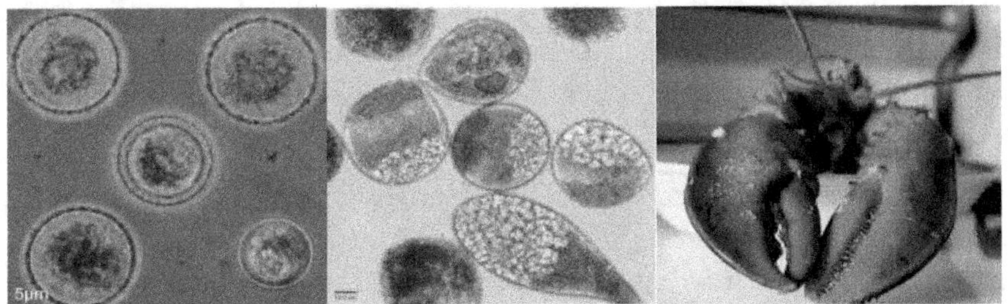

Algae cells laden with carotenoids and carotenoid eaters

Carotenoids serve two key: they absorb light energy for use in photosynthesis, and they protect chlorophyll from photo damage. Algae use carotenoids to make retinal, (provitamin A) which allows the plant to convert light into metabolic energy.

In humans, carotenoids deposit in the macula and are vital in protecting the retina photoreceptors and retina pigment epithelium from harmful damage by ultra-violet and blue wavelength light sources. Carotenoids also enhance vision by decreasing chromatic aberration and photosentivity. These compounds improve glare recovery time and contrast sensitivity through a reduction in blue-light scatter.

Carotenoids are powerful antioxidants that improve health by enhancing provitamin A activity. β-Carotene is used as a yellow-orange food coloring and may help prevent certain types of cancers. Astaxanthin, the most powerful carotenoid, protects against oxidation of essential polyunsaturated fatty acids and protects skin from adverse UV light effects.

Astaxanthin can repair damaged tissues and slows and sometimes blocks the proliferation of cancer cells. The strong antioxidant regulates immune functions. Astaxanthin acts as a free-radical scavenger and an immunomodulator. It is a medicinal ingredient against degenerative diseases such as cancer, skin related illness, and heart disease.

Astaxanthin is more stable compared to other carotenoids and offers higher antioxidant capacity, roughly 10-times higher than beta-carotene, and 500 times more than a-tocopherol. The product offers value in drug delivery since it easily crosses the blood brain and the retina barriers. It appears to protect the brain and nervous system from neurodegenerative diseases such as cerebral thrombosis and stroke as well as premature aging. Astaxanthin also has high tinctorial ability, as it adds to or restores natural color. Astaxanthin acts as a chain-breaking antioxidant that protects lipid-rich cell membranes from degradation. It traps more free radicals than any other antioxidant. It also amplifies the action of other antioxidants such as Vitamin E and C.

Astaxanthin protects nucleic acid components of DNA, avoiding mutations to genetic material due to oxidative stress and protects muscle cells from damaging effects of active oxygen produced upon swimming upstream. Astaxanthin has been documented to prevent age-related macular degeneration, and to enhance immune functions.

Antioxidants

Antioxidants protect human health with compounds that inhibit the oxidation of other molecules. They act as a modulator of redox, (reduction-oxidation) and a modulator in signal transduction pathways. Oxidation transfers electrons or hydrogen from a substance to an oxidizing agent, which often produces free radicals. Free radicals constantly start chain reactions that can damage or kill cells. Antioxidants terminate these chain reactions by removing free radical intermediates, which prevent further oxidation reactions. Carotenoids enhance the immune system because they are efficient free-radical scavengers.

Four carotenoids act as antioxidants in humans, beta-carotene, alpha-carotene, gamma-carotene and beta-cryptoxanthin. They operate singularly or in concert to synthesize retinal, which is critical for eyesight. Other carotenoids such as lutein and zeaxanthin also help eyesight by absorbing damaging blue and near-ultraviolet light. Light absorbtion protects the macula of the retina, which is critical for sharp vision. Diabetics often have vision problems that may be related to their inability to produce sufficient retinal. People consuming diets rich in carotenoids are healthier and have lower mortality from a broad array of chronic illnesses, including diabetes.

Antioxidants such as beta-carotene moderate blood sugar levels in pre-diabetics and diabetics. Antioxidants may help return blood sugar levels to their normal range in diabetes patients. Evidence suggests that the antioxidants selenium, zinc, vitamin E, vitamin B-6 and biotin help control blood sugar. The best-known carotenoid, carotene, give carrots their bright orange color. The pink color of flamingos and salmon, and the red coloring of cooked shrimp and lobsters come from carotenoids. Flamingos, salmon, shrimp and lobsters get their pigments from algae or algae eaters. Each kg of algae contains eight times the carotene provided by an kg of carrots.

Epidemiologic evidence suggests that carotenoids are potent antioxidants and play a protective role in the development of chronic diseases including cancers, diabetes, cardiovascular disease and other inflammatory diseases. The role of antioxidants in the pathogenesis of diabetes mellitus may be related to the anti-inflammatory effects and the ability to reduce oxidative stress.

Randomized human trails in a series of studies showed that serum carotenoids are inversely associated with type-2 diabetes and impaired glucose metabolism. Currently, it is unclear whether the biological effects of carotenoids in humans are a result of their antioxidant activity or other mechanisms.

The Third National Health and Nutrition Examination Survey, (1988–1994), examined 8,808 US adults over 20 years with and without the metabolic syndrome. People with the metabolic syndrome had lower carotenoid levels, which was probably due to their lower consumption of fruits and vegetables. Adults with the metabolic syndrome had suboptimal concentrations of several antioxidants, which partially explain their increased risk for diabetes and cardiovascular disease.

The carotenoid lycopene acts as both an anti-inflammatory and antioxidant. It has been found to be effective in the inhibition of angiotensin-converting enzyme, ACE activity, an important indicator of diabetes-related complications.

Algae probiotics

Gut flora, (microbiota, or gastrointestinal microbiota) is the complex community of microorganisms that live in the digestive tracts of humans and other animals. The gut metagenome is the collection of all the genomes of gut microbiota. Microbiota inhabit and are active in several body functions besides the intestines, such as the skin. Probiotics supplements add to gut flora. Probiotics are live microbes such as bacteria, algae and yeasts that are good for health, especially for the second largest body system: digestion. A person's body may host 2,000 types of microbes, both good and bad. Probiotics are often called "helpful" because they work to keep the gut healthy.

Probiotics such as yogurt, miso soup, kimchi, Spirulina and Chlorella have proven effective in supporting immune function and healthy digestion, as well as beautiful skin. Healthy microflora produces vitamin B12, butyrate and vitamin K2. They produce enzymes that destroy harmful bacteria and crowd out bad bacteria, yeast and fungi.

The immune system protects the body against pathogens, such as bacteria or viruses. The gut immune system does not eliminate microbiota but instead nourishes rich bacterial communities and establishes advanced symbiotic relationships. Gut microbiota are essential for nutrient processing, production of vitamins, and protection against pathogens. They are also responsible for the development and maturation of the immune system.

Microflora stimulate the body to secrete IgA and regulatory T-cells. Secretory IgA cells serve as the first line of defense in protecting the digestive track from toxins and pathogenic microorganisms. Regulatory T-cells play a critical role in maintaining immune tolerance. T-cells work through IgA to regulate the diversity and composition of microbiota. Poor and unbalanced microbiota induce inflammatory T-cells and IgGs, which can lead to inflammatory bowel syndrome.

Prescription antibiotics, antibiotics in some foods and highly chlorinated water can kill good gut microflora. Probiotics supplements or probiotic-rich foods can help replace the gut metagenome. Improving gut microflora improves digestion and builds a stronger immune system that resists colds and flu. It increases energy from production of vitamin B12 and can heal leaky gut syndrome and inflammatory bowel disease. Probiotics improve skin health because the microflora naturally treat eczema and psoriasis.

Algae cosmeceuticals

Algae adaptations in extremely bright ocean environments explains their value in cosmetic ingredients. Algae had to develop ultraviolet, (UV) adaptation strategies as well as high protein and antioxidant capabilities to survive. Planktonic organisms floating near the surface of the ocean thrive without shade and without getting sunburned. They had to produce antioxidants to prevent oxidation and severe damage from free radicals. Their cellular structure materials allow the cells to survive in a high-salt environment while retaining their cellular water.

Algae are cellular biofactories that produce an extremely rich source of valuable cosmeceuticals complexes. Algae oils and pigments are used today as skin moisturizers, similar to aloe and jojoba oil.

Algae cosmeceuticals have been used for thousands of years in Asia, Africa, Europe and the Americas. Indigenous people used algae for natural treatment for skin moisture, bruises, burns, (sun and fire), bites, stings, cuts, wounds, joint pain, headaches and indigestion.

The use of algae in cosmetics for pigments and dyes pre-dates Julius Caesar. The dominant red color of Roman military tunics came from pigments extracted from the lichen urchilles. Algae grow in the protection of fungi as symbionts in lichen. Roman women valued the pigment and used it as rouge, to give their faces a sensual color.

Caesar's armies carried dried sea vegetables for their horses because they improved the luster in the horse's coat, improved stamina, accelerated recovery from injury, and gave the horses better night vision. The vision benefits probably came from carrageen, which is also found in carrots, but in far less nutrient density.

Novel bioactive substances from natural sources such as algae are safer and are perceived by consumers as more effective than artificial substances. These compounds have highly active properties for therapeutic use and low potential toxicity. They have high concentrations of proteins, peptides, amino acids, vitamins, minerals and trace elements. Algae provide rich structurally diverse, biologically active compounds that display antioxidant, anti-inflammatory, antiallergenic, antiaging, anti-wrinkle effects, and UV protection.

Cosmeceuticals include a broad array of algae-based advanced compounds to moisturize, smooth, protect, and repair skin. Many cosmetic products today have aloe vera as a base. Algae emulsions will replace aloe vera because the tiny algae delivery package, only about 5 μ across, are so easily absorbed through the epidermis and dermis layers of the skin. They are also easily absorbed in the hair and scalp. Algae nourishment is made up of tiny droplets of algae oil dispersed in water.

Algae will replace many cosmeceuticals made currently from traditional terrestrial plant-based sources. Algae offer substantial advantages because algae nutraceuticals can be grown with abundance methods that use primarily renewable resources. Algae can provide a least an order of magnitude faster growth, harvesting and processing cycle. Algae does not require cropland and can be cultured in wastewater, with cycled nutrients. Unlike terrestrial plants, algae cosmeceuticals have no pesticide residue, no reactive pollens and no allergens.

Salmon, lobsters, crab, shrimp, other shellfish and some colorful birds get their skin, meat or feather coloring from algae astaxanthin. Flamingos eat brine shrimp that are what they eat – algae nutrients rich in astaxanthin.

This flamboyance gets their beautiful color from algae's astaxanthin
Source: – National Geographic

About 80% of modern cosmetics already contain algae extracts including agar, carrageenans, alginate and astaxanthin. Agar is mainly used as a preservative and as a gelling agent. Carrageenans are used for colorings and as a stabilizing agent in lipstick, eye liners and other cosmetics. Alginic acid is used as a thickening, stabilizing and emulsifying agent in lotions, skin creams and hair products.

The same compounds used in functional foods promote skin regeneration and produce antioxidants and oils for anti-aging formulations. Algae cosmeceuticals may be taken orally or used topically. Algae's natural defense mechanisms prevent microorganism growth in cosmetics. Algae thickening agents provide polymers that change and stabilize cosmeceutical product consistency.

Algae fragrances, colors, and pH stabilizers add sensory value to cosmetics. Algae moisturizers repair dry, burned, or scaly skin. Shampoos and soaps clean with surfactants, surface-active agents. Algae stabilizers make lipstick water insoluble, which is critical for formulating lipstick. Algae can provide imitation tans and change color on contact with skin.

Algae provide omega-3 fatty acids and astaxanthin that reduce the appearance of fine lines and wrinkles. They also prevent dryness and fight skin problems such as eczema and acne. Algae regulate the production of sebum, which moisturizes and prevents skin dehydration.

Algae offer antioxidant properties that reduce free radical damage, which is the primary cause of skin aging. Algae antioxidants fight free radicals and also promote the production of collagen and elastin, which are essential to having firmer skin. Algae are loaded with essential minerals and vitamins that provide regenerative, protective and intense rejuvenating properties. Algae cosmeceuticals slow the aging process and systematically repair skin damage.

Algae-based imitation tans change skin color. The active ingredient in most fake tans, dihydroxyacetone, is a colorless compound that darkens when it reacts with the amino acids in the top layer of skin. The color change is permanent, but because skin cells are constantly being shed, the tan usually goes away after about a week.

Summary

Algae are nano-cell biofactories that rapidly produce carbohydrates, proteins, minerals, oil, fats and polyunsaturated fatty acids. Algae compounds serve many functions that improve the state of health and vitality and protecting against disease, and slowing aging.

Algae compounds enhance the functionality and efficiency of functional foods, nutraceuticals, and cosmeceuticals. These bioactive compounds plus additional benefits will drive consumer adoption of algae foods.

Saving our planet, lifting people out of poverty, advancing economic growth... these are one and the same fight. We must connect the dots between climate change, water scarcity, energy shortages, global health, food security and women's empowerment. Solutions to one problem must be solutions for all.

– Ban Ki-moon

Algae have a well-earned reputation as the #1 food on the planet. Nearly every animal favors algae, algae feeders, or bigger fish that feed on algae feeders. It is abundant because algae produce about 40% of the global biomass every day. Fortunately, algae's many consumers reduce the biomass or the earth would be over populated by biomass. They also naturally cycle algae nutrients for the next generation of algae and algae consumers.

Algae provides the highest nutralence of any food source, with higher nutrient quality, density, diversity and bioassimilation efficiency. Each nano cell delivers a very tiny package containing all the essential nutrients for life, health and vitality. In addition to providing superior nutrition, algae deliver bioactive antioxidants, soluble dietary fibers, proteins, minerals, vitamins, phytochemicals, and polyunsaturated fatty acids. As these components are integrated into foods, they will provide consumers with all the exceptional therapeutic properties for health and disease management discussed in prior chapters.

Algae, the food of emperors, offers excellent opportunity for human food. Members of the Chinese Court, numbering around 1,100, harvested and reserved a single algae cultivar for the Chinese Emperor. The Japanese reserved another variety expressly for the Samurai, the Japanese nation's fiercest warriors. Today, Chinese Olympic athletes consume algae daily because, like the Samurai, algae nutrients enable them to train harder and longer. The diverse therapeutic compounds provided by algae allow the athletes to recover faster from training and injuries.

Algae foods

Humans have embraced algae foods for themselves and their animals since antiquity. Spirulina supported of the nutritional needs of our ancient ancestors. Early hominoids that lived around the lakes of the great Rift Valley in Eastern Africa are believed to have consumed Spirulina. As they harvested and consumed aquatic algae feeders, fish, birds and reptiles, they benefited from algae nutrients. The women in Chad harvested Spirulina in the 9th century and dried it into cakes, which are still available for purchase in local markets today. The Aztecs cultivated and consumed Spirulina in Lake Texcoco from the 10th to the 16th century. A soldier in Cortés' army described how the Aztecs used algae as food.

Algae nutrition has saved human societies through numerous historical famines. Nostoc, (*Cyanophyta*) was consumed for human survival in China as early as 2,000 years ago. Today, Nostoc is considered so valuable, several companies have patented Nostoc for its high nutralence, flavor and robust growth. These patents have ignited intense tiffs and litigation over whether a private company can patent a natural plant. It seems unlikely that companies will be successful trying to enforce a patent on a public gift – nature.

Written records show the Chinese have harvested sea vegetables for more than 2,000 years. Modern people around the Asian Pacific rim collect and eat over 200 species of red, green, brown and blue-green algae for nutritional and health benefits. Cooks use them for flavorings, colorants and thickeners.

Both sea vegetables and microalgae are incredibly diverse. Algae naturally contain 40–70% proteins, 12–30% carbohydrates, 4–20% lipids, 8–14% carotene and substantial amounts of vitamins B1, B2, B3, B6, B12, E, K, and D. Unlike terrestrial plant foods that may exhibit hidden hunger, (nutrient deficiencies), due to lack of macro and/or nutrients in the soil, each algae cell delivers a full set of the essential nutrients for life.

Sea vegetables have such high demand, nearly all natural stands have been harvested and consumed. Most algae today are commercially cultivated and represent a sophisticated global industry valued in excess of \$12 billion a year. Current microalgae production focuses on a relatively few species, but with very diverse nutrient and unique varietal expressions.

Chlorella, Spirulina, Dunaliella, Nannochloris, Nitzschia, Cyanophyta, Crypthecodinium, Schizochytrium, Tetraselmis, and Skeletonema have earned their position as favored cultivars.

New species or new expressions of current types are finding niche markets. Most algae cultivars can be trained through hybridization, mutagenesis, or genetic engineering to express more or less of specific desired target proteins, nutrient, oil or bioactive compound.

Human health

The number one goal for food producers should be **health**. MIA has flunked Health101 by producing foods with hidden hunger and empty calories. Food processors compound farmers' errors by removing natural fibers and inserting carbohydrates, sugar, fats and salt.

Farmers produce for yield, based on weight, not on nutrition. GMO seeds are genetically modified to produce more weight – often at the cost of nutrition. The USDA reports that over 90% of the corn, soy and cotton grown in the US are monocultures that use GMO seeds.

Modern farmers produce cheap, calorie-dense food that shifts consumer costs from food to healthcare. Food costs in the US are about 9% of living expenses, but healthcare costs have doubled in the last decade to 18%. Poor child health degrades not only each child's life, but also the family, school, community and nation.

Why are children and family members not getting good nutrition? The root causes are access, hidden hunger (by nutrient deficiencies) and food prices. Many industrial foods suffer from **hidden hunger**, which results in foods with empty calories. Hidden hunger is serious. It refers to crops that need more of one or more nutrients, yet show no or few visible deficiency symptoms. The nutrient content may be above the deficiency symptom zone needed for passable appearance, but below the zone for optimal crop health. Farmers practicing industrial agriculture grow the same crop year-after-year, to maximize profits. Unsurprisingly, systemic extraction wears out the soil nutrients.

The appearance of produce with hidden hunger can be deceiving. Field tomatoes look bigger today than they were 30 years ago, but the taste and texture has degraded substantially.

Vegetables, grains and fruits need a full complement of micronutrients to incorporate into the fruit of the vine, which farmers harvest as food. When micronutrients, minerals, vitamins and trace elements have been extracted from the field and not replaced, the crop suffers from hidden hunger. Clear proof comes from the taste difference between heirloom and field tomatoes.

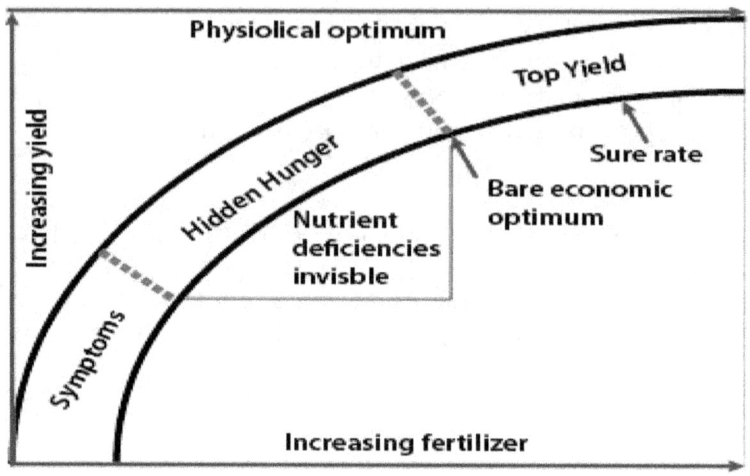

Hidden hunger in modern foods

Crops allow farmers a wide zone, where withheld nutrients (as fertilizers), show no visual effects. Farmers know that extra nitrogen creates larger produce, even when multiple micronutrients are low. Consumers are attracted to larger produce. Few consumers suspect that the extra weight comes from water; not nutrient-rich biomass.

Farmers are paid by weight, not nutritional density, quality, diversity or bioavailability. Consequently, many MIA foods are nutrient deficient because farmers hold back fertilizer, especially micronutrients, to save money. Most farmers do not add micronutrients to fields because those formulations may not be available, or are too expensive. Applying just the macro fertilizers, NPK, may represent 40% of the cost of the crop.

Hidden hunger in foods transfers directly to hidden hunger in people. The lack of micronutrients results in empty calories; produce that delivers few nutrients per bite. Processing food with extra sugar and fat make food attractive to children, but amplifies empty calories.

Calorie-dense but nutrient light foods have created a global obesity epidemic. In 2015, more than 2.2 billion people globally are overweight or obese and suffer health problems because of their weight. People affected by obesity has doubled since 1980. The US has the most obese adults, with 80 million, followed by China with 57 million.

While produce with hidden hunger may not show visible effects, hidden hunger in people often results in both visible, (stunting, obesity and diabetes) as well as behavioral problems, (inability to concentrate). The cost of diabetes in 2012 was $245 billion, an increase of 41% over 2007. The CDC predicts that 1 in 3 children born after 2000 will become diabetic, about 45 million more children.

Diabetes drag alone should motivate consumers to take action. But food suppliers continue to sell foods that are calorie dense, but nutrient poor.

Algae biofertilizers can reduce or eliminate hidden hunger in field crops, which will improve health for consumers. Algae biofertilizer can reduce the fertilizer cost to farmers by 50%, which represents a major savings. Field produce grown with algae biofertilizer receive the full set of micronutrients, vitamins and trace elements crops need to thrive. The results give the farmer higher yields and produce with superior sensory perception and nutralence.

Empty calories impose a heavy health burden on consumers who feel continually hungry, (nosh demand), because their stomach signals the brain that they are nutrient short. Algae-based foods are nutrient dense and calorie light. They expand to create a feeling of fullness. The high nutralence creates a satiety signal to the brain to stop eating. Appetite control paired with better nutrition will help millions of children avoid obesity and diabetes.

Social justice

After health, the most important goal for food production should be **social justice**, to assure everyone has access to good food. MIA has failed this goal. Food production per section of land has not kept pace with population growth for decades. Per-capita cropland production has fallen by more than half since 1960. Per-capita production of grains, 80% of what people eat, has been falling globally for 20 years.

Many Americans do not enjoy food justice, with access to affordable good food. Several factors are responsible for hunger and food insecurity that algae foods and bioproducts can solve.

Food insecurity. America, gifted with the best farmland and finest climate in the world, experiences severe hunger. Over 49 million Americans struggle to get enough food. The USDA subsidizes school lunches for over 31 million kids, because they are hungry. More than 1 in 5 US children is food insecure and at risk of hunger. Among African-

Americans and Latinos, 1 in 3 are hungry. Eight states have food insecurity rates above 15% of households.

Food deserts. The USDA estimates 23.5 million people live in food deserts with limited access to fresh, healthy food. Residents are forced to rely on fast food and convenience stores with no fresh produce. The USDA administrates SNAP and has mapped food deserts in the US.

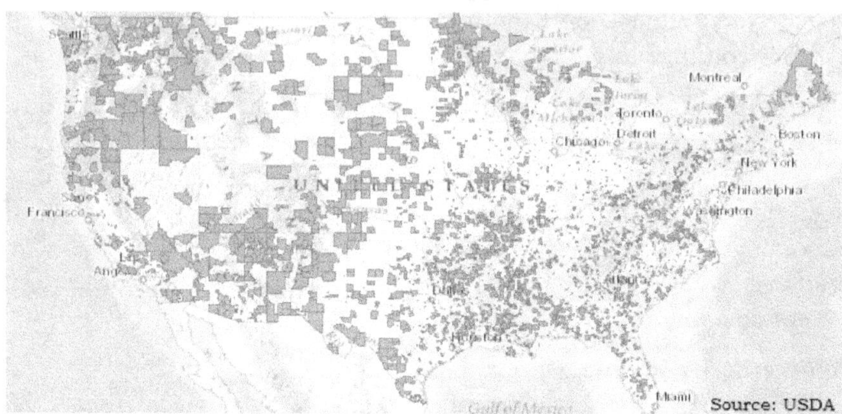

Families that live in these areas spend more on food but get poorer nutrition. Poor nourishment has caused a severe epidemic of obesity, diabetes, cardiovascular disease, osteoporosis, high blood pressure, cancer, acne, gout, depression, and diseases caused by vitamin and mineral deficiencies. Kids often have trouble in school because their brains are under developed due to lack of nutrients and constant hunger causes fatigue and irritability. These kids spend more time in hospitals, have higher medical costs and die earlier than more fortunately people who live in neighborhoods with access to healthy food.

Algae can improve the **nutralence** in agricultural produce and end hidden hunger and empty calories. Algae biofertilizers and biofeeds will improve not only the nutrition in produce and animals, but also taste, color, aroma, texture and quality. Algae bioproducts will make the animals happier and healthier too. Research shows they display more vitality, have higher stress tolerance and grow faster. Their higher stress tolerance endows them with higher survivability.

Food costs prohibit many from obtaining good nutrition. Food costs rise with the cost of fossil resources, especially fuel and fertilizers. Food prices increase when climate change causes diminished yields or crop failures. Transportation costs also escalate the cost of food. The average American foodstuff travels an estimated 1,500 miles before being consumed. Algae biosystems can reduce the cost of food production for farmers, which should benefit consumers with more nutrition access and lower costs.

Peace microfarms distributed in food deserts across America could create food justice and give all children food security and health. Microfarmers could feed their families and communities. Microfarms would enable growers to produce 80% of the food needed in US and global cities, such as LA, Paris, NY, Beijing, Jakarta and San Palo.

The Green Friendship Bridge project published in *Algae Industry Magazine* describes how peace microfarms could be built across America, Mexico and Central America for only 2% of the projected cost of President Trump's proposed wall with Mexico. The Green Friendship Bridge project examines the substantial health, social, economic, environmental and ecological of distributed microfarms.

Today, over 4 billion people endure water scarcity. While millions go thirsty, agriculture uses over 90% of available freshwater in Africa, Asia and the Americas. Algae can reduce water consumption for animal production by 70% by growing biofeeds that do not consume fresh water. In addition, algae biosystems can clean polluted water, which recycles the water for people, animals or crops.

World hunger

One of the highest values MIA can provide is sufficient, affordable good food for all people. MIA does not deliver affordable food. Over 842 million people suffer from hunger globally, 12% of the world's population. Over 9 million people die of hunger each year; more than the death toll for malaria, HIV/AIDs and tuberculosis combined. Hungry people consume fewer than 2,000 calories a day.

Global hunger figures understate the much larger number of people who are malnourished due to the lack of quality food or who suffer from micronutrient deficiencies. Half the people on earth, **3.6** billion, are food insecure, without reliable access to good food.

Over 60% of the hungry are women, who have limited access to food resources. The physical requirements, heavy equipment and serious injury risks required for industrial agriculture defeat social justice. Even in the US, where 1 in 5 children are food insecure, women do not have **access** to food production. A recent USDA analysis showed that more than 92% of the 2.1 million US farmers are non-Hispanic, white men.

Ana Feeds Our World

The average US farmer is over 58 years old. Farmers in the US not only discriminate against women, but also young men and non-whites.

The high prevalence of hunger among women has led to malnutrition becoming the leading cause of death for children. About 3.1 million children die from hunger each year. In 2013, poor nutrition accounted for roughly half the deaths for children under five.

Polluted water or not enough water was the other culprit in a majority of child deaths. Half of the world's hospital beds are filled with people suffering from a water-related disease. More than 750 million people lack adequate access to clean drinking water. In developing countries, about 80% of illnesses are linked to poor water and sanitation conditions. Roughly 1 out of every 5 deaths under the age of 5 worldwide occurs due to a water-related disease. Diarrhea caused by inadequate drinking water, sanitation, and hand hygiene kills an estimated 842,000 people every year, 2,300 people per day. Clean and safe water is essential to healthy living.

Malnutrition remains the primary symptom of hunger. Among preschool children in developing countries, 40% are estimated to be anemic due to iron deficiency. Anemia occurs when the body does not make enough red blood cells. Symptoms include fatigue, weakness, pale or yellowish skin, irregular heartbeats, shortness of breath, dizziness or lightheadedness, chest pain and headache. Anemia causes 20% of all maternal deaths.

An estimated 350,000 children go blind from Vitamin A deficiency every year. WHO classifies vitamin A deficiency as a serious public health problem affecting about one third of children in 2013. In sub-Saharan Africa and South Asia, about 45% of children are impacted.

Protein-energy malnutrition, (PEM) causes stunting, slowing of linear growth and incomplete growth of major organs. In 2013, about 165 million children under 5 were stunted, and another 51 million were wasted, with low weight for the child's age. Behavioral changes occur such as irritability, apathy, decreased social responsiveness, anxiety, and attention deficits that lead to problems in school. The early childhood effects of malnutrition are irreversible.

Clinical signs and symptoms of micronutrient deficiencies include:

- **Iron** - Fatigue, anemia, decreased cognitive function, headache, glossitis, and nail changes.

- **Iodine** - Goiter, developmental delay, and mental retardation.
- **Vitamin D** - Poor growth, rickets, and hypocalcemia.
- **Vitamin A** - Night blindness, xerophthalmia and poor growth.
- **Folate** - Glossitis, anemia (megaloblastic), and neural tube defects (in fetuses of women without folate supplementation).
- **Zinc** - Anemia, dwarfism, hepatosplenomegaly, hypogonadism, and acrodermatitis enteropathica.

Malnutrition in children

Undernourishment amplifies poverty. It deepens poverty by reducing capacity for work and resistance to disease. Poor nutrition degrades children's mental development and educational achievements. Physically and mentally weak children create a massive drag on society in education, family life and health care. Over 75% of the world's poorest grow their own food. This causes widespread food insecurity and nutrient deficiencies due to climate change that causes crop failure. Nearly half of the world's population, more than 3 billion people, live on less than $2.50 a day. When their family crop fails, they have no way to buy food.

Peace microfarm solutions

Peace microfarms preserve natural resources by cycling waste streams, which may avoid conflict or war over land, water, fuel or fertilizer. A peace microfarm can clean wastewater and/or provide all the essential nutrients to avoid malnutrition for a community.

Local microfarms can eliminate malnutrition and micronutrient deficiencies, in rural and urban areas. A single 50 m² microfarm can deliver enough Spirulina to cure **1,350 children** and/or pregnant mothers from the curse of malnutrition. That is a worthy goal because it helps not only the kids, our next generation, but their families, schools, medical facilities and communities. Stronger kids grow up to be better citizens and can take their rightful place to be strong contributors to local economic prosperity.

Algae microfarm

Example: 50 m² (544 ft²) microfarm, (surface area), About 3m by 17m. Volume about 15142 L (4,000 gallons) at 15 cm depth. Microfarm yields about 135 kg of Spirulina a year. Antenna research shows that an 8-week Spirulina treatment with 100 g (total) resolves child malnutrition.

Microfarms grow microcrops that produce healthy protein 30 to 70 times faster than field crops such as food grains. A microfarmer can harvest about 30% of the algae biomass daily, or choose to harvest a higher percentage every two days during sunny weather. Growers can produce algae food and bioproducts year-round in many regions.

Each microfarm may employ several people. Microfarms will not make them rich, but they will have the means to provide healthy food for their family and food to sell in their community. An estimated 100 small spirulina producers are growing food locally in French spirulina microfarms as far north as Normandy. The school at the CFPPA Center in Hyères continues to train more growers.

Robert Henrikson tends an algae microfarm of his design. Robert created an excellent "Getting started checklist" for creative people interested in building a microfarm. He also wrote a 5-part series on algae microfarms for *Algae Industry Magazine*.

Robert manages several free websites dedicated to promoting algae microfarms, Spirulina and our global society; SmartMicrofarms.com, SpirulinaSource.com and AlgaeCompetition.com. Recent books also provide considerable guidance for microfarmers. Henrikson's *Algae Microfarms: for home, school, community and urban gardens, rooftop, mobile and vertical farms* provide the value proposition for families, farmers and community microfarms.

Ana Cultivates Algae Foods

Peace Microfarms: A green Algae Strategy to Prevent War, (Edwards & Henrikson), explains how algae microfarms give growers the freedom to produce food, feed and other valuable bioproducts locally. Peace microfarms avoid war by producing food and other forms of energy with minimal fossil resources. Resources saved eliminates the need to fight over scarce food production resources.

Microfarms can provide social justice, since only modest physical labor is required and there is no dust, pesticides, heavy machinery or poisons. Women, physically handicapped and elderly people can grow highly nutritious food locally. Some microfarms have been designed for Wounded Warriors who have lost limbs in war. Families can support themselves and stay in the communities they love. A microfarmer may cultivate one of many algae species, and may choose to dry the product or sell it fresh locally. Fresh or frozen algae may be eaten directly without any processing or cooking.

As growers learn better production techniques, microfarm productivity will rise and probably triple within 10 years, to benefit growers and communities. Experience and sharing innovations will broaden the range of algae biofertilizer, biofeed, foods, functional foods, nutraceuticals and medicines grown, which will enhance microfarm expansion opportunities and profitability.

Peace microfarms can produce healthy food independent of altitude, latitude, climate or geography. Production systems can be sited on empty lots, rooftops, urban gardens, rail right-of-ways and balconies. Microfarmers can grow enough food in cities to feed the entire city. Microfarms will create good jobs for families that live in inner-cities, slums, food deserts and rural communities. Urban microfarms can significantly reduce transportation costs and black soot pollution from diesel truck engines because local food production nearly zeros out transportation. Microfarms can also cycle nutrients and grow excellent biofertilizer and biofeed for urban farmers and family animals.

Microfarms reduce production risk from climate events for growers because they grow independent of weather. Microfarms do not compete with field crops for land, since they can be sited nearly anywhere. In some settings, the ability of microfarms to clean water may be more valuable to the community than the rich biomass.

Global warming amplifies water shortages that are addressed with deeper wells. Deeper wells tend to increase levels of heavy metal poisons, especially iron, lead, mercury and arsenic. Eating nano-cellular foods allows the body to bioabsorb the tiny algae cells that chelate with heavy metals. The body sluffs them off and passes them out of the body in the urine. In regions plagued with heavy metals in drinking water, (e.g. Bangladesh, China and communities near mines), the ability of algae to detox heavy metal poisoning can save millions from painful and ugly death.

Pesticide pollution imposes a terrible toll on pregnant mothers, fetuses and young children. Recent research shows a connection between pesticide exposure by pregnant mothers and autism spectrum disorders in children. Pesticides cause serious health impacts such as headaches and nausea and chronic impacts like cancer, reproductive harm, and endocrine disruption. People exposed to these poisons in crop fields, in the drinking water of local communities, and even pesticide residuals on produce suffer terrible health risks. People may experience acute nerve, skin, and eye irritation, nerve or eye damage, headaches, dizziness, nausea, fatigue, and systemic poisoning.

Additional research suggests that spirulina eaten normally can chelate with the poison molecules, similar to their attachment to heavy metals, and flush the poisons from the body.

The next section examines the critical question: "Will consumers adopt algae-based foods?"

*My goal is to go from the industrial food system toward a
real food system where you understand what you are eating.*

– Kimbal Musk

Algae foods have not been adopted today because they have not been available. Consumer behavior will change quickly when algae foods arrive because they provide people with so many benefits.

Everett Rogers' well-researched model, *Diffusion of Innovation,* explains how, why, and at what rate new ideas, such as algae-based foods move from trial to acceptance. Rogers found that many innovations, such as hybrid seed corn, contraceptives, and microwave ovens took 20 years before they were widely adopted and became self-sustaining. Algae foods may take 20 years before they are widely adopted. Consumer adoption will be accelerated by a series of actions: breaking myths, packaging, new channels, algae stars and new metrics.

Changing people's eating habits is non-trivial. Few behaviors are more ingrained and rigid than food choices. A popular food myth goes like this: "Consumers like **tangible** food. They want to be able to **see,** touch and crunch their food. They want to **go to the store** and select the **best fresh produce,** in just the right **packaging.**"

Twenty years ago, pundits forecasted that everyone wanted a physical newspaper. Today, few Millennials subscribe to a newspaper. They digest their news from online sources and social media. Convenience and personalized news changed behaviors – quickly.

Convenience and personalized nutrition will change consumer food choices and shopping behaviors. Twenty years ago, Kroger's did not dedicate twenty feet of shelf space to meal replacement bars, powders and drinks. Even the produce area has been invaded with breakfast drinks and smoothies. Meal replacements, power bars and snacks are among the fastest growing food marketing segments.

Until July, 2017 Amazon.com did not own Whole Foods. Amazon invested in extensive consumer research, and knows what people want, speed. Consumers want to save time. They want to talk into their personal assistant, probably on their wrist, and order food for supper. Food will be delivered to their door, probably by drone, within the hour.

The wish to select the best "fresh" produce may give way to better benefits. Personal selection of fresh produce comes with two costs; time and waste. Shopping requires driving, walking or biking and parking, before shopping begins. Fresh foods are perishable. Consumers waste more food after it arrives home than was lost in the entire food production channel. The USDA estimates that consumers waste over 30% all food, 133 billion pounds, worth $161 billion a year.

What if good foods were not perishable? Imagine the savings from algae foods that do not need an expiration date. Fresh produce, dairy products and meats are attacked by microorganisms such as molds, yeasts and bacteria. Microbes grow rapidly and degrade the quality of the food. Spoilage bacteria cause foods to deteriorate and develop unpleasant color, odor and taste.

Fresh algae spoils even faster than fresh produce, because algae contain more protein and sugar, which actively attract microbes. Growers remove the water from algae, which gives these foods a nearly unlimited shelf-life. When consumers re-hydrate dried algae foods, their beautiful original colors typically reappear.

Food technology will allow algae-based foods to retain desired tangibility. They can take any desired form, color or shape. Algae flour makes the perfect feedstock for 3D printers. Natural Machines recently introduced the "Foodini." This mini manufacturing plant deploys edible ingredients squeezed out of stainless steel capsules. Foodini is capable of printing a wide range of dishes, from sweet to savory.

Processing soy is difficult because the raw product is hard, bitter, starchy, beany and nutty. Processing algae is not difficult because the natural product is soft, savory and sweet. Alfu, algae-based tofu, can be made into anything made with food grains.

Food packaging

Food packaging slows the spoilage process and waste. The National Resources Defense Council found that food waste consumes 25% of U.S. freshwater and 4% of US oil consumption. Plastics have become the champion to slow spoilage, but foul the environment.

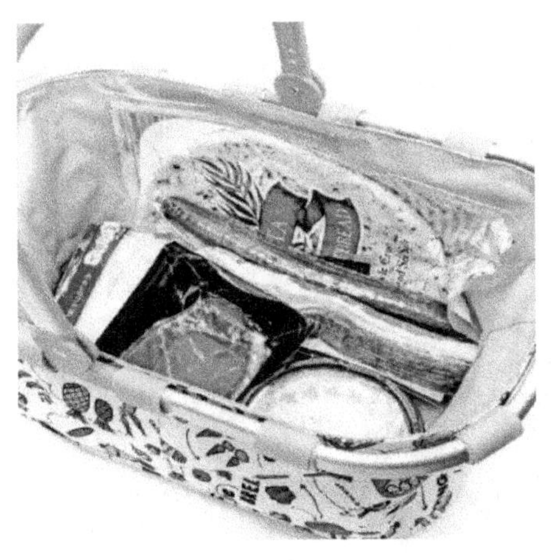

Plastic food packaging has become ubiquitous. It may have 6 to 10 hi-tech layers to protect against oxygen and microbes. Cucumbers sleeved in polyethylene film, have 3 to 14 day longer shelf life. Chopped, colorful ready-to-eat salads and fruits in polyethylene terephthalate bags last twice as long. Vacuum-packed meats are an expanding presence in meat department cases.

Fresh food loses some of its luster when packaging costs to consumers and our planet are considered. Depending on the item, packaging may add 10% to 60% to the price. Many plastic pages are relatively new, which means no long-term health studies are available.

In addition to creating safety problems during production, chemical additives that give plastic products desirable performance properties also have negative environmental and human health effects. These effects include direct toxicity and carcinogens. They can cause endocrine disruption, which can lead to fertility problems, birth defects, immune system suppression and developmental problems in children. The Ecology Center maintains the *Adverse Health Effects Grid*, which provides a list of commonly used plastics and their known health effects.

The Ellen MacArthur Foundation released an excellent study on the impacts plastics have on the health of our planet. *The New Plastics Economy: Rethinking the Future of Plastics*, report details the scale of the packaging waste problem. In 2013, industry produced 78 million metric tons of plastic packaging worldwide. Of that, 40% was landfilled and another 32% was "leaked" to the environment, polluting land and sea.

The "great Pacific garbage patch," located between Hawaii and California, spans 3.5 million square kilometers, (1.35 million square miles). The MacArthur Foundation report predicts there will be more plastic than fish in the oceans by 2050 unless urgent action is taken.

Algae can provide the needed urgent action by producing all the foods in the shopping cart below. Algae can also produce the sustainable and biodegradable packaging too.

ALGIX supports sustainable fish farms in Mississippi for the combined production of fresh fish and algae biomass. Algix's process cleans the fish wastes from the fish ponds and grows algae with the waste nutrients. Their bioplastic technology blends aquatic feedstocks with commercial polymers to reduce cost and dependence on fossil-fuel and food-based plastics.

Algae-based food containers will push the adoption of algae foods. Imagine a pet food container were the pet eats the food, then eats the container for desert.

Food labeling

Today food producers put a tiny bit of information useful to health on packaged foods due to FDA requirements. Algae foods will revolutionize food labels as food marketers will actively invent incredibly useful labels readable on smart phones, smart glasses, and personal assistants. The extended food labels will provide the key metrics for nutralence and other valuable nutritional information. They might say: "Eating one portion of this food three times a week gives the consumer a 90% chance of avoiding heart disease, based on nutrition." Another might say: "The bioactive compounds in this algae food will reduce the common cold by three days, or disrupt asthma in three to five days, without other medicines."

New algae foods

Champions of plant-based diets include extraordinary people, including: The Buddha, Confucius, Pythagoras, Leonardo da Vinci, Leo Tolstoy, Gandhi Gaudi, Percy, Bysshe, Shelly, George Bernard Shaw and Paul McCartney. Each might have migrated down the food chain to algae, but algae foods were not invented yet. The vanguard of algae foods has already arrived – but remains unequally distributed.

Why does the number one rated restaurant in the world, NOMA, serve algae? Because algae foods are choice! Rene Redzepi chef, forager, and owner of NOMA in Copenhagen, made the cover of *Time Magazine* for his excellent innovations in locally sourced and foraged cuisines, which include local sea vegetables. His superb NOMA cookbook shows beautiful pictures of algae garnishing and supporting his world-class servings. The human tongue has five taste buds: sweet, sour, bitter, salty and umami. Umami, the savory or hearty taste comes from taste buds in the middle of the tongue that give a savory or hearty taste – not to just the food eaten directly, but also to the accompanying food.

Rene Redzepi and the Umami Burger

Many upscale restaurants in Europe, Australia and Asia offer algae foods directly or with accompanying hors d'oeuvres and main courses. One of the most popular new restaurant chains in Los Angeles, Umami Burger, has found sustained success promoting the umami taste in their beef burgers with algae flavonoids. The umami sensation comes from the detection of glutamate in specialized taste buds present on the human tongues. Food technologists estimate 52 peptides are responsible for detecting umami taste. Its effect balances taste and rounds out the overall flavor of a dish and enhances the palatability of a wide variety of foods.

Amazon.com offers many books on vegetarian lifestyles, many of which provide value propositions for algae foods. Over 20 books describe the benefits of sea vegetables and sea greens. *Seaweeds: Edible, Available, and Sustainable* by Ole G. Mouritsen provides a comprehensive description of edible seaweeds. Mouritsen uses science and his fascination with Japanese cuisine, as he champions sea vegetables as a staple food. He simultaneously explains algae, its biology, ecology, cultural history, and gastronomy

Mainstream food stores such as Safeway, Van's and Kroger have installed sushi bars where shoppers can lunch on nori, laver, wakame and sea vegetable salad, Hiyashi Wakame. Epicurious.com and AlgaeCompetition offer recipes using various forms of algae. Edible San Francisco, Edible Boston and other communities offer fresh and pre-prepared algae dishes sourced locally.

Barbara and John Stephens ~Lewallen have been edible seaweed wild-crafters since 1980. They run public seminars on foraging. They gather at Greenwood Beach in northern California and provide a lunch of fresh sea vegetables, then talk about cookery and therapeutics. 

Smart Microfarms in Half Moon Bay, California produces fresh, frozen and dried Spirulina for the San Francisco area. SpirulinaSource.com offers wonderful recipes that incorporate Spirulina into foods.

Alnuts are an algae food under development. Alnuts provide an allergen-free algae flour that can be made into nearly any food that currently uses food grains, seeds or nut oils. Alnuts can be made into snacks similar to corn-nuts, food ingredients, similar to sesame seeds or functional foods such as energy shakes or power bars. Alnuts flour can be made into pasta, bread, pastries, cookies or snacks.

One of the most interesting food innovations belongs to the Girl Scouts and palm oil. Two Girl Scouts created an initiative to end the use of palm oil in Girl Scout cookies. Palm oil farming causes rainforest deforestation, endangers thousands of animal species. Over 70,000 people signed their petition to stop the use of palm oil in Girl Scout cookies.

Two Girl Scouts ended Palm Oil use in Girl Scout Cookies

The two girls have been featured on numerous news and talk shows, and they were recently honored with the United Nations Forest Heroes Award for their work in saving rainforests.

As companies look for sustainably sourced oils, algae oils will become popular rapidly because the value proposition has already been communicated to consumers – sustainable, healthier oil.

Soylent offers an algae-based food replacement in drinks, power bars or powder. Soylent had a supply issue and the products now use considerable land terrestrial plant protein. They are designed to maximize nutrition and contain a complete blend of protein, carbs, oils and nutrients.

Soylent is positioned as a meal replacement, targeted to busy people who do not have time to shop for a full set of vegetables and fruit. The company has a mix of products, more with soy protein than algae. In a recent review of meal replacements, Soylent did not make the top 10.

Whole Foods Market carries dozens of nutritious and healthy sea vegetables for snacks and food ingredients, including dulse, laver, kelp, wakame, nori, agar, as well as Spirulina and chlorella. Algae foods are found in several sections, including sea vegetables, snacks, nutrition bars, shakes, and powders.

TerraVia, based in San Francisco's motto is "Harnessing the power of algae, the mother of all plants and earth's original superfood." TerraVia, now owned by Corbion makes a range of algae products, food ingredients, foods and cosmetics. Thrive, the Culinary Algae Oil, is targeted to home cooks. Thrive is high in monounsaturated fats that are heart-healthy and fight inflammation. Thrive is low in polyunsaturated fats, which cause oils to smoke.

Avoidance of legacy foods

Many consumers will adopt algae foods in order to avoid the health problems with modern foods that inflict people with all the diseases associated with the Western Diet. These include heart disease, obesity, hypertension, type 2 diabetes, cancers, autoimmune diseases, and osteoporosis. Considerable research suggests the Western Diet contributes to chronic degenerative diseases, as well as brain and neurological disorders. Consumers interested in promoting their own health and their family's health and longevity will become algae food adopters. Algae foods will provide the extra years of life proven by vegetarian diets, without the threat of empty calories or allergens.

Millions of people have allergic reactions to food and treatments costs US families over $25 billion a year. Food allergies can cause severe reactions and may be life-threatening. The FDA recommends **strict avoidance** of food allergens. They note that early recognition and management of allergic reactions can prevent serious health consequences. The FDA and the University of Nebraska maintain sites that go into extensive detail regarding the occurrence and severity of food allergies. The FDA requires the 14 major food allergen sources to carry food label warnings.

FDA research reports there is no cure for food allergies. Algae nutrients can replace all the nutrients in 14 allergen foods with no allergens. Algae sit on the lowest rung on the food chain and produce no known allergens. Harmful algae blooms (HAB), can produce toxic substances, e.g. red tides. Extensive research has led to a classification of which species and under which conditions these toxins are created. Algae food producers avoid those species and cultivation conditions.

New meat allergies have arrived, and this tick carries a very nasty one. The lone star tick cometh to change or terminate lives for thousands. Red meat contains several protein-linked saccharides: galactose-alpha-1, 3-galactose, and alpha-gal. Symptoms include itching with angry hives blossoming, stomach cramping, fainting and for some, death.

Lone Star tick

Algae organic and vegan meats will provide a safe alternative that will continue to give the familiar texture and taste sensations that make animal flesh attractive. Smart consumers will see the benefit of foods that do not cause allergic reactions, for themselves and for their children. Any parent that has taken a child to do a series of 28 anti-allergy shots will become an enthusiastic supporter of algae food. After each shot, the child must be monitored for 30 minutes for possible reaction. In 2010, Americans lost more than 6 million work and school days to allergies and made 16 million visits to their doctor.

One of the most popular arguments against algae foods is: "I want to know what I am eating." If this were true, consumers would never eat chicken nuggets, hotdogs or other processed meats. Much of those meats are offal, organ meats, and entrails.

New metrics

A new set of nutralence metrics will help consumers understand the value in their food. Nutralence differentiates algae from industrial food; both plants and meat. These metrics will test the degree of difference provided by any novel food alternative. The nutralence model provides a path for food technology scientists to create metrics that benefit consumers.

Nutralence Attribute	Algae compared to land plants or meat	Criticality
Nutrient density and quality	10x to 100x	No empty calories. More nutrients per bite.
Nutrient diversity	100x to 1000x	More micronutrients, vitamins and trace elements.
Bioactive compounds	100x to 1000x	More disease protection. More disease therapeutics.
Bioavailability	10x to 100x	Faster and more reliable assimilation into the body.

Consumer behavior scientists use over 20 sensory attributes for taste, because taste is so complex. Nutralence is even more complex. The nutralence *estimates* here, e.g. 10 times superior nutrient quality, may be validated, (or invalidated), over the next decade by food scientists. No terrestrial foods currently offer any of the key nutralence metrics, because the numbers would be so poor.

Nutrient quality is problematic in terrestrial plants because the nutrient value of each food depends on the elements in the soil that are bioavailable to the roots in the current growing season. Many years of constant production strip the cropland of organic material, humus and micronutrients. The produce may look good, but have hidden hunger, due a lack of micronutrients, vitamins, minerals and trace elements.

Industrial foods often deliver negligible nutrient diversity because the crops have been bred for yield (weight), not nutrient diversity. The nutrient diversity of algae foods, including over 100+ micronutrients, vitamins, trace elements and 200+ enzymes, work together to improve health and vitality. Modern foods are practically devoid of measurable levels of bioactive compounds because the crops have been bred for thousands of years for maximum yield in terms of weight, rather than health. These food components include antioxidants, soluble dietary fibers, proteins, minerals, vitamins, phytochemicals, and polyunsaturated fatty acids. Bioactive compounds operate individually, or more often in concert, to assist the body's defenses and protect from threat vectors such as viruses and bacteria, (antiviral and antibacterial). When the body does become infected, they work to neutralize or expel the pathogens, (e.g. anticancer) and repair tissues and organs. Algae foods provide a diverse array of bioactive compounds.

Ingredient	Algae source	Applications
β-carotene	Dunaliella salina	Antioxidant, (food) pro-vitamin A
Astaxanthin	Haematococcus pluvialis, Chlorella	Pigmenter, antioxidant
Canthaxanthin	Chlorella spp., other green algae	Pigmenter, (food, aquaculture, poultry)
Zeaxanthin	Chlorella ellipsoidea; Dunalielle salina	Antioxidant, food pigmenter
Lutein	Scenedesmus spp.,	Antioxidant
Phytoene	Dunaliella	Antioxidant, cosm.
Echinenone	Botryococcus braunii,	Antioxidant
Fucoxanthin	Phaeodactylum tricornutum	Antioxidant
Phycobilins, phycocyanin, phycoerythrin	Cyanobacteria, Rhodophyta, Cryptophyta,	Natural pigment fluorescent conjugates, antioxidant
Arachidonic acid	Parietochloris incisa	Nutritionals
Sterols	Many species	Nutraceutical
Squalene	Aurantiochytrium sp	Cosmetics

High-value bioactive ingredients from microalgae
– Adapted from Michael Borowitzka

Bioavailability includes both nutrient bioactivity and bioaccessibility. Bioaccessibility refers to the release from the food matrix, transformations during digestion, and transport across the digestive epithelium. Bioactivity encompasses uptake into tissues, metabolism, and physiological effects.

Chocolate cake provides a delightful pallet and nutralence comparison for many consumers. Industrial agriculture produces a chocolate cake with many disadvantages, which are apparent when compared with an cake made with algae-based oil and flour.

Chocolate Cake Mix - Boxed vs Algae Cake Mix

Ingredients	Industrial cake	Algae cake
High saturated fats and cholesterol	Yes	No, 80% less
GMO food and empty calories	Yes	No, 100% less
Preservatives and pesticide residues	Yes	100% fewer
Micronutrients and bioactive compounds	Few	400% more
Nutrient quality, density and diversity	Low	100% higher
Nosh, hunger pangs	Amplifies	No, moderates

Land plants have cells that are 2 to 20 times larger than algae cells, which often makes them less bioavailable. Even though algae cells are small, their strong cell walls create a challenge for digestion. Algae food providers use a variety effective methods to break down the cell walls, which make the algae nutrients substantially more bioavailable than many foods made from land-based crops.

Nutralence limitations

A cautionary 2017 review article on algae nutrition and functional foods, by Mark Wells and team, points out that algae nutrients, (quality, density, and diversity), may or may not be assimilated efficiently, especially seaweeds, by different consumers. People in Asia have evolved stomach enzymes that break down foods that are not bioavailable in the West. The team notes correctly, that considerably more interdisciplinary research needs to occur to improve knowledge about the actions of bioactives compounds and nutrient bioavailability with various methods of algae processing.

New technologies

Individualized medicine will push adoption of algae foods for purely nutritional reasons. Precise or personalized medicine designs diagnosis and treatment to each patient to optimize care. The process uses a person's unique genetic code to more effectively and precisely diagnose, treat, predict and eventually prevent disease. Researchers at Mayo Clinic Center for Individualized Medicine are exploring ways to analyze a person's gut microbiome and then design a diet to maintain a person's health and avoid the development of disease.

A July 2017 weight loss **biomarker study** published in the *American Journal of Clinical Nutrition* found that fasting blood sugar and/or fasting insulin can be used to select the optimal diet and to predict weight loss, particularly for people with prediabetes or diabetes. The research analyzed clinical data from three trials which collectively looked at more than 1,200 individuals. The findings suggest that for most people with prediabetes, a diet rich with vegetables, fruits and whole grains should be recommended for weight loss and could potentially improve diabetes markers. For people with type-2 diabetes, the analysis found that a diet rich in healthy fats from plant sources would be effective for weight loss. These diets may be effective independent of caloric restriction.

DayTwo Inc., works in concert with Mayo Clinic, and completed a study examining the impact of changes in diet on blood glucose levels in the blood. Investigators developed a mathematical model to predict how people's glucose level would change after eating a variety of foods. Based on that model, they were able to create customized diets appropriate for each person and control glucose levels. Researchers also provided participants with suggested meals and snacks to maintain their health.

Orig3n is one of many new companies that offer a private $150 DNA test. Some offer results and dietary guidance on a smart phone. Orig3n claims the 24-gene profile reveals how a person's body responds to food. The smartphone app helps a person discover which foods to choose.

The profile may indicate micronutrient or vitamin deficiencies or how a person's genes impact weight. Other companies betting on DNA tests and nutrition or fitness include Dnafit, DnaNutrition and Precision Nutrition. Campbell's Soup believes in individualized medical nutrition. The company is investing $32 million in Habit, a nutrition focused startup that uses data from a test kit to make personalized food recommendations tailored to an individual's unique DNA.

Personalized food coming soon

Imagine that in 10 years, you walk into **NutraU,** which offers the full array of morning power drinks. You make polite small talk to *N-Dow*, the *NutraBot*, and then indicate the nutrients you want. You might name a diet, or show *N-Dow* your smart phone app that highlights the diet that an intelligent system recommends for you. You talk about the form, taste and texture you like. *N-Dow* might lift some fresh fruit into your smoothie. She is likely pull some algae components for healthy protein, micronutrients, bioactive compounds and enzymes.

N-Dow's friend, the 3D food printer bot, *N-Joy*, may make you a to-go basket with an algae-based shrimp ceviche for lunch and a healthy and tasty algae umami burger for supper. Alternatively, *N-Genius* can make you a healthy surprise meal that fits your pallet and your health profile.

Personalized foods, made to order immediately to match your DNA will be very attractive. Algae ingredients will make these foods easier to prepare and avoid the packaging and waste associated with fresh produce.

Smart nano sensors will help consumers monitor their biomarkers and microbiome. A major factor holding back consumer's access to algae based foods is the cost of medical research. In order to prove that an algae bioactive compound actually does what medical research theorizes it can do, the FDA requires studies in three phases. The human trials are likely to cost $50 million or more. Forbes Magazine did a study on the cost of bringing a new drug to market. Their conclusion was a minimum of $1.3 billion. The average drug developed by a major pharmaceutical company costs $4 to $11 billion. No algae company has the resources for these kinds of studies.

Smart nano sensors can cut animal and human medical trial costs by at least 10x. Scientists are developing nano sensors that enter the body, similar to an algae cell, and are transported normally throughout the body. The sensors are designed to detect biomarkers, such as enzymes, antibodies or specific cellular compounds. The sensors do their job and then pass out of the body in the urine, where they are assessed regularly by robotic urinalyses. Early sensors will detect a single biomarker, while later tools will monitor several.

Similarly, continuous non-invasive testing of body compounds from saliva, sweat or hair composition will allow fast, low cost medical tests. Subjects might wear an appliance like a FitBit that constantly monitors several body functions, including an array of non-invasive blood tests. Smart sensors create a flood of data that needs to be filed and tracked. Technologists will rely on Big Data and the IofT, (Internet of Things).

Implanted chips have already arrived. The first in the US, Three Square Market in Wisconsin, offered voluntary implanted chips to all of their employees in August 2017. The RFID chip, from BioHax International in Sweden, allows employees to make purchases in the micro market, open doors, login to computers, use the copy machine, etc. The next step will use similar sensors to monitor body functions for medical purposes.

The FDA could play a pivotal role in algae food adoption by actively conducting human trials on 10 algae bioactive compounds. These trials would create the metrics to assess their value in functional and medical foods. Then food companies could use their creativity to deliver excellent foods. The FDA would continue its role in monitoring producer quality. The Global Organization for EPA and DHA Omega-3s, (GOED), has done an excellent job of organizing the medical research on Omega-3s.

Machine learning paired with **artificial intelligence** holds promise to reduce the cost of medical research. Smart nano sensors may feed big data to computer systems that use machine learning to assess medical impacts. A key question in the use of bioactive compounds from algae is the upper and lower threshold for a therapeutic dose. Machine learning could make those determinations and frame follow-up questions for effective medical protocols.

Clear nutritional impact on health metrics will help. People have trouble making healthy food decisions because they are unaware of the health consequences of the decisions they make. A 2013 study, which followed more than 95,000 men and women in the US from 2002 to 2009, found vegetarians had a 12% lower risk of death than non-vegetarians. Other studies suggest vegetarians live 4 - 6 years longer.

New impact metrics might give consumers a YouTube video illustrating realistic body functions after eating a beef hamburger compared with vegan meat made from algae. Similar impact metrics on the ecological footprint of foods, such as water, land and energy consumption may be persuasive to consumers. A clear impact metric on residual pesticide poisons may have a substantial impact on consumer choices.

The Environmental Working Group, (EWG), led by Ken Cook, has done great work on the environmental, social and health impacts of MIA. EWG's analysis of tests by the USDA found that nearly 70% of samples of 48 types of conventionally grown produce were contaminated with pesticide residues. The ERG's Dirty Dozen begins with strawberries, spinach, nectarines, apples, and peaches.

Improving nutrition and aggression metrics that clarify and quantify the well-known link between poor early childhood nutrition and adolescent and adult aggression, will help focus public policy on nutrient value. A comprehensive list of studies connecting diet to aggression and ADHD symptoms may be found at Fiengold Research. Since one out five American children are food insecure, the President should declare a national emergency to fix the problem. Peace microfarms distributed in food deserts across America could reduce child malnutrition by half. The full distribution of peace microfarms would cost less than 5% of President Trump's proposed wall on the Mexico border.

Many of yesterday's malnourished children involuntarily invoked their aggression and were sent to prison. The Bureau of Justice Statistics reported in 2013 that 2.2 million adults were incarcerated in US – about nearly 1% of all adults. Another 4.7 million Americans were on probation or parole.

A recent study published in the *New York Times* found that NYC paid $167,731 to feed, house and guard each inmate in 2012.

Imagine the value of investing a fraction of that "housing cost" in early childhood nutrition. The US could end malnutrition in all children for less than the cost of housing NYC inmates.

The research is clear that early childhood malnutrition stunts brain development and results in low IQ, antisocial behavior, and lack of impulse control. Peace microfarms placed in every prison could reduce operating costs, supply inmates with healthy omega-3 foods, and train them in green jobs. The omega-3 foods should reduce the firestorm in their brains and restore their mental and physical health.

Similarly, clear metrics on the contribution of algae bioactive compounds in the **reduction of symptoms** of brain disorders such as PTSD, dementia and Alzheimer's disease, will spur adoption of algae foods. The military might lead this line of algae medical research focused on the critical problem of PTSD, depression and suicide among service personnel and veterans.

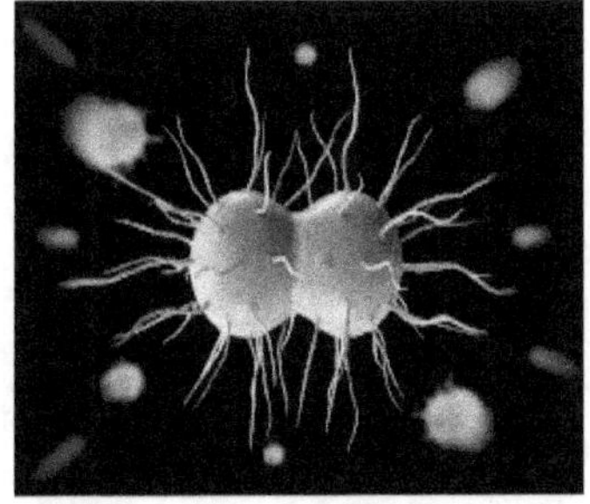

Virus defense methods represent a critical challenge, but also present an opportunity for medical solutions from bioactive algae compounds. The UN WHO issued a warning in July 2017, that bacteria causing gonorrhea (left), resist treatment via antibiotics. In several countries, gonorrhea strains are now untreatable.

Gonorrhea is reported by over 820,000 Americans each year. Many more people have the virus, but do not show symptoms. A broad-spectrum algae-based virus defense and treatment would benefit millions. Several studies have shown algae antivirus compounds have slowed or eliminated symptoms of HIV-AIDS and the highly pathogenic avian flu. Other viral vectors await algae antivirals; cholera, Ebola, West Nile and Lyme. These illness sicken children and adults and substantially reduce the people available to grow healthy food.

Summary

Algae foods offer significant value for improved human health compared with MIA field crops. Algae foods are healthier because they deliver superior nutralence. MIA crops suffer from hidden hunger, empty calories, pesticide residue, and a wide array of potential allergens.

Algae foods can address global poverty and hunger in a manner not possible with MIA. Distributed microfarms can resolve malnutrition for millions of children, mothers and the elderly. Microfarms reduce food production risk for everyone, especially the poorest who have to go hungry when their field crop fails. New algae foods are finding niche markets, especially in upscale food retailer such as Whole Foods, Trader Joe's, Kroger, Edeka Zentrale in Germany and Woolworths in Australia. Food retailers in Asia have carried algae foods for decades.

Algae foods are being adopted and will benefit consumers with enhanced nutritional metrics, production technologies and medical research. Algae foods set the stage for the next major breakthrough in the global food supply; freedom foods. But first, a note on algae and sex.

12. Algae and Sex: Can Algae Give Life?

Superior sex outcomes: ability to have children when it seemed impossible, and smart children, without birth defects too. This miracle has yet to be performed, but algae scientists can make it happen.

Algae has already performed incredible miracles, some of which were discussed previously, and others are shown in Appendix I. Algae biofertilizers have demonstrated their ability to bring dead sterilized soil back to life. Algae biofeeds increase animal stress tolerance, health and survivability, but those come from the benefits of superior nutralence. Better nutrition is amazing, but not truly miraculous.

The same is true for algae's bioactive compounds, which improve health and vitality for people. Algae medicines will extend and save lives, but some may argue that is not gifting the miracle of life. Algae's ability to overcome sex challenges may actually give life to couples where having children appears impossible.

Sex offers an potentially catastrophic human problem where algae can perform another miracle. No published research studies yet, show algae foods or algae bioactives improve sex quality or the experience.

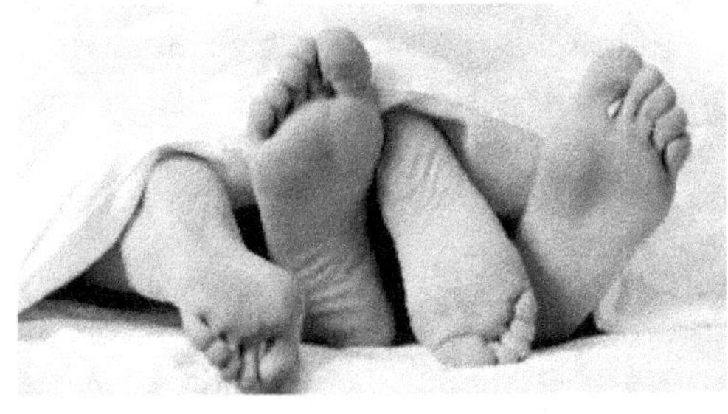

The exception may be omega-3s that reduce CHD symptomology, and improve the sex experience for men with chronic heart conditions.

Sex self-destruction

Will continuing human actions that raise levels of atmospheric CO_2 diminish or destroy sex? This theory, "sex self-destruction," has not been proposed before in the scientific literature. Certainly, more research will be required to prove whether we could be so irresponsible to allow business as usual, ignore climate change, and destroy sex.

The **sex self-destruction** theory: The collapse of vital dietary nutrients in food crops due to global warming contributes significantly to the catastrophic collapse in male sperm counts, which threatens to destroy successful sex for our next generation. Knowledge of sex self-destruction may transform many climate deniers into climate evangelists.

Sperm collapse

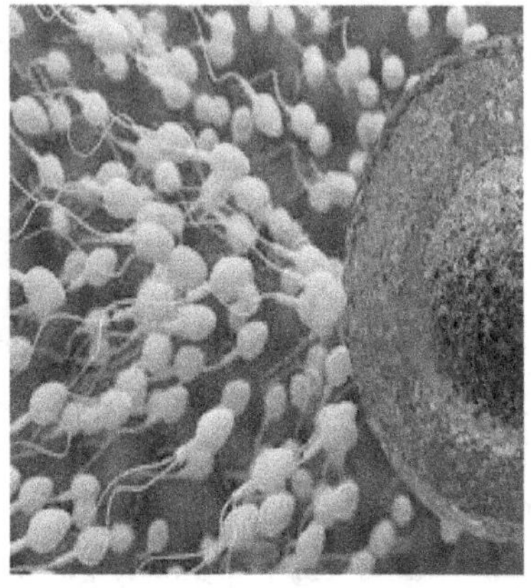

A July 2017 international study lead by a Harvard team indicates that human that sperm counts have declined 59% over the last 40 years for men in North America, Europe, Australia and New Zealand. Lower sperm counts degrade or destroy the purposes of sex for many couples. Evidence indicates that a sperm concentration below this threshold is associated with a "substantial decreased probability of conception."

Many men may discover they are infertile. Infertile means a pair have practiced sex regularly without protection for over a year without creating pregnancy. Men with low sperm counts may also have weak sperm motility (ability to move), or abnormally shaped sperm. The sperm may not contain sufficient enzymes to penetrate the outer layers and properly fertilize the egg.

Some men may not worry about low sperm count, because they assume the problem applies to others. Nearly 1 in 6 couples in the US currently confront fertility problems. Just in time, the *New York Times* reports that a new cell phone app will allow men to accurately check their sperm count for about $5. When Millennials realize their ability to procreate is damaged by a tainted food supply, they will want solutions – quickly.

Low sperm count impacts health in several ways beyond infertility. The economic and societal burden of male infertility is high and increasing. Reduced sperm count predicts increased chronic medical conditions including increased mortality and morbidity. Reduced sperm count is associated with cryptorchidism, hypospadias and testicular cancer, suggesting a shared prenatal etiology. Sperm count sensitively reflect the impacts of the modern environment on male health throughout the course of life.

Algae and Sex

Rising levels of atmospheric CO$_2$

Rising levels of anthropogenic atmospheric CO$_2$ are causing significant loss in vital dietary nutrients in food crops, especially protein, zinc and iron. Food crops have only so much energy. The extra CO$_2$ does increase growth rates and size, but most of the extra weight composition creates more retained water, sugar and starch.

The plant does not have enough energy to balance nutrient intake with valuable micronutrients, vitamins, minerals and trace elements. Higher CO$_2$ levels create deficiencies of protein, zinc and iron, which imposes many adverse health impacts, including lower sperm counts and depressed sperm motility. Low iron also reduces red blood cell production, which diminishes energy.

Considerable research shows that reports about climate chaos that impact human health and happiness create a significantly stronger response in people than environmental destruction. Climate deniers may dismiss environmental losses thinking the damages will only impact others.

Among human life desires, positive sex ranks near the top. Successful sex and procreation are vital to human health and the important feeling of fulfillment. The sex self-destruction theory may add another label to climate deniers – sex destroyers.

Sex serves several of life's core purposes, including pleasure, stress reduction, identity formation, intimate connection and procreation. The evidence in this scientific mystery offers fascinating leads and indicators. The implications are catastrophic, and even potentially more severe than climate change.

Several independent reports, including WHO, estimate that in 2017 over 2 billion people already suffer from zinc and iron deficiencies. These deficits result in a loss of 63 million life years annually from malnutrition. The loss of zinc, iron and protein in food crops represents the most significant health threat yet shown to be associated with climate change.

Zinc and iron

The Linus Pauling Institute estimates that the global prevalence of zinc deficiency today at 31% of the global population. Higher concentrations of atmospheric CO2 will expand zinc deficiency to possibly double that number. Zinc deficiency currently ranks as the fifth leading disease risk factor worldwide, causing 176,000 diarrhea deaths, 406,000 pneumonia deaths and 207,000 malaria deaths, due to weakened immune systems.

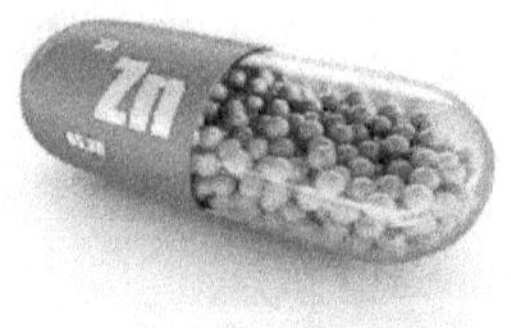

Zinc has earned the label as the "essential trace element" for all forms of life. All living things need this nutritionally essential mineral for catalytic, structural, and regulatory functions in the body. The mineral zinc is present in every cell, organ, bone, tissue, and fluid. Zinc plays an important role in activating enzymatic reactions, wound healing and normal immune function.

Zinc is especially prominent in the male prostate gland and must be present to make sperm. The zinc RDA for adult men and women is 11 mg/day and 8 mg/day, respectively.

Zinc deficiency can cause impaired growth and development in children, (dwarfism) and slow or incomplete development of major organs, especially the brain. Women with zinc deficiency face a wide range of pregnancy complications, including miscarriages and newborns with severe development disorders. Zinc deficiency causes immune and neurological dysfunction and increased susceptibility to infections. The structure and function of cell membranes are regulated by zinc. Loss of zinc from biological membranes increases their susceptibility to oxidative damage and impairs their function.

Research funded by the Bill & Melinda Gates Foundation and the International Zinc Nutrition Consultative Group estimate the total number of people at new risk of zinc deficiency by 2050 in the hundreds of millions.

Another report estimated that more than one billion mothers and 354 million children live in countries where dietary iron is projected to drop significantly. Iron deficiency will exacerbate the already widespread public health problem of anemia. Anemia occurs when the body fails to make enough red blood cells, which require iron. In infants and young children, signs of anemia include poor appetite, slowed growth and development, and behavioral problems.

Adult symptoms of iron deficiency include fatigue weakness, irregular heartbeats, dizziness, chest pain, cold hands and feet, headache, heart arrhythmias, enlarged heart and heart failure. Men and women suffering from iron deficiency lack the energy and stamina for successful sex.

Algae and Sex

Nutrient sources

Food grains, (e.g. rice, soy, corn and wheat) make up about 80% of the world's food supply today. Most global citizens depend on food crops for nourishment because they cannot afford meat. These people are at increasing risk from zinc, iron and other micronutrient deficiencies due to increasing concentrations of atmospheric CO_2. Field trials with ambient CO_2 levels projected for 2050 showed a significant decrease in zinc, iron, and protein in food grains – 9.3%, 5.1%, and 6.3% respectively.

These losses may seem trivial. They are not for the 2 billion people who live on less than $2 a day. The poor need more nutrients per bit, not fewer. In addition to elevated levels of CO_2, climate chaos causes extreme temperature spikes, drought and fierce storms that further diminish food production and the micronutrients in all types of food.

Food grains are highly susceptible to drought and temperature spikes. Lack of soil moisture from drought or temperatures outside a narrow "acceptable" growing temperature around 85°F, (25°C) can produce crop losses of 3% to 8% a day. Elevated atmospheric and ocean heat are igniting more fierce storms.

Hurricane Irma caused a 75% loss to the $10 billion citrus industry in Florida. While many farmers lost their crop, others lost their entire orchards to high winds and rain. Many farmers feed their families with their farm production and the revenue generated by their produce. When their crops fail, their family goes hungry.

The combination of nutrient loss from higher atmospheric levels of CO_2, climate chaos caused temperature spikes and more severe storms will leave families very hungry and nutrient deficient. In addition to higher CO_2 emissions destroying sperm, pesticides amplify the problem.

Pesticides destroy sex too

EPA's *Annual use of Pesticides in the U.S. Report* shows that American farmers apply 1.1 billion pounds of toxic chemicals into the environment and our food supply each year. Farmers in the US apply over 90 million pounds of Organophosphates (OP), neurotoxins that silently build up in the bodies of Americans and degrade male sperm. Plants may absorb less than 0.1% of each applied pesticide. The 99% residual enters the local ecosystem where it degrades the brains, neurons and bodies of birds, amphibians, fish farm animals, farm families and their neighbors.

Pesticide residuals also remain on the crops after harvest. The use of OPs continues to expand because so many insects have become resistant to other pesticides and alternatives are not available. OPs have contributed to a devastating human sex problems, including male infertility, female fertility problems,

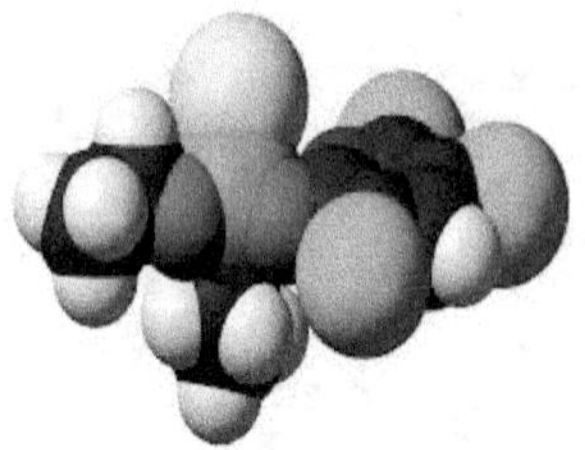

Organophosphate molecule

miscarriages, severe birth defects, impaired brain development and dysfunction, lowered IQ, and neurological development problems.

Exposure to OPs in the environment and in and on food and in water have contributed significantly to the collapse of men's sperm counts. When men do not have enough sperm, they become infertile and women do not get pregnant. Procreation stops. While the collapse in sperm counts may associate with other factors, such as higher levels of CO_2 and micronutrient deficiencies, pesticide exposure from the MIA food supply chain appears to be a primary driver.

Children are Uniquely Vulnerable

Children are not small adults. They have key neurological, physical, developmental, and behavioral differences from adults that make them uniquely vulnerable to chemical exposures. By size and weight, children drink more, breathe more, and have more skin surface area to body weight relative to adults, making their bodies more sensitive to pesticides and other chemicals. Their brains and nervous systems are still making connections and maturing, processes that are particularly sensitive to interference by pesticides. Children come into contact with pesticides daily through air, food, dust, and soil, and on surfaces through home and public lawn or garden application, household insecticide use, application to pests, and agricultural product residues

Epidemiologic studies associate pesticide exposure with adverse birth outcomes, including preterm birth, low birth weight, congenital abnormalities, pediatric cancers, neurobehavioral and cognitive deficits, asthma and autism spectrum disorder, (ASD). The evidence is especially strong linking pesticide exposure with pediatric cancers and permanent neurological damage. Some birth cohort studies of American children have found associations between pesticide exposure and neurobehavioral and cognitive defects like lower IQs, autism, and attention deficit disorders.

Algae and Sex

The International Agency on Research on Cancer found that organophosphates increase the likelihood of cancer. OPs may cause DNA or chromosomal damage, and can cause non-Hodgkin lymphoma, or cancer of lymph nodes. Conditions linked to these endocrine-disrupting chemicals ALS, diabetes, obesity, and CHD.

Organophosphates are used on a massive scale to produce modern industrial foods. They are neurotoxins used in both nerve gases, (which are outlawed), and insecticides. They work by disrupting the nervous system of insects, a mechanism that also affects the human nervous and reproductive systems, when people are exposed.

An endocrine disrupter, Atrazine, (herbicide), is one of the most widely used pesticides in the world. This poison can be transported by wind or water more than 1,000 km from the point of application to other farms, cities and remote habitats.

Over 80 million pounds of Atrazine are applied in the US annually and has become the number one pesticide contaminant in water. Like other OPs, it causes complete feminization and chemical castration in male frogs, fish, birds, rodents and **human cell lines.**

Atrazine not only disrupts sex by preventing the production of sperm, but destroys sex as we know it. The pesticide causes animals to become "intersex." The chemical causes a "chemical castration," causing males to develop female sex characteristics. Researchers hypothesize that atrazine signals the conversion of testosterone to estrogen, demasculinizing the animal. A recent USGS study of male bass showed that 85% of male smallmouth bass across Northeast National Wildlife Refuges demonstrate characteristics of the opposite sex – including eggs located where testes should be. In some water bodies, the pesticide-driven sex changes collapsed the entire fish population.

Russ Hauser at Harvard School of Public Health and a team of 18 international researchers found that exposure to endocrine-disrupting chemicals cost the European Union more than €150 billion, ($209 billion), a year in health care expenses and lost earning potential. Pete

Myers, founder of Environmental Health Sciences and team, performed a similar analysis in the US and found the annual cost of endocrine-disrupting chemicals in the US exceeds $340 billion; 2% of the US GDP. Pesticide exposure in the US causes an estimated 2 million lost IQ points and another 7,500 intellectual disability cases annually.

These pesticides create appalling damage during fetal and infant life and lead to severe, lifelong brain and neurological problems, including ASD. The prevalence of autism in the US has increased 119% since 2000 and one in 45 children in the US are born with autism. Autism costs $268 billion a year and costs are projected to rise to $461 billion in 2025, if autism's prevalence remains the same as 2015.

Pesticide application

The thirstiest part of a food crop is the edible fruit, vegetable, seeds or nuts. In produce treated with OPs, all the juicy, crispy, pulpy or leafy flesh carries the chemical residue. The pesticide is present throughout, and cannot be removed. The EWG's 2017 *Shopper's Guide to Pesticides in Produce* provides useful guidance, but also clear warnings for consumers to beware.

Russ Hauser at Harvard School of Public Health and a team of 18 international researchers found that exposure to endocrine-disrupting chemicals cost the European Union more than €150 billion, ($209 billion), a year in health care expenses and lost earning potential. Pete Myers, founder of Environmental Health Sciences and team, performed a similar analysis in the US and found the annual cost of endocrine-disrupting chemicals in the US exceeds $340 billion; 2% of the US GDP. Pesticide exposure in the US causes an estimated 2 million lost IQ points and another 7,500 intellectual disability cases annually.

The EPA decision to approve modern OPs was driven by the belief that the pesticide breaks down quickly and loses its toxicity. Apparently, the EPA made a bad decision. A recent study compared expired OP pesticides with fresh products. The expired OP pesticide formulations exhibited **higher toxicity** than the corresponding unexpired pesticides. A USGS study of male bass showed that 85% of male smallmouth bass across Northeast National Wildlife Refuges demonstrate characteristics of the opposite sex – including eggs located where testes should be.

The Environmental Working Group found more than 40,000 water systems had detections of known or likely carcinogens exceeding established federal or state health guidelines. These are levels that pose real health risks, but are not legally enforceable. Many water systems contained chemicals associated with brain and nervous system damage, developmental harm to children or fetuses, hormone disruption and male and female fertility problems. The accumulated knowledge regarding agriculture chemicals poisoning drinking water were to be regulated by the EPA's Clean Water Rule.

Clean Water Rule killed

In July 2017, EPA Secretary Scott Pruitt caved to pressure by the pesticide lobby to allow agribusiness to continue using known endocrine disruptors, despite irrefutable scientific evidence that shows how exposure, even at the smallest levels, can harm children's brains. President Trump and Pruitt announced that they killed the Clean Water Rule – a safeguard that protects drinking water for an estimated 117 million Americans. The EWG and the American Academy of Pediatrics, called on Trump and Pruitt and the EPA to reverse course, and put a full-scale ban of the brain-damaging endocrine disruptors.

Trump's "swamp of scitards" (advisors who are too mentally weak to understand science – so they deny facts), impose a horrific price on families. Trump probably does not know that killing the clean water bill will create thousands of "ghost children," kids who are visualized by their parents but not are born due to pesticide-caused fertility problems. Trump and his swamp of scitards will kill thousands of unborn children with miscarriages. Additional thousands will be born with severe birth defects, which will add substantial drag to families and the economy.

Can algae restore male fertility?

In addition to the miracle of giving life, this green algae strategy has the potential to recover 2 million IQ points for American children each year. It may cut birth defects and births with autism spectrum disorder, (ASD) by 50%. Currently, 3.5 million people in the US live with ASD. This miracle begins with an understanding of root cause, plus an important feature in common with men's testes and brains.

The first algae miracle for restoring men's sperm and fertility is quick. But fertility provides an incomplete solution. Currently, their male offspring will have a 1:42 chance of ASD. The other solutions are more difficult but equally valuable; bioremediation of pesticides from surface and ground water, and flushing pesticide poisons from the body.

DHA rescues sperm count

Male DHA levels are generally highest in the testes and brain. Low DHA levels are linked to poor sperm quantity and quality and decreased fertility. Simple DHA supplements can create a miracle, and restore men's fertility. Validation comes from knockout mice and stallions.

Manabu Nakamura, at the University of Illinois and team, created the knockout mouse, which was genetically modified so that it was not able to make its own DHA. The mice without DHA could not make sperm and were infertile. Fertility returned when their diet was supplemented with DHA. The team determined that DHA plays critical role in the formation of a structure called the acrosome on the head of the sperm. The acrosome is a pointy caplike structure containing enzymes that break through the egg's outer layers, enabling the sperm to fertilize it. The acrosome on top of this cone head is a gigantic sack containing lots of enzymes. When the sperm meets the egg, the acrosome bursts and releases enzymes, which help the sperm penetrate into the egg.

Racehorse breeders know this trick too. Stud fees for Kentucky's finest racehorses can reach $300,000. Arabian studs in Arizona may demand $500,000. Breeders want to be sure their stud does his job, because next year's stud price depends on a successful sire. What have elite horse breeders given their prized stallions for decades? Breeders know DHA supplements improve sperm counts,  motility and quality in stallions. Stallions are crazy, so no claim can be made for the DHA improving the animal's brain, but DHA does improve testes function. Prize bulls also get DHA supplements to improve their sperm metrics, but most bulls do not get the privilege of directly breeding cows. Most cows are artificially inseminated, but a person must collect viable semen.

Algae bioremediates pesticides

Only about half of the prescription drugs and few pesticide contaminants in sewage are removed by treatment plants. Sewage treatment plants are not designed to remove pesticides. Although the EPA regulates and monitors several drinking water contaminants, most pesticides are not regulated contaminants. When pesticides contaminate water, the levels often vary widely from month to month, and from season to season. Pesticides are applied to canals, rivers, lakes and streams to control pests such as mosquitoes, weeds or invasive fish.

The USGS National Water-Quality Assessment Program found that 100% of US streams have detectable levels of at least one pesticide and 56% of streams contain one or more pesticides that exceed at least one aquatic-life benchmark. About half of shallow wells have detectable levels of pesticides. About 90% of the 139 municipal water systems sampled by EPA contained detectable levels of atrazine, an endocrine-disrupter.

T. P. Ca´ceres and team at the University of South Australia tested five green and five blue-green algae for their ability for biodegradation of an OP pesticide, fenamiphos. They found all 10 species had the ability to detoxify fenamiphos and bioremediate the pesticide and its toxic metabolites. This research adds to the substantial reasons to use algae bioremediation of wastewater to reduce exposure in animals and people.

Algae flush toxins

The same algae bioactive compounds that biodegraded OP pesticides in wastewater in the University of South Australia study can do the same in people or animals. (Note: no citation exists for this, but it is logical.) Failing direct evidence, related research on algae chelation with heavy metals supports this premise.

Spirulina has been shown to chelate with heavy metals such as arsenic and remove them from the body. Mir Misbahuddin and team at the Medical University, Dhaka, Bangladesh performed a series of studies showing spirulina chelated effectively with arsenic and removed most of the poison from animal body tissues. The team did a double blind and placebo test on forty-one chronic arsenic poisoning patients who were treated orally by placebo or spirulina, (250 mg) plus zinc, (2 mg) twice daily for 16 weeks. The spirulina extract plus zinc removed 47% of the arsenic from scalp hair, while the placebo did not. Spirulina extract had no noticeable side effects. Results showed that spirulina plus zinc offers a natural treatment of chronic arsenic poisoning.

Summary

The **sex self-destruction** theory suggests that the collapse of vital dietary nutrients in food crops due to global warming contributes significantly to the catastrophic collapse in male sperm counts, which threatens to destroy successful sex for our next generation. Sex self-destruction also occurs with the application and lack of regulation of pesticides, especially organophosphates. Exposure to OPs in the environment, drinking water and in and on food have contributed significantly to the collapse of men's sperm counts.

Algae omega-3 fatty acids can remediate male sperm count loss, in many cases, and restore successful sexual function. However, algae supplements can overcome the terrible price fetuses and infants pay for pesticide exposure.

Algae can clean pesticides from water, which will reduce potential exposure for millions of consumers. Avoiding pesticide exposure can save thousands of ghost children and additional thousands from birth defects. Algae foods can be used to chelate with heavy metals and pesticides, to cleanse the body of poisons. Early removal of poisons can substantially improve newborn growth, development and vitality.

Algae offer several other novel solutions discussed previously to reduce exposure to OPs and other pesticides. Algae biofertilizers enhance crop stress tolerance and induce plants to produce natural biopesticides, which reduces or eliminates the need for pesticides. Algae crusts can hold topsoil and prevent or mitigate migration of poisons by winds. Algae-based animal feeds are pesticide free and are natural, diverse and GMO free. Algae foods offer an alternative that are grown without pesticides and leave no poison residuals in or on foods or in food supply ecosystems.

Algae nano medicines will accelerate the adoption of algae foods. Consumers are smart and when bioactive algae compounds become commonly available in medicines, algae foods are the next logical application.

13. Ana Cultivates Nano-Medicines

Ana's quest for food justice began with an integrated plan to lift industrial agriculture and, in addition, provide algae compounds for food ingredients, functional foods, cosmeceuticals, nutraceuticals and algae foods. On her path to food justice, Ana discovered that medical justice needs considerable work. Why not restore health to millions of people with bioactive compounds from algae?

Prediction: By 2040, companies will have earned ten times more wealth in algae medicines than with any other algae bioproduct category, including food. Bioactive algae compounds offer preventive and therapeutic solutions for 90% of the diseases humanity faces today.

Roughly 70% of medicines currently come from terrestrial plants or animals. Many of those will be replaced because algae can produce the same or better therapeutic compounds substantially faster, cleaner and at a higher quality. Consumers will rejoice at the freedom to choose natural compounds that do not impose the high financial costs and heavy drag of undesirable drug side effects that are common today.

The development and conveyance of algae medicines represents the most credible action to support algae food adoption by mainstream consumers. Today, people tend to think of food and medicines separately because they are marketed in different stores. Tomorrow, those lines will blur. Amazon, Target, Kroger and others will build supply chains that deliver food, medicines, pharmaceuticals and cosmeceuticals. Consumers will have the freedom to choose foods that prevent illnesses and other foods that treat diseases.

Market research shows that people strongly prefer following the advice of Hippocrates: "*Let food be thy medicine in the medicine be thy food.*" Algae already support our global food system as useful ingredients, valuable compounds for functional foods, and in some cases, algae food. Tomorrow consumers will choose algae foods for their extensive medical benefits as well as freedom from allergens and empty calories.

Craig Venter's keen observation on "normal" having no meaning is, unfortunately, true. People cannot relate to normal, which simply means average. Even if they did, normal is not the place a smart person wants to be when the CDC reports that 71% of the US population is overweight or obese, and over half of adults over 50 have one or more chronic diseases.

Algae offer novel biosolutions. Algae photoautotrophic cell factories that provide an efficient means of converting solar energy into biomass composed of fatty acids, lipids, vitamins, carbohydrates, antibiotics, antioxidants, proteins and bioactive compounds that can battle disease.

Algae prevent disease

Algae compounds prevent disease by providing the essential nutrients for sustained health and vitality. Algae contain high multiples of the nutrients that cause the major nutrient deficiencies globally. Algae contain several times more beta-carotene, (provitamin A) than other foods. Algae are rich in antioxidant vitamins, (C and E), in concentrations far higher than any land plants. Vitamin C provides protection against immune system deficiencies, CHD, prenatal health problems, eye disease, and skin wrinkling. Vitamin E moderates neurological problems due to poor nerve conduction and anemia due to oxidative damage to red blood cells. Algae are a good source of all seven B vitamins. Algae offer a unique as a plant source of vitamin B12.

Algae provide a mineral profile superior to that of land plants, milk, eggs or soybeans. Terrestrial foods such as food grains have minerals such as iron bound up in phytic acid complexes, limiting their bioavailability. These complexes cannot be absorbed into the blood stream and pass through the body. Studies show iron absorption significantly higher for algae compared to rice, other food grains or beef.

Algae are rich in iodine and selenium, critical trace elements that are highly variable in food supplies by geographic region. These minerals have been associated with endemic deficiency disorders throughout history. Algae concentrate these trace minerals in one tablespoon of dried algae, which provides sufficient levels of these nutrients when introduced into the diet. Algae have a high content of glutamic acid that stimulates taste receptors with umami, (savory or hearty).

Umami amplifies taste differentiation and increases the desire to consume algae for taste.

Algae medical treatments

Algae offer therapeutic protection or treatment for many diseases. A web search of algae and ______, typically turns up relevant recent research. Peer-reviewed scientific research provides algae-based medical solutions for the following health challenges.

Deficiencies	Major organs	Major systems	Diseases
Vitamins	Brain	Cardiovascular	Blood pressure
Minerals	Eyes	Digestive	Hyperlipidemia
Elements	Heart	Endocrine	Bleeding gums
Antioxidants	Lungs	Immune	Infections
Hormones	Kidneys	Respiratory	Inflammation
Disorders	Skin, hair, nails	Circulatory	Cancers
Mood	Liver	Urinary	Immune
Anxiety	Blood	Nervous	Viral infection
Psychotic	Pancreas	Muscular	Bacterial infection
Personality	Hypothalamus	Integumentary	Injuries
Sexual	Pituitary	Reproductive	Diarrhea
Development	Thyroid	Skeletal	Diabetes
Brain	Nerves	Lymphatic	Obesity

Algae prevent or remediate nutrient deficiencies, which inflict pain and development disorders on nearly half of the world's people. Algae compounds offer medical treatments to restore healthy functioning to major organs and major body systems.

Algae have therapeutic properties that improve health and prevent disease that are not found in terrestrial plants. Algae evolved in incredibly harsh environments and developed hundreds of bioactive compounds that defend against predators and disease. Land plants invest their energy in roots and physical structure. Algae do not.

Algae bioactive compounds include anticancer, antiobesity, antidiabetic, antihypertensive, antihyperlipidemic, anticoagulant in anti-inflammatory. Other bioactive compounds are immunomodulatory, antiestrogenic, thyroid stimulating, neuroprotective, antiviral, antifungal, antibacterial and tissue healing properties. Active compounds include sulphated polysaccharides, phlorotannins, carotenoids, (e.g. fucoxanthin), minerals, peptides, and sulfolipids, with proven benefits against the generative metabolic disorders.

Allergies

The onset of allergies in children has tripled in one generation. Over 40% of all US children now suffer from allergies. Allergic diseases such as eczema, asthma and allergic rhinitis in infancy and childhood involve immune dysfunction. These hypersensitivity disorders involve strong inflammatory responses and the production of antibodies called IgE.

Omega-3 fatty acids manage cellular membranes and moderate inflammatory allergy responses. Omega-3s do not cure inflammatory conditions, but can bring substantial symptom relief. High proportions of DHA and EPA in maternal and infant plasma phospholipids are associated with less IgE-associated disease and a reduced severity of the allergic phenotype.

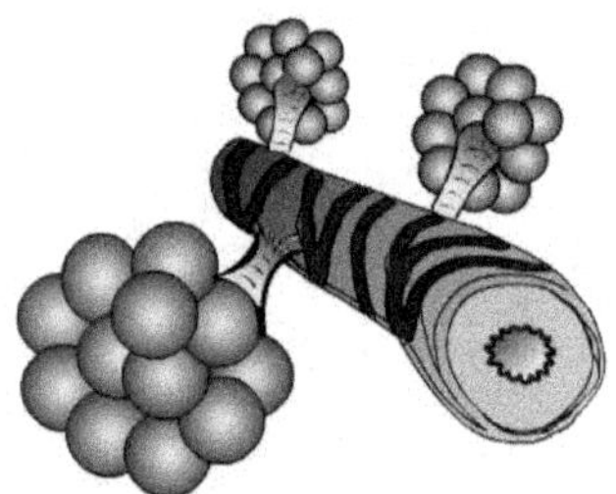

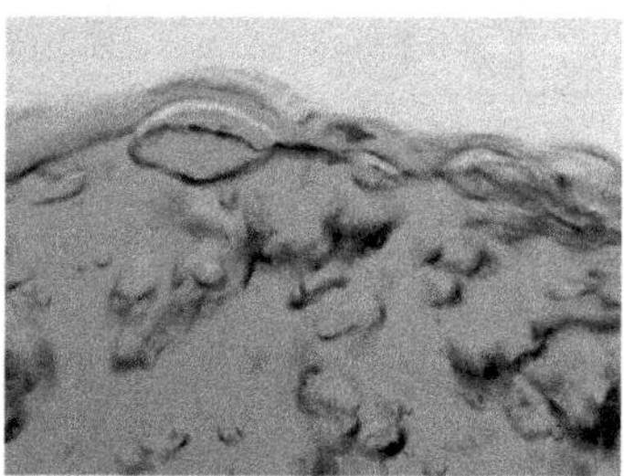

Asthma Irritation   *Omega-3 fatty acids in algae*

Studies show diet supplementation with omega-3 fatty acids, Zn and vitamin C significantly improves the asthma control test, pulmonary function test and pulmonary inflammatory markers in children with persistent bronchial asthma. Research results on EPA supplements alone have been mixed, possibly due to a high background intake of omega-6 fatty acids, the kind found in most vegetable oils. Medical research supports a diet with increased omega-3 fatty acids and reduced omega-6 fatty acids to protect children against symptoms of asthma and a litany of other autoimmune disorders.

Studies show supplements rich in EPA and DHA reduce asthmas symptoms compared to children who took placebo. Other studies found evidence for a modulatory effect of the dietary omega-6: omega-3 fatty acid ratio on the presence of asthma in children. These studies provide evidence that a diet with increased omega-3 and reduced omega-6 protects children against asthma and can treat symptoms.

Exercise-induced asthma may cause bronchoconstriction from airway inflammation following exercise. A diet rich in pro-inflammatory omega-6 fatty acids and low in anti-inflammatory omega-3 fatty acids tends to **amplify airway constriction**. Researchers sampled mucus taken from participants found omega-3 supplements—3.2 grams of EPA and 2 grams of DHA daily—resulted in reduced amounts of pro-inflammatory cells and markers. A team at Indiana University found adults with persistent asthma that took an omega-3 supplement daily for three weeks improved their post-exercise lung function by 64%. Breathing improvement allowed a 31% decrease in the use of inhalers.

Another promising line of research uses algae bioactive compounds to interrupt and stifle the allergy progression. Allergies are caused by an exaggerated reaction of the immune system to environmental substances, such as animal dander, house dust mites, foods, pollen, insects, and chemical agents. The initial event responsible for the development of allergy is the generation of allergen-specific CD4+ Th2 cells. Th2 cells produce a cascade of events that initiate the production of allergen-specific IgE, (immunoglobulin E) by B cells. Allergic reactions are induced upon binding of the allergen to IgE, which is tethered to the high affinity IgE receptor on the surface of mast cells and basophils. The algae inhibitors can block IgE cells from binding, inhibit histamine and cytokine production and release and suppress production of Th2 and IgE cells. These actions effectively disrupt the allergy progression, which gives relief to the patient.

Algae medical tactics

Many disorders follow a known sequence that builds one step at a time to create the chronic condition. Algae apply the disruption tactics, which they have evolved over eons, to break the sequence and defeat the condition before it becomes chronic.

The graphic illustrates that algae inhibitors apply multiple tactics to fight disease. They block, tackle, suppress, disrupt, gum and engulf. The gum and engulf strategies are not shown in the graphic, but algae compounds can gum up receptors, similar to the IgE cells, which prevent invasive cells from binding. Algae lipids can the stimulate production of macrophages that engulf foreign substances, microbes, allergens, cancer cells, and anything else that does not have healthy compounds.

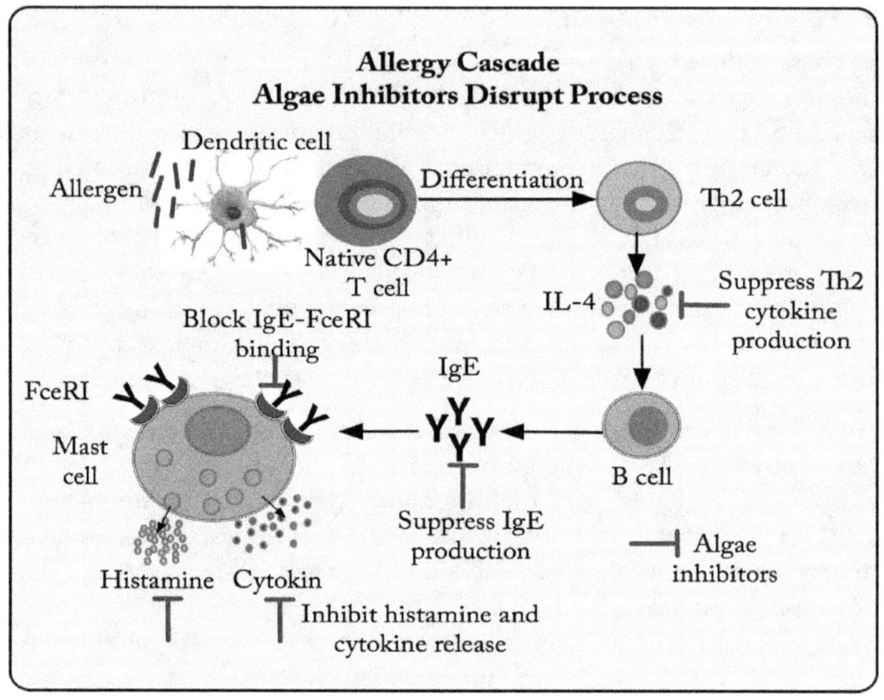

Allergy Cascade adapted from Thanh-SangVoa, et al.

Current allergy drugs, such as antihistamines or corticosteroids, do ameliorate symptoms, but do not stop the disease progression. These drugs may cause serious side-effects, particularly in children and the elderly. Natural bioactive compounds from algae offer the development of new generation anti-allergic therapeutics, which can disrupt the disease cascade and impose fewer side-effects. Natural algae anti-allergy compounds have been used in Asian folk medicine for centuries.

Hepatic inflammation

Human longevity rise has been accompanied by growing incidences of other devastating age-related pathologies. Aging is a progressive functional deterioration associated with frailty, disease, and death. Stress and immune responses deteriorate during aging, causing low-grade inflammation and increased susceptibility to infections, which collectively lead to chronic disease. The liver is the second largest organ in the body and processes everything people eat and drink. It filters out harmful substances from the blood, and it is responsible for helping the body fight off infections.

Age-related hepatic, (liver) degradation occurs, such as an increased hepatocyte size, an increase in the number of binucleated cells, and a reduction in mitochondrial number. These changes significantly affect liver morphology, physiology, and oxidative capacity. Aging predisposes patients to hepatic functional and structural impairment, inflammation and metabolic risk, which can cause non-alcoholic fatty liver disease, (NAFLD). No validated treatments of NAFLD exist beyond weight loss or comorbidity management. Spirulina may provide a solution.

Spirulina is one of the most important healing and prophylactic nutritional ingredients of the 21st century due to its nutrient profile, its therapeutic effects, and its lack of toxicity. Spirulina may protect the body from hypertension, inflammatory diseases, insulin-resistance, diabetes mellitus, non-alcoholic fatty liver disease, malnutrition, anemia, allergic rhinitis, cancer, and reduction of drug toxicity.

Emerging evidence shows extensive interaction between the gut microbiota, the immune system, and inflammatory pathways that influence aging in humans. The aging process can seriously affect the composition of the gut microbiota. Constipation is common symptom of aging. This uncomfortable indicator results from decreased intestinal motility and slower intestinal transit. This event chain reduces bacterial excretion, alters the gut fermentative processes and negatively affects the composition of intestinal microbiota. Counteracting inflammation occurring in the liver and intestines through gut microbiota modulation, may be a key factor for healthy aging.

Audrey Neyrinck and team at the Louvain Drug Research Institute in Belgium, found that oral feeding of spirulina improves several immunological functions. They assigned mice to three groups. Young three-month-old mice were fed with the standard diet, and old mice of 24 months were fed a standard diet supplemented with or without 5% spirulina for six weeks. The 5% addition of spirulina to the diet of old mice modulated immune function involving, among others, the TLR4 pathway.

Oral consumption influenced both gut immunity and systemic sites, including the liver. This suggests that spirulina's immune action goes beyond the gut immune system. The team found improvement of the homeostasis in the gut ecosystem, which is essential for the gut health. They concluded that spirulina improved gut microbiota in the elderly mice. It seems to be an effective dietary supplement for preserving a healthy gastrointestinal microbial community, in addition to its beneficial effects on immune function.

Metabolic syndrome

A cluster of conditions causes metabolic syndrome — increased blood pressure, high blood sugar, excess body fat around the waist, and abnormal cholesterol or triglyceride levels. These tend to occur together, increasing risk of heart disease, stroke and diabetes. The incidence of the metabolic syndrome is increasing worldwide, with notable exceptions of some Asian countries where seaweeds are consumed. Several studies show that diets that include only 6 g/d of sea vegetables improve the critical inflammation biomarkers and blood lipids.

Sodium alginate from sea vegetables is used in culinary physics, or molecular gastronomy, at some of the best restaurants in the world. Molecular gastronomy investigates the physical and chemical ingredient transformations that occur while cooking. The study includes the social,

artistic and technical components of culinary and gastronomic phenomena such as spherification of juices and other liquids. Chefs combine sodium alginate with calcium lactate to create spheres of liquid surrounded by a thin jelly membrane. High-end restaurants present these spheres (left), with different internal liquids for cocktails, appetizers, side dishes and desserts.

Alginic acids are made up of hydrophilic colloidal polysaccharides that deliver complex molecules such as peptides, proteins, nucleic acids, oligonucleotides, and plasmids across biological surfaces. The delivery capability makes alginic acids ideal carriers for obesity, diabetic and related medicines. Many weight loss medicines use alginate as an appetite suppressant. The mechanism includes the absorption of water to create the feeling of satiety or fullness. Researchers at Newcastle University found that dietary alginates can reduce human fat uptake by more than 75%.

Sodium alginate acts as a natural chelator for metals and is sold in the nutraceutical industry as a detoxifier for removing heavy metals from the body. Research shows that sodium alginate pulls heavy medals including radioactive toxins from the body, such as iodine-131 and strontium-90. Spirulina has also been proven to chelate and remove both heavy metals such as mercury and lead and radioactive toxins from human tissues.

The effect of soluble fiber on the blood glucose response seems related to its ability to increase the viscosity of a meal. Viscous fibers slow the gastric emptying rate of a meal in subjects with and without diabetes. Alginate fibers offer a source of viscous dietary fiber in algae-based foods. The main constituents of alginates are uronic acids (mannuronic and guluronic acids), which give the alginate characteristics similar to pectin (galacturonic acid).

Hypertension – blood pressure

The CDC reports that high blood pressure affects over 75 million Americans and adds \$94 billion a year in medical costs and lost work days. Progression of hypertension results in cardiac and vascular abnormalities, such as endothelial dysfunction, peripheral resistance, altered contractility, and vascular remodeling.

Hypertension increases the force of the blood against artery walls and eventually causes health problems, such as heart disease, strokes, kidney damage, organ damage and heart failure. High blood pressure is called the "silent killer."

Omega-3 supplements have been shown to lower total blood fat, which lowers blood pressure. DHA and EPA supplements can also cut elevated triglyceride levels. Omega-3 fatty acids also appear to lower the overall risk of death from heart disease. Omega-3 may reduce arrhythmias and slow the development of plaques in the arteries. Omega-3s moderate inflammation and help sustain tissue pliability. Patients who take omegae-3 supplements after a heart attack cut their risk of having another heart attack significantly.

Ben-Gurion University researchers in Israel isolated a microalgal strain, which can accumulate up to 15% dry weight of a polyunsaturated fatty acid, PUFA called DGLA (Dihomo-γ-Linolenic Acid).

Andy Ayers, ex-CEO of Algae Biosciences in Arizona developed a natural algae mutant strain that produced over 30% dry weight of EPA oil. Some algae strains produce predominately DHA, EPA or DGLA, while others produce a mix of two or more PUFAs.

Hyperlipidemia

Cholesterol and triglycerides are critical blood fats and lipids. Cholesterol is an essential component of cell membranes, brain and nerve cells, and bile, which helps the body absorb fats and fat-soluble vitamins. Cholesterol is a waxy substance that can build up as plaque on blood vessels. Foods containing cholesterol, saturated fat, and trans fats can raise blood cholesterol levels, such as dairy products, fried and processed foods and red meat. Lowering harmful cholesterol levels reduces the risk of heart attack, stroke, and other problems.

The Mediterranean diet, rich in vegetable foods, contributes both quantitatively and qualitatively to essential fiber compounds that decrease lipids and lower blood sugar levels. These include cellulose, hemicellulose, gums, mucilages, pectins, oligosaccharides, lignins. Scientists believe that dietary algae fibers may make it possible to lower dosages of hypolipemic drugs, which decreases possible side effects.

Microalgae produce a variety of bioactive metabolites that can be used in managing hyperlipidemia, microbial infection, and oxidative stress. Several studies have demonstrated that peptides derived from algae proteins possess antioxidative and antihypertensive properties. Elevated levels of reactive oxygen species can cause oxidation of biological macromolecules, ultimately leading to pathological conditions that include endothelial dysfunction and hypertension. Oxidative stress is not only a causative factor of hypertension, but acts as an important mediator in the imbalance between vasoconstrictor and vasodilator mechanisms. Oxidative stress-mediated events are basic factors in the development of hypertension, which can be moderated by algae antioxidant peptides.

Other lines of research demonstrate algae's ability to decrease lipids and lower blood sugar, which improve cardiac and diabetic symptoms. Algae polysaccharides, such as carrageenan, are excellent sources of dietary fiber that moderate hypoglycemic events and lower cholesterol and lipids. Algae extracts produce low-density proteins in blood cholesterol, which helps regulate lipids.

Alginic acid has been shown to exhibit antioxidant and angiotensin-converting enzyme, (ACE) inhibitory activities. Alginic acid reduces tension on blood vessels, lowers blood flow and causes dilation of blood vessels, which results in lower blood pressure. ACE inhibitors are used to treat hypertension, cardiac failure, diabetic nephropathy and renal failure. These soluble polysaccharides act as prebiotics, stimulating growth of beneficial bacteria in the colon.

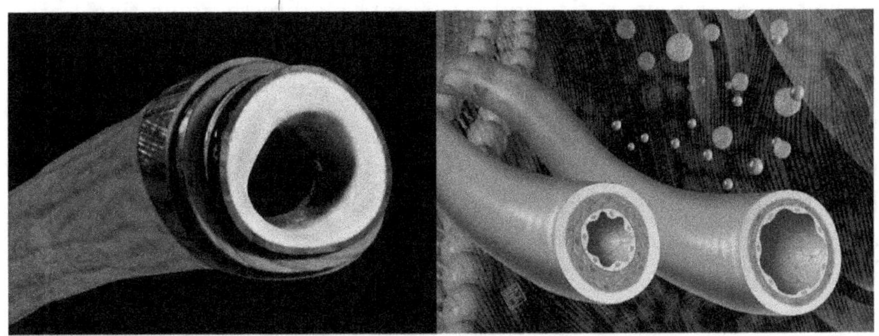

ACE inhibitors relax blood vessels

Anticoagulants

Anticoagulants are substances that prevent blood coagulation, (clotting). These substances occur naturally in leeches, blood-sucking insects, and some algae species. Algae offer a broad array of novel sulfated polysaccharides with diverse chemical characteristics that produce a variety of natural anticoagulants useful for various medical conditions.

Anticoagulants and antiplatelet drugs reduce the risk of blood clots. They are often called blood thinners, but these medications do not thin blood. They help prevent or break up dangerous blood clots that form in blood vessels or on the heart. Without treatment, these clots can block circulation and lead to a heart attack or stroke. They are often the first medication prescribed by doctors following a stroke. By reducing the ability of the blood to clot — and thereby reducing the likelihood of coronary or vascular emboli — anticoagulants are frequently used in patients who are already at high-risk for stroke. Unfortunately, these drugs can cause serious side effects. Natural anticoagulants from algae are likely to perform well, but do not induce unfavorable medical events.

Phlorotannins and sulfated polysaccharides, such as fucoidans in brown algae, carrageenans in red algae, and ulvans in green algae have been recognized as effective anticoagulant agents.

Both freshwater and marine algae offer a large number of natural anticoagulant polysaccharides that have been isolated and characterized. Algae polysaccharides typically exert anticoagulant activity through antithrombin III and/or heparin cofactor II. These are important endogenous inhibitors, called SERPIN.

The anticoagulant mechanism occurs when heparin, heparin sulfate and dermatan sulfate exert their activity. Some algae anticoagulant polysaccharides exert anticoagulant activity by directly inhibiting fibrin polymerization and/or thrombin activity. New functions of algae anticoagulant polysaccharides have been discovered recently.

Heparin and its derivatives play important roles in many biological processes. It biostimulates the body to produce natural compounds that keep the blood flowing smoothly. Algae anticoagulant polysaccharides activate the fibrinolysis system and modulate endothelial cell functions. Biologically active compounds in algae have displayed anti-platelet and anticoagulant proteins and fibrinolytic enzymes.

Cancer

Cancer is a complex set of diseases in which abnormal cells divide without control and invade other tissues. Cancer cells can spread to other parts of the body through the blood and lymph systems. Many of the more than 100 different types of cancer are named for the organ or type of cell in which they start. Cancer that begins in the colon is called colon cancer, while cancer that begins in melanocytes of the skin is called melanoma. In 2016, 1.7 million new cases of cancer were diagnosed in the US and about 600,000 people died from the disease. Direct medical costs for cancer were about $125 billion in 2011. Death rates for the least educated are 2½ times higher than the most educated.

Medical tests on algae compounds have addressed more than 70 types of cancer. Therapeutic strategies use algae compounds, such as astaxanthin and metabolites, including zonaquinone acetate and flabellinone that create growth inhibitory effects on cancer cells. The natural algae compound fucoxanthin has strong antioxidant and cytotoxicity against breast, lung and prostate cancer. Algae sulfated polysaccharides have been shown to inhibit cell proliferation and to induce apoptosis by inhibiting IGF-IR signaling in several cancers. Other algae metabolites operate as antioxidants and protect against DNA damage.

Medical scientists are working to develop novel targeted therapies in human cancer treatments, which are capable for selectively killing cancer cells, but are not harmful to normal cells. New anti-cancer therapies selectively target molecular pathways thought to be critical for tumor survival, growth, and metastases.

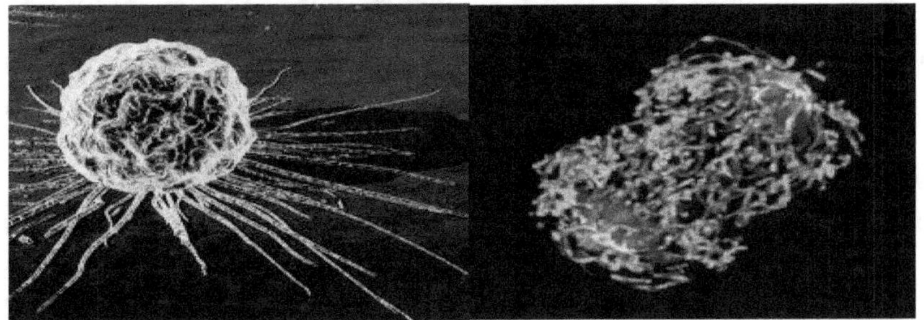

Cancer tumor and skin melanoma

Some algae-derived compounds modulate multiple cellular mechanisms, including cellular cytotoxicity, inhibition of invasion and the eradication of cancer cells. These potent, naturally occurring anticancer compounds effectively prevent tumorigenesis. Fucoxanthin, a carotenoid found in diatoms and brown seaweeds exhibit anticancer activity, of cancer cells along with the induction of cancer suppressor genes and cell cycle arrest, but not apoptosis, (cell death).

Sung-Suk Suh and team demonstrated with in vitro experiments that an extract from the Antarctic freshwater microalga, *Chloromonas sp.*, exhibited high anti-oxidant capacity and triggered anticancer activities, including anti-proliferation, anti-invasion and apoptotic cell death in cancer cells through the modulation of apoptosis-related genes.

Metastasis, the leading cause of cancer mortality, occurs with a sequence of events, including invasion. In the invasion process, malignant tumor cells are able to become dissociated from the primary tumor and invade the surrounding tissue through the modulation of proteins involved in the control of cellular motility and migration. Algae extracts can significantly inhibit the invasion process of cancer cells at low doses, relative to those with anti-proliferative effect. The algae extract in the study had sufficient antioxidant activity to induce apoptotic cell death in cancer cells *in vitro*, through the caspases dependent pathway.

Algae also produce steroids that inhibit both cancer cells and cancerous tumors. Scientists are discovering new bioactive steroids in algae species such as Sargassum that exhibit cytotoxic activity (toxicity) against various cancer cell lines. A new promising line of research focuses on cancer vaccination, to make cells immune from the onset of cancer. One of the most successful approaches has been working with genetically modified tumor cells that are introduced into a patient's body. Algae toxins enable researchers to harvest natural toxins that strengthen the immune response, which is the critical path to human trials.

No other recombinant protein production system can accumulate these complex eukaryotic toxin molecules as soluble and enzymatically active proteins. These traits set algae apart from other expression platforms. The potential of immunotoxins as potent and specific anticancer therapeutics is enormous. The use of antibody drug conjugates, using small-molecule drugs, to target and kill cancer cells and to minimize the exposure of healthy cells is already a reality. Some expensive therapies are in late-stage clinical trials or are already approved by the FDA.

Protein toxins are effective in inhibiting cancer-cell proliferation, but their production is limited to bacterial expression platforms that require the protein to be denatured and subsequently refolded. The process increases production time and cost substantially.

Algae provide a faster, less costly production platform that adds the ability to create more complex molecules than presently can be produced in bacterial systems. Although additional work needs to be done to determine whether larger or smaller immunotoxins are more effective for specific cancers, the αCD22PE40 and αCD22HCH23PE40 produced by the UCSD team demonstrated that *C. reinhardtii* chloroplasts can create complex immunotoxins and provide an effective platform to produce next-generation cancer therapeutics.

Stephen Mayfield and the UCSD Laboratory team developed a novel therapeutic anti-cancer strategy, which may be called "search, find, and kill." The team developed a genetically engineered designer alga for the production of special compounds for both searching for cancer cells and then killing them. The first step introduces an antibody that hunts down a cancer cell, and then lights it up. The algae toxin is sent to find the cell based on its heat signature. The toxin follows and kills the "hot" cancer cell, while leaving healthy cells uninjured.

Mayfield calls these "dual-domain drugs," which offer better cancer therapy. These drugs are currently produced through a complex process so costly that a course of treatments for lymphoma can cost over

$100,000. The new algae-based production method should the cut treatment cost by possibly 90%.

Stephen Mayfield's team studies beautiful therapeutic proteins

The UCSD team demonstrated that the green algae *Chlamydomonas reinhardtii* are capable of expressing, folding, and accumulating a range of human therapeutic proteins in the chloroplast. They also showed that recombinant proteins could be secreted from algae. Cost is a critical factor in the production of protein-based therapies. Algae reduce production costs because growing algae requires only fertilizer, trace minerals, and sunlight.

Algae have the potential to produce a wide variety of recombinant proteins for various therapeutic applications. An algae platform can produce desirable classes of therapeutically relevant proteins quickly. Algae offer the potential to produce a number of novel proteins due to the unique biochemical environment of the chloroplast.

Algae's unique ability to fold, assemble and accumulate multiple domain proteins as soluble molecules offers significant advantages. The attributes that truly distinguish algae from other recombinant expression platforms are the presence of chloroplasts and the ability to produce and accumulate immunotoxin proteins in these compartments. Chloroplasts of higher plants such as tobacco could theoretically provide a viable option for expressing immunotoxins. Algae offer far better quality control because cultures can be grown in closed systems, avoiding problems from cross-contamination with native species.

Blindness

Over 15 million people suffer from some form of blindness, with the most common conditions being retinitis pigmentosa and age-related macular degeneration. Both of these conditions occur when disease or age damages photoreceptors in the eye. Photoreceptors are responsible for transforming light entering the eye into electrical impulses, but when damaged, the brain is unable to receive this information.

Algae have 3.7 billion years of evolutionary experience with light. Since algae use light for energy, early algae evolved a gene that helped algae recognize the path toward light. Algae's ability to recognize light offers several lines of fascinating research that show promise for sight restoration. Retinitis pigmentosa is an eye disease in which there is damage to the retina. The retina is the layer of tissue at the back of the inner eye that converts light images to nerve signals and sends them to the brain. Retinitis pigmentosa is a genetic disease that causes first tunnel vision, then night blindness and eventually blindness. The disease plaques over two million people a year.

The disease degrades the outer retina's rod cells, which are highly sensitive to light and allow night and peripheral vision. Some patients lose only night vision. Others lose daylight vision and some go blind completely. The color-sensing cone cells of their inner retinas slowly degenerate. Although scientists do not clearly understand the pathway, the disease makes cone cells unresponsive to light but may not kill the cells. This phenomenon leaves a time window where the cone receptors are still there, but not functioning properly. Human solutions first had to recover sight for three blind mice.

A fascinating series of studies at Johns Hopkins, Harvard, and Stanford proved that inserting algae pigments into blind mice allowed the mice to first detect light, then see the direction of light, and finally see enough light to successfully navigate their way out of a maize.

Neuroscientist Alan Horsager, at the Institute of Genetic Medicine at the University of Southern California is working with the gene responsible for making Channelrhodopsin-2, (ChR2) in algae. This gene can detect light projected to the patients' eyes. This form of gene therapy is not yet approved for humans, but is likely to offer applications for eye diseases like macular degeneration and retinal damage due to diabetes.

Human blindness

Algae are photosynthetic and very sensitive to light because photons provide their energy. Neuroscientists plan to use the same cells algae use to seek out sunlight for photosynthesis to replenish damaged cell equivalents in the human eye.

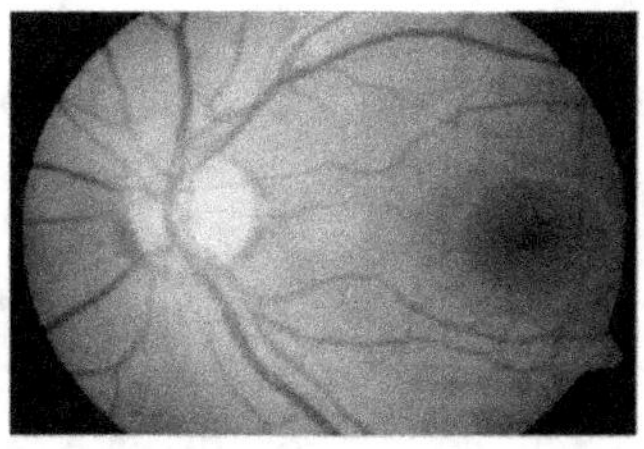

Another approach uses optogenetics, which is a neuroscience technology designed to precisely control the activity of nerve cells. It works by adding DNA instructions for channelrhodopsin, which algae use to sense sunlight and move toward it. Added to a nerve, it causes the cell to fire when exposed to a specific wavelength of light. The photosensitive protein helps direct algae toward a source of light. The team led by E.G. Govorunova at Moscow State University, believe they can replace damaged cells in the retina with cells found in algae.

Eye health products also continue to advance. Valensa International, recently received a patent covering its eye health cosmeceutical, EyePro MD. The formula includes lutein, zeaxanthin and astaxanthin mixed with omega-3 essential oils from krill, algae or perilla seed.

Arthritis

Rheumatoid arthritis is one of many autoimmune diseases where PUFA supplements make a substantial difference. Most clinical studies examining omega-3 fatty acid supplements for arthritis have focused on rheumatoid arthritis (RA), an autoimmune disease that causes inflammation in the joints. Three meta-analyses of randomized controlled trials in RA patients found that omega-3 supplementation significantly decreased the number of painful and tender joints. Several studies show that omega-3 supplementation creates decreases in pain intensity and shortens the duration of morning stiffness. Omega-3s do not appear to slow progression of RA or to mitigate joint damage, only to treat the symptoms.

Diets rich in omega-3 fatty acids (and low in the inflammatory omega-6 fatty acids) may help people with osteoarthritis. Omega-3 supplements have been reported to reduce joint stiffness and pain, increase grip strength and improve walking pace for people suffering with osteoarthritis. Analysis of 17 controlled clinical trials examined the pain-relieving effects of omega-3 fatty acid supplements in people with

RA or joint pain caused by inflammatory bowel disease and painful menstruation. The results show that omega-3 fatty acids, along with conventional therapies, help relieve joint pain occurrence and severity.

Inflammation

Algae produce strong omega-3s, which can benefit people with a wide spectrum of inflammatory diseases. Their high protein content provides a rich source of diverse biologically active peptides. Select bioactive peptides provide potent inhibitory effects that moderate, disrupt or shut down the production of inflammatory mediators. Natural biologically active peptides protect cells by modulating the effects of oxidative stress. Oxidative stress creates inflammatory reactions that cause endothelial failure (lining of blood vessels), lung disease, carcinogenesis, and atherosclerosis.

The versatility of algae solutions appear to derive from their high concentration of bioactive metabolites. Bioactive metabolites include brominated phenols and oxygen heterocyclics, nitrogen heterocyclics, kainic acids, guanidine derivatives, phenazine derivatives, amino acids and amines, sterols, sulfated polysaccharides, and prostaglandins.

Fucoxanthin, a type of xanthophyll and an accessory pigment in algae chloroplasts, has also shown beneficial antioxidant, anti-inflammation, anti-cancer and anti-obesity activities. Many algae species contain antioxidants such as astaxanthin, which scavenges free radicals and protects the body against oxidative damage. Astaxanthin moderates the lipids that raise LDL-cholesterol and strengthens cells and their membranes and tissues.

Edible vaccines

Infectious diseases account for more than 54% of total mortality in developing countries. Vaccines are the most effective means of prevention, but many are too expensive or too difficult to administer for broad-scale use. Expiration dates and refrigeration requirements inherent for nearly all commercial vaccines demand constant attention to the pathogen contained in such vaccines. This increases control, distribution and application costs. Vaccine degradation after stomach acid digestion and possible allergic reactions, also add constraints.

Edible vaccines offer an alternative method of vaccination that overcomes many of the disadvantages of current vaccines. Edible vaccines do not require an extensive framework for their production, purification, sterilization, packaging, or distribution. This reduces costs up to 90% compared to traditional vaccines

Edible vaccines in functional foods provide nourishment, but their real value is their action to immunize the consumer against a disease. Upon oral ingestion, the outer wall of alga cell protects the antigens from degradation by gastric secretion. The antigens are delivered to the intestinal mucosal surfaces, where they are absorbed by different mechanisms and stimulate a strong and specific immune response.

Edible vaccines are developed with an antigenic protein introduced into the algae cell by genetic engineering. The antigen must elicit a strong specific immune response. The gene encoding for this antigen must be cloned into a transfer vector carrying an antibiotic-resistance gene. The vector carries the antigen into the algae cell. The edible malaria vaccine developed at UCSD provides a field-tested example.

Malaria vaccine

The parasitic, mosquito-borne, infectious disease malaria threatens nearly half of the global population. Many of the over 3 billion people most vulnerable to malaria are children and families that are extremely poor. Eradication of malaria requires low-cost, easily administered vaccines that work in concert with current control methods. Current medicines require refrigeration, which is difficult and expensive in hot rural areas. A short, low cost supply chain and ease of administration are essential components of a malaria vaccine, because malaria is endemic to regions that often lack an adequate healthcare infrastructure.

Mayfield's team collaborated with a medical team led by Joseph Vinetz in the UCSD School of Medicine, to create the precursor to a low-cost algae-based malaria vaccine that does not need refrigeration. Recent work has focused on identifying specific parasite antigens that elicit the desired cellular and humoral immunity. These subunit vaccines are generally made in recombinant systems, purified, and delivered via injection. Production and purification of subunit vaccines are often complex and expensive. Bacteria, yeast, insect, and mammalian cells are most commonly used for producing recombinant proteins but they are slow to produce and extremely expensive to extract.

James Gregory, Stephen Mayfield and their team developed an inexpensive malaria vaccine from plants and algae. Their expression platform is capable of producing a recombinant antigen that precisely mimics the native protein structure. This ensures that the immune response confers protection to the corresponding pathogen. This is difficult to achieve because predicting whether a heterologous platform can replicate the three-dimensional structure of a foreign protein is nearly impossible, particularly for unique or structurally complex antigens. The authors describe mosquito stage vaccines, called transmission-blocking vaccines, (TBVs) which focus on antigens from sexual stage parasites.

Antibodies to several of these proteins block parasite sexual development when taken up with *Plasmodium* gametocytes during a mosquito blood meal. This prevents mosquito infection and subsequent transmission to the next human host. Antibodies raised in mice to TBV candidate antigens have successfully blocked transmission in both animal models and standard membrane feeding assays, but have not advanced beyond safety tests in human clinical trials.

The malaria parasite life cycle includes a sequence of potential points for vaccine intervention. The mosquito introduces sporozoites into the bloodstream. They invade the liver and then are released into the circulatory system via the lungs. Thousands of sporozoites travel to the mosquito salivary glands when the oocysts burst.

The parasite life cycle repeats after being transferred to a new human host via the mosquito.

The UCSD team produced Pfs25 and Pfs45/48 in the chloroplast of the green alga *Chlamydomonas reinhardtii*. They demonstrated that alga-produced Pfs25 (CrPfs25) elicits TB antibodies. *C. reinhardtii* is an extensively researched single-celled eukaryotic alga that has only recently been exploited as a platform for producing recombinant proteins. Algae have been used to produce industrial enzymes, vaccine antigens, and complex immunotoxins on an academic scale. Depending on the desired posttranslational modifications, transgenes can be expressed from the nuclear or chloroplast genome. The ideal malaria vaccine must be extremely inexpensive, heat-stable and easily administered.

UCSD Center for Algae Biotechnology

Currently, oral vaccines are available for polio, rotavirus, cholera, and typhoid, but these vaccines are based on attenuated or heat-killed pathogens. Novel strategies are necessary to overcome the obstacles that block orally available subunit vaccines, especially for pathogens like malaria that cannot easily be cultured and affect poor regions.

The UCSD team investigated a strategy for using the whole *C. reinhardtii* cells. CTB-Pfs25 was produced as a fusion protein in chloroplasts and orally delivered to mouse pups in freeze-dried whole cells. This strategy was not sufficiently effective, but the team learned insights helpful for a future oral malaria medicine.

Genetically modifying algae

Food consumers are concerned about GMO food ingredients. In Europe, GMO foods are not allowed. Algae are at the same time the most abundant and diverse, yet the smallest and simplest organisms. These characteristics make algae cells ideal for genetic modification, but preferably with a required GMO label. Interestingly, some transgenic engineering is allowed under the USDA Plant Protection Act and current EU regulations.

Four genetic manipulation methods are allowed in the EU without classifying an organism as a GMO.

1. Introduce a gene from the same genus as the one being manipulated. In biological classification, genus comes above species and below family.

2. Edit the location or presence of genes in the same organism. This is often called gene knockin or knockout.

3. Genetically cross breed, which creates hybrids like nearly all modern non-GMO foods.

4. Mutagenesis and selection, which intentionally nudges the organism to mutate. The best mutants are then selected for the next round of mutagenesis.

Genetic manipulation is not the only road to discovery. Many medical and other valuable biocompounds can be found by bioprospecting, but the process requires time and patience. Texas A&M's Nano Biosystems Lab is developing a chip that can screen natural algae cells quickly to determine certain parameters, such as growth speed and oil content.

New chip screens will enable algae diversity can be exploited as a unique source of bioactive compounds like carotenoids, fatty acids, sterols, mycosporine-like amino acids, phycobilins, polyketides, pectins, halogenated compounds, toxins, and others. Algae are cost-effective and safe hosts for expressing a wide array of recombinant proteins, including human and animal therapeutics, as well as industrial enzymes.

Biomanufacturing

The ancient process of biomanufacturing uses living organisms as raw materials to convert into desirable bioproducts, such as beer, wine, cheese, and bread. Advances in biotechnology have expanded the scope of bioprocesses, enabling the use of gene editing for recombinant proteins and small molecules. Current transgenic techniques with terrestrial plants and animals shows merit, but suffer from high costs, low expression levels for complex proteins, and unstable cell lines.

Algae provide a superb biomanufacturing platform for the production of recombinant proteins and small molecules for a range of industries including bioenergy, biopharmaceuticals, biomaterials, nutraceuticals, agriculture, health, cosmetics and personal care. Biomanufacturing with algae allows low cost production, safety, metabolic diversity, and scalability.

Recent studies have demonstrated algae's ability to express, fold, post-translationally modify, and secrete complex mammalian and other eukaryotic proteins. Beth Rasala and Stephen Mayfield published an informative recombinant table showing various proteins, their function, expression host, genome and notable results. Rasala and Mayfield note that recombinant proteins display promising results for the production of orally available vaccines and gut-active biologics, as well as complex unique anti-cancer therapeutics.

New gene editing tools like CRISPR, (Clustered Regularly Interspaced Short Palindromic Repeats), allow some genetic manipulation without requiring a GMO label. CRISPR allows researchers to target specific stretches of genetic code and edit DNA at precise locations, modifying select gene functions. The Broad Institute posts a good video illustrating how CRISPR works. A novel approach to resolving blindness provides a good example.

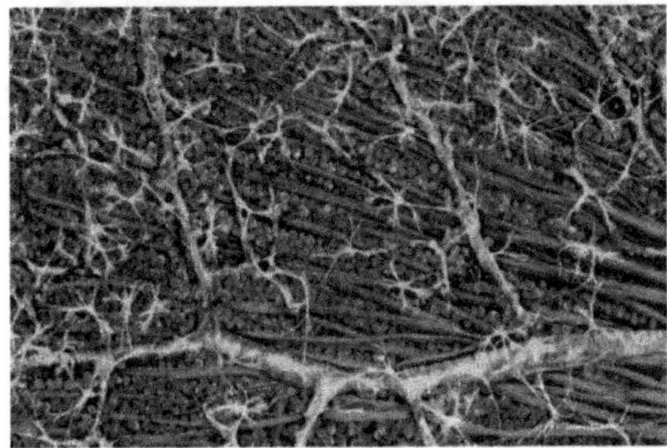

Retinitis pigmentosa is a group of inherited vision disorders caused by mutations in more than 60 genes. The mutations affect the eyes' photoreceptors, specialized cells in the retina (left), that sense and convert light images into electrical signals sent to the brain.

There is no treatment for RP and disease progression results in blindness. A team led by Kang Zhang, Institute for Genomic Medicine at UCSD School of Medicine, used CRISPR/Cas9 to deactivate a master switch gene called *Nrl* and a downstream transcription factor called *Nr2e3* to restore sight in mice. They reprogrammed mutated rod photoreceptors to become functioning cone photoreceptors, reversing cellular degeneration and restoring visual function in two mouse models with RP. Zhang said their strategy used gene therapy to make the underlying mutations irrelevant, resulting in the preservation of tissue and vision.

A UCSD study led by Javier A. Gimpel used metabolically engineered algae as production platforms for metabolites. The team changed one gene to enhance the metabolic algae pathways to improve photosynthetic growth and achieved trophic conversion. Trophic conversion allows algae to thrive on exogenous glucose, in the absence of light.

The major concern about outdoor production of GMO algae is that the cells may run amok. The fear is that the genetic modifications may invade natural habitats and change indigenous algae or other nearby microorganisms. Scientists at UCSD and Sapphire Energy successfully completed the first EPA-approved outdoor field trial of genetically engineered algae. They found that cultivating the algae outdoors did no harm to nearby populations of wild algae. Sapphire Energy is developing algae for use as biofuel, while UCSD researchers led by Stephen Mayfield, are researching algae as a source of food and drugs.

The team tested the freshwater algae *Acutodesmus dimorphus* for 50 days in outdoor pools. The algae were genetically engineered by adding two genes; one for enhanced fatty acid biosynthesis, and one to make a green fluorescent protein. Unmodified algae from the same species were also grown. Neither the GMO nor unmodified algae were able to outcompete algae native to the area.

Summary

Algae medicines, with and without genetic modifications, will transform both disease prevention and treatment. Medical bioactive compounds can be found and grown in algae faster, at lower cost and with higher quality than terrestrial plants.

Individualized medicines will advance algae biofactories with compounds tailored to the DNA of each consumer. Development times for land plants take far too long for individualized medicine. Algae production platforms are able to produce bioactive compounds quickly and efficiently to support individualized medicine.

The next section explores new types of foods, freedom foods, that have not yet been produced anywhere on the planet. Yet, these foods are critical for the future of human survival. The Coral Sead'aster uses novel variables to convey the value proposition.

14. Ana Cultivates Miracles: Freedom Foods

Hungry, hot and thirsty consumers will need Freedom Foods before 2040.

Neither Ana nor anyone else has produced a meal made of freedom food – yet. Freedom foods are different from MIA production because they are healthier, use no fossil resources, and repair rather than degrade ecosystems. Freedom foods use abundance production methods that recover and recycle nutrients to produce affordable and sustainable food. Several organizations are racing to be the first freedom food producers, because these foods are going to be needed – ASAP!

Global food supply models reveal that societies on every continent will need all the food production available by 2040. These models use the scarce fossil resources that have been discussed previously. The case for freedom foods here uses metrics from a different set of variables that lead to the same conclusion – freedom foods are critical for survival. These variables driven by climate chaos may be called the **"Coral Sead'aster,"** which begins with people voting, as they like to do, with their feet.

Human migration

Roughly 45% of the world's population, over 3 billion people, live within 100 km, (60 miles) from a coastline. People prefer to live near water and migration to coastal cities has become a stampede. Over 1,000 people arrive in China's large coastal cities each day, and similar numbers move to the coasts in Vietnam, the Philippines, and India. In 1991, there were 10 megacities, with over 10 million people. The UN anticipates 41 megacities by 2030, with 36 on coastlines.

Sea levels have risen an average of 40 cm, (1.3 ft), over the past 100 years. NOAA's models predict the rate of sea level rise to increase – substantially. Sea levels will continue rising even if the climate has stabilized, because both the atmosphere and ocean react slowly.

The billions of people living along coastlines are highly vulnerable to sea level rise. People in megacities may be astonished to discover they must move because they are too thirsty and hungry, before they are pushed out by seawater floods over seawalls. The Coral Sead'aster reverberates with the sound of surprise.

Underestimating the velocity of change

"OMG! I didn't think it would happen this quickly. I didn't think it would happen here." These lines will be repeated so often in the next decades that journalists will quit printing them. Astonishment will become trite. Why are climate events happening at a faster rate than expected? Five factors account for this frequent mistake; conservative bias, accelerants, old metrics, convenient metrics, and lag effects.

Major climate reports, including the Paris Accords, are written by a team that must gain **consensus**. The consensus must include the judgment of the most conservative team member. Published journal articles and international NGO reports may appear to have great face validity, due to the credibility of the authors, but they often understate the true threat. The consensus is often swayed by a single extremely conservative member. The Delphi decision process moderates this effect by deleting the extreme votes before reanalysis to reduce bias. Olympic scoring has become standard for many sports due to the inherent bias from judges from an athlete's own country. Scientific policy documents have not followed suit. Consequently, both the estimates and the language reflect the conservative bias.

Accelerants break the "slow and steady" rules that climate models tend to follow. For example, the USDA uses a metric for soil loss of 6 tons per acre per year. Yet one severe storm can carry away 100 tons per acre in two days, 16 times more than a full year average. The displaced soil adds more sediment to reservoirs, substantially reducing water storage capacity and threatening dams earlier than predicted. Other accelerants include volcanoes, earthquakes, wild fires and other natural disasters.

Old metrics may be way out of date. For example, livestock methane emissions in 2011 were 11% higher than estimates based on 2005 data from the UN's Intergovernmental Panel for Climate Change. Why? Because the models used old data and assumed cows had stayed the same size. Julie Wolf led a research study for the USDA and found cows have increased in size and food intake. The larger animals belch and fart at least 11% more methane. A 2017 NOAA study used new sensors and discovered fossil fuel recovery adds 60% more methane to the air than previously thought. A second independent NOAA analysis of methane in the atmosphere with new sampling tools found the methane impact on global warming is 100% higher than predicted by older data. Similar new metrics are finding stronger effects for CO_2 and other GHG.

Convenient metrics are not necessarily an indication of slothful behavior. The repeated mistake made by those designing and running models is that they grab the "top line metrics," such as atmospheric and ocean temperatures that are reported continuously by NOAA. These easy metrics fit well and look good in mathematical scenarios. Modelers are likely to leave out variables that are hard to measure or difficult to explain. Metrics such as the loss of coral reefs may be ignored because, until recently, there were no metrics for the status of coral reefs.

Lag effects occur because environments are surprisingly resilient. Scientists may dismiss or fail to understand how much damage has already been inflicted on an ecosystem. After rising slowly from 2000 to 2006, the concentration of methane in the atmosphere has climbed 10 times more quickly in the last decade. This 10x acceleration occurred because both the number and size of cows were underestimated and there was no metric for loss of permafrost and covering ice. When the tipping point occurs, things happen far faster than anyone expected.

Coral reefs are typically in neither climate change nor food supply models, yet coral reefs have a titanic impact climate, water and food.

Loss of coral reefs

Coral reefs are one of the most beautiful and diverse, yet delicate ecosystems on the planet. Zooxanthellae algae supply coral with biofeed from photosynthesis; glucose, glycerol, and amino acids. Corals live in nutrient-poor tropical waters and algae's ability to recycle of nutrients give coral life.

Corals get their beautiful colors from their symbionts; algae pigments

About 90% of the organic material produced by the *zooxanthellae* is transferred to their host's tissues. Coral uses these products to make proteins, fats, and carbohydrates, and to produce calcium carbonate for their structure. Coral's structure provides the algae with a protected environment, similar to fungi's structure in lichen on land.

A study by an international team of scientists revealed that coral reefs protect hundreds of millions of people along coastlines and river deltas from rising sea levels and damaging wave action. The mechanical ability of reefs to protect coastal cities, croplands and river deltas is incredible. A study in the journal *Nature Communications*, reviewed 255 studies on the protective nature of coral reefs. The team found that reefs **reduce wave energy by 97%** and **wave height 84%**. Over 200 million people are protected by reefs today, but billions will be vulnerable tomorrow.

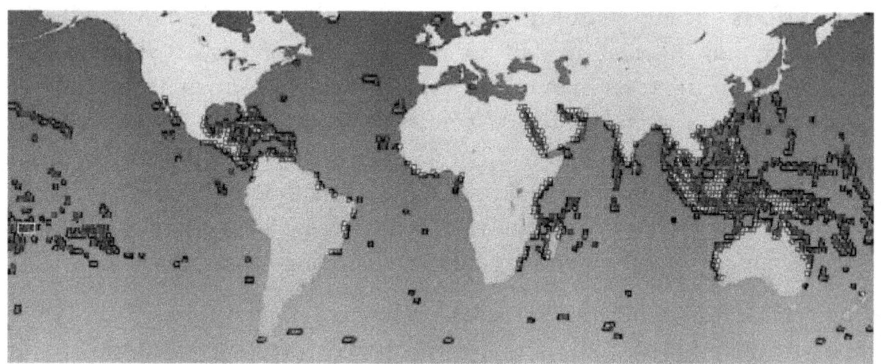

Coral reefs protect thousands of miles of coastlines from storm surge

Heat creates the primary threat to corals. Global warming and increasing levels of CO_2 in the atmosphere transfer directly to the oceans. According to *Reefs at Risk Revisited,* by the World Resources Institute (WRI), 75% of the world's coral reefs are at risk. At least 30% of coral reefs have already been damaged beyond repair, and if human business continues as usual, WRI projects that 90% of coral reefs will be in serious danger by 2030, and most lost by 2040.

A 2015 report led by Ove Hoegh-Guldberg, Director of the University of Queensland's Global Change Institute, found that reefs support 500 million people across 50 nations. The loss of coral reefs caused by rising sea temperatures will cost in excess of $1 trillion a year.

Corals are extremely sensitive to temperature swings. A rise of a few degrees can lead to illness, and eventually to a tippling point; death. The oceans absorb 93% of the heat from the atmosphere and are now warmer than at any time in recorded history. The top ten feet of the ocean hold as much heat as the entire atmosphere. A recent article in *Science* found that the Pacific Ocean warmed 15 times faster in the last 60 years than it did during warming cycles in the previous 10,000.

For thousands of years, the Great Barrier Reef off the coast of Australia has thrived. The scenic reef is the largest living structure in the world. However, a recent photographic project shows that in the past 18 months, two-thirds of the coral along the reef turned white and died. The breathtaking Netflix documentary *Chasing Coral* provides time lapse video showing the death process.

A report from Australia's Climate Council projects that the loss of Queensland's Great Barrier Reef would cost that region a million visitors a year, imperiling 10,000 jobs, and draining $1 billion from the economy. Coral reefs are endangered by natural phenomena such as hurricanes, El Nino, and diseases. Local threats take a toll too, including overfishing, destructive fishing, coast development, pollution, and careless tourism.

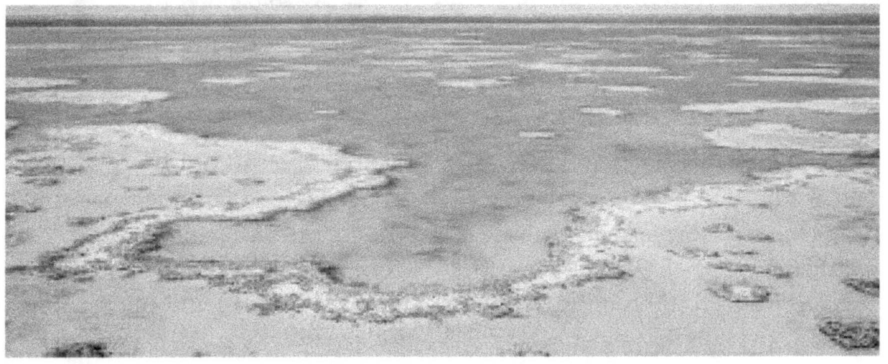

The Great Barrier Reef in Australia is dying – quickly

Coral reefs and food

Much of the world's food is produced in the rich soil of coasts and river deltas. These vital croplands are threatened by expanding cities that sprout high rises instead of food. These fertile areas are also vulnerable to rising sea levels, storm surges and seawater invasion.

Coral reefs protect hundreds of millions of people and farms along coasts. As the reefs degrade or die, storm surge amplifies destruction. Shorelines are eroding, putting millions of people at risk. In the US, 60% of the Pacific and 35% of the Atlantic Coast shoreline are eroding at a rate of over a meter every year. NOAA estimates coastal erosion in the US causes over $500 million a year in property loss. More than 80,000 acres of coastal wetlands are lost annually—the equivalent of seven football fields disappearing every hour of every day.

Storms like hurricanes Harvey, Irma, Maria, Katrina, Sandy, Camille, Allen, and Andrew eroded shorelines at 100 times the normal rate. The U.S. Geological Survey estimated that hurricane Katrina destroyed 220 square miles of wetlands, killed 1,245 people and caused over $152 billion in damage. Katrina killed or damaged 320 million large trees, which led to accelerated erosion.

Beach erosion – New York and California

The models predict that a warming atmosphere will hold more energy and water, which will produce much stronger winds and heavier rains. The severe storms will cause more flooding and runoff, carrying fertilizer that will increase eutrophication. The predicted changes in precipitation would require a 62% reduction in nitrogen and phosphorus input to prevent an eutrophication (below).

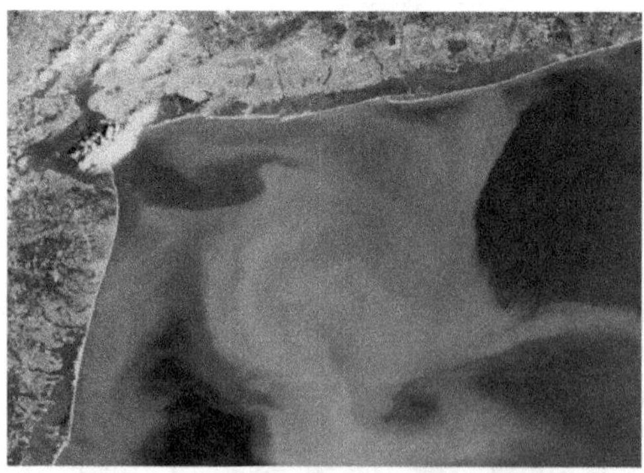

A study in *Science* validates the new normal of more severe storms. The researchers examined threats to water resources by using projections from 21 climate models, each of which was run for multiple climate scenarios. More rainfall from extreme events will occur in the future, even in some regions that will experience a drying trend.

River deltas

River deltas make up less than 1% of the world's land, but they are home to more than a billion people. Deltas are incredibly fertile ecosystems that aggregate nutrients from the river's course. They harbor mangroves, wetlands and marshes. Deltas support much of the world's fisheries, forest products and agriculture. They serve as food baskets for many nations. Similar to coral reefs, river deltas provide a natural protection to lowlands from storm surges and seawater invasion.

Coral reefs have protected deltas for eons, but now storm surges are damaging deltas with erosion and salt. Deltas are being destroyed even faster than coral reefs. Half of the world's coastal deltas have been lost in the 20th century, as were over half of all mangrove forests.

Human actions rob deltas of their lifeblood: water and sediment. Globally, people have diverted more than 40% of river discharges and 26% of river sediments into large reservoirs. Much of the sediment has been cut off from deltas across Asia. India has experienced substantial sediment reductions to their primary deltas; 50% for the Brahmani, 74% for the Mahanadi, and 94% for the Krishna. Imagine the effectiveness of a sea wall that lost over 50% of its size.

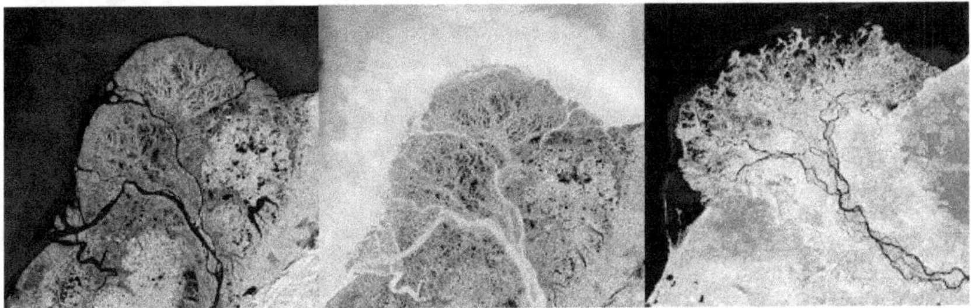

River deltas are fertile yet fragile

The Nile River Delta has been known for millennia as the bread basket of the world. A recent multi-year National Geographic study concluded that the Delta soon will not be able to support Egypt. The Nile Delta plain sits just one meter above sea level. The northern third of the Delta is falling by up to 8 millimeters a year, while the sea level is rising over 3 millimeters. Soon, much of the Delta plains will be under water. Years before sea water covers the delta, salt-water incursion in the delta's freshwater aquifer will have ruined the land for crops.

A single storm surge can apply enough salt from sea water to ruin cropland indefinitely. Seawater intrusion into aquifers eliminates water available for people and irrigation. Many deltas are sinking at a faster rate than sea levels are rising. Upstream farmers demand dams and irrigation. Rivers do not flood, which means deltas are starved.

Deltas suffer from decreased water flow, less sediment, rising sea levels, and saltwater intrusion—all of which damage food production and fresh water supplies. The Community Surface Dynamics Model System tracks delta losses and involves hundreds of researchers and students in 500 institutes in 68 countries. The community is watching the disastrous accelerating loss of river deltas.

Saltwater intrusion

Fresh water resources are scarce. Only 2.5% of all water on Earth is fresh, with less than 0.05% dissolved salts. About half the water stored in the earth is brackish, more saline than fresh, but not as salty as seawater, which contains 35 grams of salt per liter. The largest available source of fresh water lies in aquifers because surface water has become nearly extinct in many areas in the world. As water tables drop, springs, rivers, lakes and reservoirs drain.

Most coastal regions rely on groundwater as their main source of fresh water for domestic, industrial and agricultural purposes. As coast cities continue to expand, fresh water supplies are being sucked from aquifers, causing saltwater intrusion. Saltwater intrusion occurs when saline ocean water invades freshwater aquifers. Water extraction drops the level of fresh groundwater, reducing its water pressure and allowing saltwater to flow further inland.

Freshwater contaminated with just 5% of seawater can no longer be used for common purposes, such as human use or agriculture. Saline water has a higher mineral content than freshwater, which makes it denser and gives it a higher water pressure. The hydrostatic pressure

allows saltwater to push inland beneath freshwater aquifers and destroy them. Human activities, especially pumping groundwater from coastal wells, have accelerated saltwater intrusion.

Ghost forests (left), dead trees along vast swaths of coastline invaded by rising seas, are one of the most obvious markers of climate change.

Extreme storm surges amplify salt intrusion in surface water and aquifers. Hurricane Katrina's 28-foot storm surge reached 6–12 miles inland, killing the native plant life.

Large salt ions clog the plants' roots, which starves the plant. Root systems are essential in holding the soil together in marshes and wetlands. Loss of plant life results in rapid erosion, which further lowers the ground level. The area becomes vulnerable to the next storm surge.

Agricultural drainage channels, natural or man-made, provide conduits for saltwater to move inland. Coastal cities cover the ground with highways, canals, concrete buildings and storm sewers, all of which prevent aquifer recharge. Constant water extraction for agriculture and cities without recharge drops the water table, making the aquifer more vulnerable to seawater intrusion.

NOAA analysis indicates that much of America's densely populated Atlantic and Gulf Coast coastlines lie less than 10 feet above mean sea level. Over half of the Nation's economic productivity is located within coastal zones. This includes 72% of ports, 27% of major roads, and 9% of rail lines. A single 23-foot storm surge in the Gulf Coast has the ability to inundate 67% of interstates, 57% of arterials, almost half of rail miles, 29 airports, and virtually all ports.

Overdrafting groundwater along all three US coasts, has caused the salt-water interface to move inland, often more than 5 miles. As salt water invades aquifers, it kills the plants above. The seawater intrusion rate in the Pajaro Valley in California is estimated to be advancing at 250 feet per year. One strong storm could push seawater forward much faster.

Seawater invades coastal aquifers worldwide, especially in North Africa, the Middle East, the Mediterranean, Spain, China, and Mexico. About 60% of Spanish coastal aquifers are contaminated by seawater intrusion. Coastal aquifers in China are being invaded by salt at the rate of 30 square kilometers a year.

Compaction and subsidence

Subsidence caused by cities and farmers pumping from aquifers or pumping oil by petroleum companies, causes the land to sink by 10 inches per year in some areas. Lowering the land surface makes it more vulnerable to ocean cruelty; storm surges and salt invasion. Dams, diversions and reservoirs in the US have created substantial delta losses on each coast.

The Mississippi River has 400 dams over 10 feet high, which have substantially degraded and weakened the delta. The Gulf delta did not protect the coast when Harvey and Katrina made landfall.

Overdrafting not only causes seawater intrusion, but aquifer compaction and subsidence. The San Joaquin Valley, one of the most productive agricultural regions in the world, overdrafts its aquifers by billions of gallons a year, which will extinguish farming in the Valley. As the aquifer compacts, the soil settles causing surface subsidence. About half the San Joaquin Valley, about 5,200 square miles, has experienced subsidence greater than a foot. Some areas, such as Mendota, the "world cantaloupe center of the world," had experienced subsidence of 28 feet, (8.5m) by 1970. Subsidence continues to reduce ground levels at a rate of one foot a year.

An aquifer stores water in layers of permeable rock, or unconsolidated materials, (gravel, sand, or silt). Overdrafting drops ground water levels. The aquifer caves in on itself as the water is extracted and causes aquifer compaction. Compaction results in permanent aquifer storage loss.

No practical technology has been proposed to restore compacted aquifers. Canals carrying water for people and agriculture are extremely sensitive to subsidence, because they move water by gravity. When one part of a canal subsides, it reduces or destroys the conveyance capacity for the water column downstream. Subsidence makes downstream farmers even more dependent on groundwater. As subsidence sinks the land, bridges and infrastructure sink with it.

Coral Sead'asters

Coral Sead'sters will cause catastrophes for coastal cities as natural protections – corals, deltas and forests – fall like dominos. Human migration to megacities along coastlines by 2030 will have consumed the land and water industrial farmers would otherwise use to grow food. The loss of coral reefs and river deltas will allow storm surges that are greater than 10 times more damaging to infrastructure, blocking food and water transportation. Cities, ports and estuaries will be surrounded by dead zones from eutrophication, eliminating the opportunity for local sea food.

Salt incursion will destroy huge areas of cropland and drinking water, leaving megacity populations very hungry and thirsty. Cities typically store less than a week's worth of food. Hurricane Maria's devastation to San Juan, Puerto Rico provides a glimpse of the future. Maria left Puerto Ricans very hot, hungry and thirsty. What can possibly mitigate hurricane and Coral Sead'ster destruction?

Following a natural disaster, fossil resources are scarce, but typically there is plentiful wastewater, botanical wastes, and solar energy. Microfarmers can practice abundance methods and use algae and solar energy to cycle nutrients from waste streams to cultivate healthy and safe food, while they clean the water.

Freedom foods

Freedom foods are special foods made from algae and other microcrops. They are extraordinary because they are the first food designed to grow free from consumption of fossil resources. Cycled nutrients provide superior nutrition, micronutrients, bioactive compounds, vitamins and minerals. These foods will deliver superior aroma, color, texture, and taste, with less than half the fat and cholesterol of foods from terrestrial crops. Their high nutralence will provide twice the protein and 10 times the total nutrients per bite. In addition, freedom foods will offer 50 times more natural biodiversity than legacy foods.

Abundance growing methods reduce production risk for growers while diminishing waste and costs. Microfarms can provide climate independent food production year-round in a city, even after a natural disaster. Abundance methods allow growers to recover and reuse nutrients from waste streams as well as clean wastewater.

Cities will have learned lessons from world leaders through the Rockefeller Foundation's 100 Resilient Cities project, and similar sustainability initiatives. The Netherlands will provide excellent guidance because the Dutch are world leaders in dikes, CEA (controlled environmental agriculture), and algae bioproducts. The Wageningen University Research Centre, Algae Parc, led by their extraordinary scientific Director, Rene Wiffels, will provide much needed solutions for algae foods, biofeed, biomaterials and energy production. Algae Parc partners with organizations globally to resolve exactly the types of challenges that will face coastal cities.

Coastal cities will become painfully aware of the coral cascade that will cause enormous storm surges that inflict devastation, displacement, hunger and thirst on one city after another. Ecosmart cities will already be growing some of their city's food in CEA vertical farms, peace microfarms, and urban gardens. These solutions will allow cities to produce most of their own food in the city. Local production of freedom foods will leave fresh water for consumers. It will increase jobs and social justice with affordable, high nutralence food.

Triple Bottom Line

Freedom foods maximize the sustainability Triple Bottom Line with social, environmental and economic solutions that benefit local and global societies.

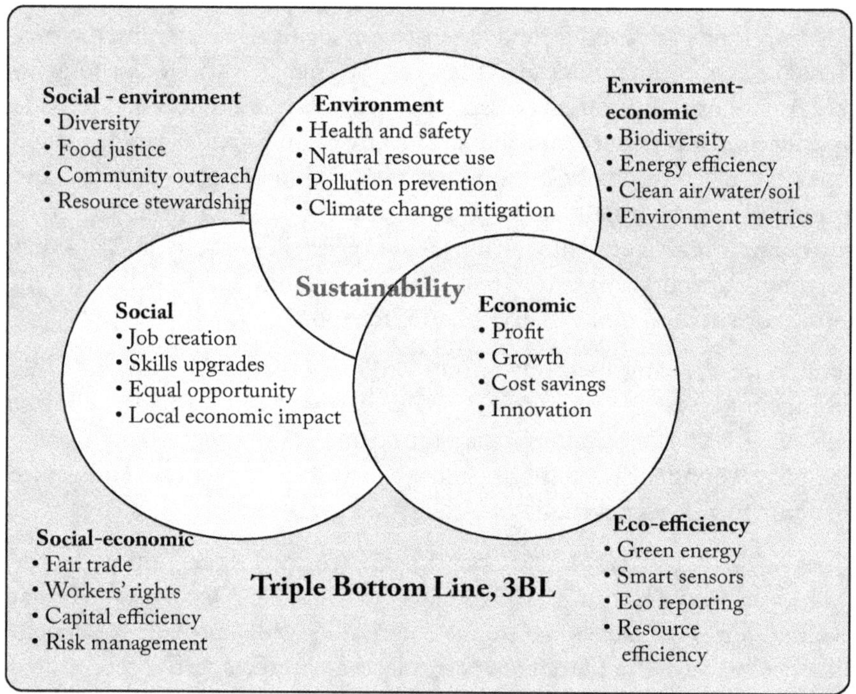

Social justice

Freedom foods allow social justice as women, minorities, young and elderly, as well as handicapped people can grow good food. Peace microfarms can eliminate hunger and malnutrition for children and the elderly, and provide affordable good food. Freedom foods free children from the plague of obesity and diabetes. People will be free to choose tasty, high nutralence produce without nutrient dilution or hidden hunger. These foods will free consumers from genetic monocultures that are refined into foods that are sugar, calorie, salt and fat dense, but nutrient light. Microfarms enhance workers' rights, because each microfarmer can choose which of many bioproducts to produce. Risk reduction improves capital efficiency and protects microfarmers against health threats, physical injuries and production loss.

Environment

Freedom foods cycle carbon and other greenhouse gasses that would otherwise contribute to global climate warming and chaos. Algae can capture carbon for sequestration or reuse. These foods improve nutrition and taste, while reducing pollution and waste. Freedom foods liberate farmers from many production risks, including crop failure due to weather, extreme physical labor, heavy equipment and exposure to agricultural dust that carries chemicals and poisons. These benefits flow to the community and local towns and cities that avoid pesticide poisoning, blowing dust that carries pathogens and agricultural chemicals, as well as groundwater poisons.

Freedom foods free growers from GMO crops that consume massive amounts of cropland, freshwater, fossil fuels, chemical fertilizers and pesticides. Farmers can avoid MIA's enormous air, water and soil pollution. These foods free our planet from the loss of biodiversity and the extinction of natural organisms. Abundance production methods preserve natural resources for our children. Microfarmers can repair and restore natural ecosystems, while leaving a positive eco-footprint.

Economic

Peace microfarms create good jobs that can be performed by people in all walks of life. Microfarms help people learn and practice sustainable food production in a fashion that improves their skills and allows them to train others. Microfarms can lift an entire community or city with employment that cultivates food that improves health and community energy. The wide set of algae bioproducts permits substantial economic growth, creative entrepreneurship and social justice. Microfarmers can support urban farmers with affordable biofertilizer and biofeed. They can produce sustainable and biodegradable bioplastics, green chemicals and building materials that benefit both the economy and the ecology.

Ana Feeds Our World

Microfarms provide a center of innovation as producers continually find methods that make bioproducts faster, easier and better. Smart sensor technologies will provide the data for eco-reporting that validates the substantial benefits that accrue to microfarmers and their communities.

Algae solves possibly the most serious problem with MIA, inefficient and one-time use of resources. Microfarms permit the recovery and reuse of resources multiple times, using the power of the sun in photosynthesis. They provide the most efficient use of resources to product food.

Ana sustains her passion for single-celled organism and loves cultivating miracles.

One question remains;

Should Ana enlarge her quest?

Without health, life is not life; it is only a state of languor and suffering – an image of death.   *– Buddha*

Ana wants to take her idea to improve our world beyond food. She has a plan to **"Make America Healthy Again"**. Her proposal includes a series of strategic steps that engage US agencies and international NGOs with responsibility for human health and life quality.

1: The first step requires identifying the top health concerns, which the CDC has already created, (see next page). Then the design team will select the top therapeutic compounds for treating each malady, using a balanced policy of natural and synthetic compounds. The team will prioritize the therapeutic compound R&D list based on those that offer solutions for multiple diseases. The list might be segmented by life stages; children, young adults, adults and the elderly.

The FDA's engagement would start with a change in charter from gatekeeper to health promotion. Rather than a role of keeping helpful drugs off the market, the new charter, health promotion, would focus on finding drugs for the market. The FDA, EPA, CDC, National Institute of Health and other agencies would work together on health promotion.

2: The USDA engagement needs to critically examine both farm subsidies and food programs, such as SNAP. Farm subsidy policy would improve with consideration for human, animal and especially environmental health. Food provision programs would focus on improving health, affordability, food justice and nutralence. Engagement of NGOs associated with health, exercise, sports medicine, aging and vitality would also be important. They will help convey the value proposition for lifestyle changes that will Make America Healthy Again.

3: Engagement with accounting firms; PWC, Deloitte, Ernst and Young and KPMG will be critical. These firms can make the credible cost/benefit analysis for investment in health promotion now in order to substantially diminish future health costs.

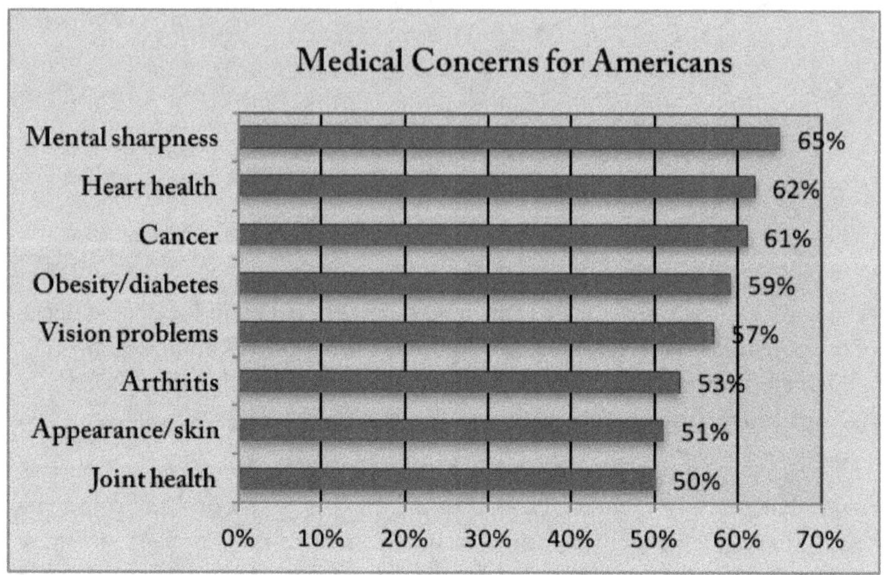

Over half of adults over 50 have one or more chronic health condition. About 25% of adults suffer from two or more chronic conditions. Seven of the top 10 causes of death were chronic diseases. Two chronic diseases—heart disease and cancer—account for 46% of all deaths.

The cost of chronic health conditions associated with the western diet is unsustainable. The these chronic conditions cost US citizens over $2.4 trillion dollars a year. These health problems create a huge drag on all parts of society, especially when factoring in lost work and school days and the tremendous number of people required to care for sick people.

The first presidential candidate that promotes a strong health promotion policy will find that a huge majority of voters will prefer making strong medicines and healthy foods over other policy alternatives.

Ana knows that creating social justice for healthy and affordable food by 2040 serves as a great opportunity. Who is willing to help Ana's quest to **Make America Healthy Again** by 2040?

Appendix I. Algae's Amazing Miracles

Algae's actions over the recent 3.5 billion years defies the imagination. She has created more than 20 times more miracles than any other organism on earth. Algae's family includes both single and multicellular organisms, which are classified as plants, bacteria, and by some scientists, as tiny animals with intelligence. Knowledge of algae's extraordinary actions can build a shared understanding for the miracles that will come next.

Algae will improve our food, health, and medicines, while repairing many of the most degraded and polluted ecosystems on our planet.

Algae:

1. Became the first plant on the planet, around 3.5 billion years ago.
2. Survived and adapted to the brutal conditions of early earth.
3. Evolved photosynthetic ability to create biomass from sunlight.
4. Used photosynthesis to capture CO_2 and release O_2 to support life.
5. Became the foundation of the food chain for plants, then animals.
6. Became the mother of all land plants 500 million years ago.
7. Provides nutrients for rootless plants; moss, lichens and corals.
8. Learned to grow 30 – 100 times faster than any other organism.
9. Does not waste energy on superfluous roots, stems or leaves.
10. Learned to survive through multi-season dormancy.
11. Act altruistically; purposely dies so progeny have sufficient food.
12. Developed the highest nutralence of any organism.
13. Recovers carbon and other nutrients from gas and wastewater.
14. Recovers heavy metals from gas and wastewater.
15. Eliminates heavy metal poisons from human body tissues.
16. Improves stress tolerance and survivability for plants.
17. Activates and supports plants' natural pest defense systems.
18. Restores life to dead soil from nutrient extraction.
19. Restores soil dead from salt invasion, back to life and fertility.
20. Restores life, germination, to many dead or non-viable seeds.
21. Improves sperm count and motility for animals and humans.
22. Saves many animals from death with higher survivability rates.

23. Activates animals and humans' natural immunity defense systems.

24. Restores sight to blind mice and blind humans.

25. Protects cells from severe damage from free radical scavengers.

Future algae miracles

Algae are not done yet providing miracles. Algae promise to improve human societies and the earth with still more miracles. Algae will:

26. Provide sufficient food to ensure social justice, where everyone has access to affordable and healthy food.

27. Provide food justice, where everyone has access food production.

28. End food deserts with access to local healthy food.

29. Allow climate independent food production, anywhere on earth.

30. Enable freedom foods, grown with no or minimal fossil resources.

31. Provide nutrients to end malnutrition and nutrient deficiencies.

32. Restore millions of IQ points for children with brain disorders.

33. Restore good health from heavy metals poisoning in children.

34. Provide food and life-support systems for deep space exploration.

35. Provide energy and medicines for space exploration.

Algae bioactive compounds protect from and provide treatments for:

36. Autism, ADHD and other brain dysfunctions.

37. Health restoration from heavy metals and pesticide poisoning.

38. Obesity and diabetes with fibers and antidiabetic biocompounds.

39. Kill cancer cells with anticancer compounds and cancer toxins.

40. Heart failure and strokes with anticoagulants.

41. CHD with antihypertensive and antihyperlipidemic compounds.

42. Arthritis and hepatitis with anti-inflammatory compounds.

43. ALS, Parkinson's and other neurodegenerative diseases.

44. Asthma and allergies with immunomodulatory compounds.

45. Yeast and fungal infections, e.g. ringworm, with antifungals.

46. Asian flu, viral pneumonia and HIV/AIDS with antivirals.

47. Degenerative metabolic disorders.

48. Brain dysfunction including dementia and Alzheimer's disease.

49. Reduction in bipolar disorders and mental illnesses.

50. Substantial reduction in depression, PTSD, and suicide.

Acknowledgements

New ideas build on the considerable research provided by prior pioneers in science and the environment, including:

- Qiang Hu, Director, Chines Academy of Science
- Stephen Mayfield, Professor, UCSD Laboratory
- Rene Wiffels, Algae Parc, Wageningen University
- Robert Henrikson, CEO, Smart Microfarms
- David and Marcia Pimentel, emeritus, Cornell University
- Jeffery Sachs, Earth Institute, Columbia University
- Fred Krupp, President, The Environmental Defense Fund
- Ken Cook, President, The Environmental Working Group

Thank you professors Bruce Rittman, James Elser and Peter Lammers, Arizona State University and Benjamin Brant, CEO, Ecoponex, for your excellent insights and content suggestions.

Science	Business, Economics	Agribusiness
E.F. Becker	Mark Allen	Jon Ewen
Rick Bellingham	David Schwartz	Richard Morrison
Amha Belay	Doug Young	John O'Hare
Lieve Laurens	Herb Roskind	Gary Wood
Christopher Lee	Liz Welch	Mike Pasqualetti
Fred Pearce	Gary Dirks	Jim Lane
Phil Pienkos	Henk deWaard	Ben Cloud
Ike Levine	Mark Ewen	Sally McNamara
James Elser	James Hershauer	Fred Boyd

Izabela Michalak and Katarzyna Chojnacka at Wrocław University of Technology, Poland, where extremely helpful as were the writings of Sandra Postel, Nobel Laureate Al Gore, Harvey Blatt, Michael Pollen, Brian Halweil, Clay Jason and Linda Graham.

Mark R. Edwards

Mark cultivates miracles to pursue food justice and resolve world hunger. He facilitates Ana's path to assure health and vitality for those in need, locally and globally. *Ana Feeds Our World* is his 16th book in the *Green Algae Strategy Series*, focused on affordable, sustainable and safe food and energy.

Mark graduated from the U.S. Naval Academy, where he earned degrees in engineering, oceanography and meteorology. Jacques Cousteau motivated and mentored his interest in the oceans and global stewardship. He holds an MBA and PhD in strategic marketing and consumer behavior and taught sustainability, food marketing, engineering, leadership and entrepreneurship at ASU for 39 years.

He served as marketing director for the Pritikin Longevity Institute, where he helped design healthy foods and lifestyles. As a director for a Fortune 50 food company, he did a series of projects designed to create functional foods with krill and farmed shrimp and salmon. He has performed extensive R&D on new foods and food adoption.

Mark founded and served as CEO of the software and assessment firm TEAMS Intl. for 22 years. He invented dozens of advanced metrics, including 360° feedback, that are used today by firms globally. He has consulted for Disney, 3M, Monsanto, DuPont, Nabisco, Quaker Oats, General Mills, Borden, Coca-Cola, Frito-Lay, GE, Intel, J&J, Merck, GM, Bank of America, and most of the food / agribusiness companies.

Mark has published over 140 articles and 26 books that span business and science disciplines. His *360° Feedback*, with partner Ann Ewen, was a business best seller. Several science books won international best science and environment awards including *Green Algae Strategy, Abundance: Sustainable fossil-free Food, The Tiny Plant that saved our Planet, Freedom Foods* and *Peace Microfarms*. Universities in over 30 countries use several of the *Green Algae Strategy* series books in food, energy and sustainability courses. He writes the popular Algae Secrets blog for Algae Industry Magazine.

The Green Algae Strategy Series focuses on creating Sustainable and Affordable Food and Energy – "SAFE" production. Teachers, professors and policy leaders use Green Algae Strategy books in schools and colleges in over 30 countries for courses in sustainability, engineering, business, politics, social entrepreneurship, food, water, energy, ecology, environment and world future.

BioWar I: Why Battles Over Food and Fuel Lead to World Hunger, 2007. BioWar I, where food is burned for fuel, must be ended by withdrawal – not of soldiers, but of damaging agricultural subsidies.

Green Algae Strategy: Engineer Sustainable Food and Fuel. 2008. Algae offer solutions for sustainable and affordable food and energy because algae are the most productive biomass source on Earth. *Best Science Book* **– 2009, Independent Publisher Awards.**

Green Solar Gardens: Algae's Promise to End Hunger, 2009. Algaculture in small but beautiful solar gardens and algae microfarms distributed globally will enable SAFE production locally.

Crash: The Demise of Fossil Foods and the Rise of Abundance. 2010. Traditional fossil-based agriculture sits precariously on a foundation of unsustainable fossil resources that will become unaffordable and then will run out. Abundant agriculture is sustainable because it uses plentiful inputs that are cheap and will not run out.

Smartcultures: Nature's tiny Genius – Algae – Reverses Pollution and Regenerates Degraded Ecosystems, 2011. Farmers may recycle farm wastes to their fields using abundance microfarms. Smartcultures give 20 – 30% higher yields by providing bioavailable nutrients at just the right time. Farmers save 30 – 40% by reducing input costs and reduce ecological pollution by 90%.

Abundance: Sustainable Fossil-free Foods with superior Nutrition and Taste; less Pollution and Waste, 2010. Abundance presents the value proposition for algae food, feeds and other forms of energy using plentiful resources that will not run out. Abundance growers can clean the air and water while they grow foods with superior nutrient density and better sensory values, including color, texture and taste. **Pinnacle Gold Medal winner 2011, Best Environmental Book.**

The tiny Plant that saved our Planet. The incredible true story of Tiny, Mighty Al. Tiny Mighty Al saved our planet by eating the bad carbon genie, which enabled the earth to cool and gave us oxygen. Al saved us again by becoming the bottom of the food chain and providing all living creatures with nutritious food. If we educate our children, maybe they will prompt us to take action — now. **Nautilus Silver Medal winner 2011, Best Children's Book.**

Abundant Agriculture: Smartcultures enable superior Nutrition and Yields from Regenerated Fields, 2010. Abundant agriculture represents the first new form of agriculture in 60 years. Abundant agriculture produces sustainable food, feed, fiber and other coproducts using primarily non-fossil resources that are plentiful, affordable and often surplus. Abundant agriculture growers use abundance methods to produce healthy, nutritional foods.

Freedom Foods: Superior Nutrition and Taste from low on the Food Chain for People, Producers and Our Planet, 2011. Freedom foods liberate consumers to make healthier food choices. Freedom foods are sustainable and grow free of fossil resources, GMO material and agricultural chemicals and pesticides.

Imagine Our Algae Future: **Visionary Algae Architecture and Landscapes,** 2012, with Robert Henrikson. See visionary images from the AlgaeCompetition.com showing how algae will change our world. Contestants from 40 countries created amazing graphics, pictures and videos showing how algae is produced today and will be used tomorrow for food, feed, biofuels, medicines and ecological repair.

Peace Microfarms: A Green Algae Strategy to Prevent War. 2015. Wars are fought over food and the fossil resources required to produce food. Peace microfarms enable growers to use abundance growing methods that use no or minimal fossil resources to produce freedom foods. Peace microfarms can avoid war and save our precious resources for future generations.